DIVERSITY IN OPEN-AIR SITE STRUCTURE ACROSS THE PLEISTOCENE/HOLOCENE BOUNDARY

DIVERSITY IN OPEN-AIR SITE STRUCTURE ACROSS THE PLEISTOCENE/ HOLOCENE BOUNDARY

Edited by

Kristen A. Carlson and Leland C. Bement

UNIVERSITY PRESS OF COLORADO
Louisville

© 2022 by University Press of Colorado

Published by University Press of Colorado
245 Century Circle, Suite 202
Louisville, Colorado 80027

 ASSOCIATION of UNIVERSITY PRESSES   The University Press of Colorado is a proud member of
the Association of University Presses.

The University Press of Colorado is a cooperative publishing enterprise supported, in part, by Adams State University, Colorado State University, Fort Lewis College, Metropolitan State University of Denver, University of Alaska Fairbanks, University of Colorado, University of Denver, University of Northern Colorado, University of Wyoming, Utah State University, and Western Colorado University.

∞ This paper meets the requirements of the ANSI/NISO Z39.48-1992 (Permanence of Paper).

ISBN: 978-1-64642-225-8 (hardcover)
ISBN: 978-1-64642-226-5 (ebook)
https://doi.org/10.5876/9781646422265

Library of Congress Cataloging-in-Publication Data

Names: Carlson, Kristen, [date] editor. | Bement, Leland C., editor.
Title: Diversity in open-air site structure across the Pleistocene/Holocene Boundary / edited by Kristen A. Carlson and Leland C. Bement.
Description: Louisville, CO : University Press of Colorado, [2021] | Includes bibliographical references and index.
Identifiers: LCCN 2021045198 (print) | LCCN 2021045199 (ebook) | ISBN 9781646422258 (hardcover) | ISBN 9781646422265 (ebook)
Subjects: LCSH: Archaeological surveying—Case studies. | Landscape archaeology—Case studies. | Landscape assessment—Case studies. | Household archaeology—Case studies. | Excavations (Archaeology)—Methodology—Case studies. | Pleistocene-Holocene boundary.
Classification: LCC CC76.3 .D58 2021 (print) | LCC CC76.3 (ebook) | DDC 930.1—dc23/eng/20211108
LC record available at https://lccn.loc.gov/2021045198
LC ebook record available at https://lccn.loc.gov/2021045199

Cover photograph: Gaillardia flower at Bull Creek site, overlooking the broad Bull Creek drainage in the Oklahoma panhandle. Photo by Kristen A. Carlson.

To authors and colleagues George C. Frison and Banks Leonard who left us before this work met completion. We hold you in our memories with gratitude for the projects we could share.

Contents

Acknowledgments

The editors extend our most heartfelt thanks to the organizers of the 73rd Society for American Archaeology meeting in Vancouver, Canada for providing a venue for the session that would lead to this collaboration. We thank each and every author and co-author for their hard work and contributions to this volume. We also extend our thanks to all the supporting players that enabled the writing of these chapters. We know that partners, children, friends, and family play a huge part in enabling us to focus on our work long enough to see it through to completion and those roles too often go unrecognized. This volume was greatly improved by the insightful comments provided by Victor Thompson and an anonymous reviewer. We greatly appreciate their time and support of this work. Lastly, we thank all of the archaeologists, theorists, and scientists on which our work builds. We stand on the shoulders of great thinkers and extend to them our gratitude as we continue to push our fields forward.

DIVERSITY IN OPEN-AIR SITE STRUCTURE ACROSS
THE PLEISTOCENE/HOLOCENE BOUNDARY

1

Introduction

KRISTEN A. CARLSON AND LELAND C. BEMENT

The late Pleistocene and early Holocene periods are globally plagued by archaeo-logical excavation bias. Predominantly, research has focused on rock shelters and caves overseas and large game kills and butchery sites in North America. Our focus in this volume shifts away from these typical discussions toward open-air sites, which are harder to locate and often more difficult to interpret because of depositional processes.

The contributors to this volume participated in a symposium at the 73rd Society for American Archaeology meeting in Vancouver, Canada. We, the editors, orga-nized that session after conversations arose surrounding the lack of data available during this period. We were turning our own attention away from large-scale kill events to an open-air site in the Oklahoma panhandle. Having spent much of our careers focused on large game hunting, we became frustrated by the scope of discus-sion that follows excavation of kill sites, the dominant focus of fieldwork on the Paleoindian period in North America. The Bull Creek site (Bement et al., chapter 8) provided new challenges, including discerning a potential camp structure, seg-regating possible activity areas, and defining which activities were contemporane-ous with other activities beyond large-scale kills. Background for such studies led invariably to the complex world associated with the investigation of the classic Late Pleistocene-age sites such as Star Carr (Legge and Rowley-Conway 1988; Rowley-Conway 2017), Ohalo II (Nadel 2001), and more recent work at Monte Verde (Dillehay and Ocampo 2015; Dillehay et al. 2008) to name just a few. Interest in

https://doi.org/10.5876/9781646422265.c001

the research of open-air sites was shared by other investigators who would join the symposium and later become contributors to this volume. Collectively, we move our focus away from caves and kills and instead focus on open-air archaeology at the Pleistocene/Holocene transition.

North American archaeology often finds itself in silos, creating groups that rarely interact with the literature or the people outside of their own region, time period, and specialization. The Paleoindian period has earned a reputation of being one of the worst for this kind of isolationism (Thompson 2018). This criticism can be extended to many scientific fields in general, but the limited scope of Paleoindian conversations has hit a breaking point in which we must reach beyond our standard conversations and analysis. We are dealing with limited data and poor preservation and it has taken researchers in the field a while to compile those data meaningfully so we can build on what we know and ask new questions. If anything, our limitations force us to look more widely for ways to interpret problematic data sets, and now is the time to push those limitations. We hope this volume provides a place for such discussions to develop, while bringing in some of the expertise in regions less affected by North American biases (Jochim, chapter 2; Terry et al., chapter 3).

As we move forward and broaden our scope of conversation to open-air sites, readers and researchers alike would benefit from thinking carefully about the entire archaeological process from site creation, abandonment, burial, possible reuse, and discovery. Taphonomic implications are considered and discussed throughout this text. Taphonomic processes impact all archaeological sites (Schiffer 1986, 1996). At open-air sites we are often looking at many events superimposed upon each other, often leaving the last event to be discovered. These sites pose a variety of challenges but also provide new information to researchers. The contributors of this volume meet these challenges in a variety of ways.

The term "open-air site" is used here to differentiate these sites from "rock shelter" or "cave" sites. This distinction is important because rock shelters and caves, in addition to having better preservation, are bounded by the natural structures that protected the inhabitants and, later, the material culture left behind. Solid, immovable walls that constrict and define activity spaces are different from sites in open settings where fewer, if any, natural borders exist. In open-air sites, the borders and delineation of activity areas result from human-made structures and cultural perceptions. In the open, the distribution and structure of activities may be organized more from cultural beliefs and institutions. This is not to imply that open-air sites can occur anywhere. There are constraints even in an open landscape. But unless the location is bounded on one or more sides by a cliff, river, ocean, or swamp, it would appear that the site could extend outward in other directions forever. And yet open-air sites do not extend forever. They do have boundaries and borders, many of which are culturally ascribed. And it is within the realm of culture that variability and diversity reign.

Natural barriers to open-air sites include abrupt landform changes: rivers, lakes, arroyos, rock outcrops, subtle soil changes; proximity of vermin, including snake dens, ant mounds; vegetation; aspect/wind direction/protection; and slope. While these perceived natural barriers might be applied to archaeological investigations, the true site boundary may circumvent or incorporate landscape features. For example, an open-air site might be bisected by an arroyo, stream, or river. On the other hand, a river may form the boundary between two culture groups. Determining which scenario is correct for a given context is the task of the archaeologist.

Cultural barriers take into consideration various factors, including anticipated length of occupancy, population size, and structures. Additional factors include situational conditions discerned by the following questions: Does the task involve meat processing and subsequent decay? Does it generate lots of detritus and is that dangerous? Does it require extensive processing or ancillary activities? Some activities might have additional requirements, including more water, fuel, or space, and more people than are normally required. Finally, consideration may include aspects of group composition: Nuclear family, extended family, fictive family, gender divisions of labor, combined genders, elderly, children, and dogs (humans are not the only inhabitants of sites, and animals can make their own contributions to the archaeological record).

In some instances, circumscribed site boundaries might change as the need arises. In other instances, site boundaries might have immovable cultural barriers established by convention or taboos. Diversity in site layout may be expressed at various scales, ranging from individual discrete tasks to cooperative tasks requiring two or more people or communitywide activities. These various activities may take place at vastly different localities, some on site, and some off. Identifying offsite activity areas may be necessary to truly understand the scale of that activity. In the past we have discussed these use areas in strict terms that link activities often to subsistence and may not accurately portray the lives of the site's inhabitants. For example, mammoth kills in the Clovis period that likely have had unexcavated camps nearby (Mackie et al., chapter 5). We try in this introduction to avoid categorizing human behavior into strict categories (camp, kill, processing area) to avoid minimizing the activities humans carry out in any given location.

As mentioned above, site formation and taphonomic processes are more challenging at open-air sites and are considered primary forces acting on site preservation and the post-abandonment movement of cultural materials. Cultural activities associated with cleaning of activity areas and trash also affect the ability to segregate discrete activity areas from refuse zones in intra-site patterning (Bamforth, chapter 9).

Conversely, at other sites, discrete hearth-side activity areas are preserved within structure boundaries (Jochim, chapter 2; Puckett and Graf, chapter 4 Mackie et al., chapter 5; Huckell et al., chapter 7; Bement et al., chapter 8; Nadel 2001). Distinguishing between intact activity areas and discard zones is one crucial step in understanding these sites.

Let us consider for a moment what evidence may allow demarcation of a discrete activity area. The recovery of flint knapping debris at the edge of a hearth might lead to the conclusion that a flint knapper reduced lithic material while sitting near the fire. An alternative interpretation is that the knapping debris was swept from the location of knapping and discarded in the vicinity of an abandoned hearth. In this scenario, the locale of actual knapping is not known. However, if the flint knapping was conducted on a dirt floor, its post-cleaning signature may be represented by a dusting of micro-debitage on the floor that escaped the cleanup. Thus, the recovery of micro-debitage could be an archaeological indicator of a discrete flint knapping area. Consider though, the ethnographic description of a flint knapper reducing lithic material while sitting on a large animal hide, then folding the hide and dumping its contents in a trash area (Gallagher 1977). In this instance, the micro-debitage is also transported and discarded, leaving nothing behind to suggest the location of tool production/maintenance activity. Which, if any, of the above scenarios accurately portrays the activity at the site? The study of site formational processes at Ohalo II (Nadel 2001) demonstrated that the flint knapping debris was in primary context. However, the ethnographic analog shows that the discard of material could also be a viable alternative. A demonstration of contemporaneity between the hearth use and knapping might include the recovery of burned flaking debris in the hearth and unburned debris outside the hearth. But again, an alternative scenario would be that the knapping debris was discarded in and adjacent to an active hearth. Which of these scenarios is correct? They all are, or, perhaps none are. Depending on the scale of observation required by the research questions being addressed, it may not be important which scenario led to the observed distribution of knapping debris. Consider, for example, that if the research question only required the *identification* of discrete tasks at the site, then the distribution of those discrete tasks might not be important. Discrete tasks identified by all of these scenarios include (1) hearth activity (cooking/heating) and (2) flint knapping (stone tool production/maintenance).

The diversity of site structure exemplified by these case studies provides the bridge to formal models that seek to capture the essence of human behavior during this important transitional time. The ethnographic literature provides both a starting point and a cautionary tale for these studies, including the often-overlooked insight that ethnographic analogies should not try to pigeon-hole all cultures but rather demonstrate that cultures are diverse in the ways they solved problems.

"One wonders why anthropologists have tried for so many years to reduce the captivating diversity in human social organization to static archetypes, which may only exist in the anthropological literature! In so doing, knowledge of the reality of hunter-gatherer variability is left to confound the archaeologist. Regrettably, the archaeologist commonly adopts the ethnographic characterizations as guides to the interpretation of the archaeological record, thereby obscuring from view the potentially fascinating variety of the past" (Binford 2006:18).

Trends in human behavior have been identified. For example, there is a tendency for distance between habitation zones and trash areas to increase proportionately in relationship to the anticipated duration of habitation (Kelly 2013; Kelly et al. 2006). The expected duration of occupation also affects decisions concerning the selection of materials for structure and hearth construction. Longer anticipated periods of occupation are linked to selection of sturdier construction materials and more formalized hearth construction (Kelly et al. 2006). Increased house size has been linked to greater length of stay (Kent 1992). An increase in the number of formalized tool classes at a site has been linked to the length of stay, as the number of activities performed at a site increase with longer site occupancy (Kelly 2013). Similarly, the number of taxa associated with a site increases with the increase in length of stay. Other factors that might affect site layout include the season of occupation, number and type of tasks performed, number and makeup of people in residency, and availability of resources.

The chapters that follow provide a dynamic discussion of the state of archaeological study into the diversity of open-air sites during the Late Pleistocene/early Holocene transition. This book reevaluates a range of topics, providing new case studies that integrate knowledge generated by generations of researchers with the latest analytical tools to tackle age-old problems afflicting the investigation and interpretation of these sites. Several of these authors examine sites that ancient people returned to many times, identifying persistent places on the landscape during a period when single occupations are often thought to be the norm (in the Americas at least). The researchers of these sites also examine topics beyond subsistence, engaging with broader conversations to expand our understanding of lives across the Late Pleistocene/early Holocene interval and connect our work more broadly to the study of anthropology.

REFERENCES

Bement, Leland, and Kristen Carlson. 2017. "Open Air Camps of the Terminal Pleistocene." Symposium chairs at the 82nd SAA Conference, Vancouver, BC, Canada, April 1.

Binford, Lewis R. 2006. "Bands as Characteristic of 'Mobile Hunter-Gatherers' May Exist Only in the History of Anthropology." In *Archaeology and Ethnoarchaeology of Mobility*, edited by Frederic Sellet, Russell Greaves, and Pei-Lin Yu, 1–22. Gainesville: University Press of Florida.

Carlson, Kristen, and Leland C. Bement. 2018. *The Archaeology of Large-Scale Manipulation of Prey*. Boulder: University Press of Colorado.

Dillehay, Tom D., and Carlos Ocampo. 2015. "New Archaeological Evidence for an Early Human Presence at Monte Verde, Chile." PLOS ONE. 10, no. 11 (November 18, 2015): e0141923. doi:10.1371/journal.pone.014192.

Dillehay, Tom D., C. Ramirez, M. Pino, M. B. Collins, J. Rossen, and F. D. Pino-Navarro. 2008. "Monte Verde: Seaweed, Food, Medicine, and the Peopling of South America." *Science* 320(5877):784–786. DOI:10.1126/science.1156533.

Gallagher, J. P. 1977. "Contemporary Stone Tools in Ethiopia: Implications for Archaeology." *Journal of Field Archaeology* 4: 407–414.

Kelly, Robert L. 2013. *The Lifeways of Hunter-Gatherers, the Foraging Spectrum*. New York: Cambridge University Press.

Kelly, Robert L., Lin Poyer, and Bram Tucker. 2006. "Mobility and Houses in Southwestern Madagascar, Ethnoarchaeology among the Mikea and their Neighbors." In *Archaeology and Ethnoarchaeology of Mobility*, edited by Frederic Sellet, Russell Greaves, and Pei-Lin Yu, 75–107. Gainesville: University Press of Florida.

Kent, Susan. 1992. "Studying Variability in the Archaeological Record: An Ethnoarchaeological Model for Distinguishing Mobility Patterns." *American Antiquity* 57: 635–659.

Legge, A. J., and P. A. Rowley-Conwy. 1988. *Star Carr Revisited. A Re-Analysis of the Large Mammals*. London: University of London, Centre for Extra-Mural Studies.

Nadel, Dani. 2001. "Indoor/Outdoor Flint Knapping and Minute Debitage Remains: The Evidence from the Ohalo II Submerged Camp (19.5 Ky, Jordan Valley)." *Lithic Technology* 26 (2): 118–137. DOI:10.1080/01977261.2001.11720982.

Robinson, Brian S., Jennifer C. Ort, William A. Eldridge, Adrian L. Burke, and Bertrand G. Pelletier. 2009. "Paleoindian Aggregation and Social Context at Bull Brook." *American Antiquity* 74 (3): 423–447.

Rowley-Conwy, Peter. 2017. "To the Upper Lake: Star Carr Revisited—by Birchbark Canoe." In *Economic Zooarchaeology: Studies in Hunting, Herding and Early Agriculture*, edited by Peter Rowley-Conwy, Dale Serjeantson, and Paul Halstead, 197–207. Oxford: Oxbow Books.

Schiffer, M. 1986. *Formation Processes of the Archaeological Record*. Albuquerque: University of New Mexico Press.

Functional and Organizational Variation among Paleolithic and Mesolithic Sites in Southwestern Germany

MICHAEL A. JOCHIM

INTRODUCTION

In Central Europe, most known sites from the Pleistocene/Holocene transition are caves and rock shelters or surface lithic scatters; excavated open-air sites are scarce, but can be extremely informative about site functions and settlement organization. However, open-air sites can present radically different archaeological pictures depending on their age, function within the settlement system and frequency of use, as well as their post-depositional history. This is evident in an examination of four sites located on a lake, the Federsee, in southwestern Germany (figure 2.1). The focus here is on the degree and nature of intra-site patterning, and how this patterning relates to what we can determine about the type and function of sites.

The Federsee was formed in the late glacial period by outwash from the alpine glacier to the south. At its maximum it measured roughly 16 by 10 kilometers in size. The lake shore was intensively occupied beginning in the late glacial and has been the focus of much archaeological research beginning early in the last century (Reinerth 1929; Schlichtherle 1980). Primarily known for its waterlogged villages of the Neolithic and Bronze Age, it has also produced a good number of Late Paleolithic and Mesolithic sites. The Late Paleolithic began during the Meiendorf Interstadial, around 14,400 cal BP, and lasted until the end of the Pleistocene, about 11,500 cal BP. This was followed by the Mesolithic, which came to an end with the appearance of the Neolithic in this area at around 7400 cal BP. The sites

https://doi.org/10.5876/9781646422265.c002

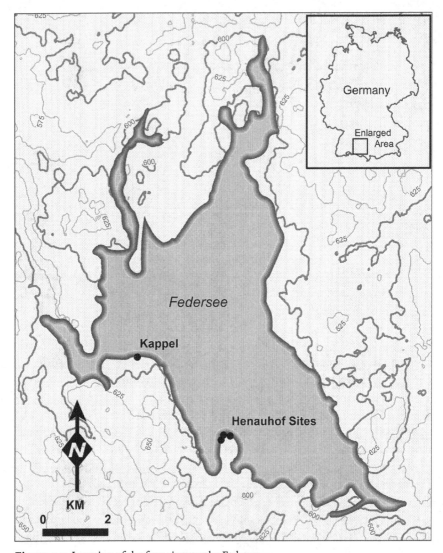

Figure 2.1. Location of the four sites on the Federsee.

to be discussed include two from the Late Paleolithic, Henauhof West (HW) and Kappel (KP), and two from the Late Mesolithic, Henauhof Nordwest 2 (HNW2) and Henauhof Nord II (HNII).

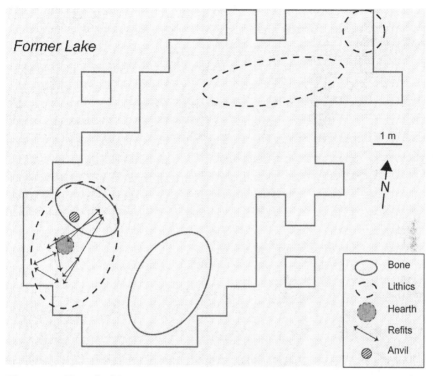

Figure 2.2. Henauhof West

THE SITES

HENAUHOF WEST

The site of Henauhof West, situated on a narrow sand spit jutting out into the former lake, was discovered by test units and 83 square meters were excavated in 1989 (Jochim 1998). Typologically, the site dates to the Late Paleolithic. The artifacts were concentrated in a sand and gravel level that forms the body of the ridge beneath the topsoil. Patterns of artifact distribution, to be discussed below, together with their elevation above the highest known level of the lake, suggest that little postdepositional disturbance has occurred.

This site's location on a very small sand spit largely surrounded by the lake shallows may have been chosen to provide maximum access to the lake, to provide a broad view for game or strangers, or to have lessened the need for clearance of dense vegetation. The small size of the sand spit (average width ca. 6–7 meters) could not have accommodated a large group. A low lithic density of 1.7 per square meter

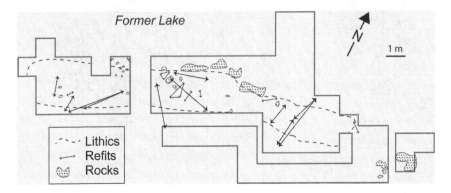

Figure 2.3. Kappel

suggests a relatively brief occupation. Lithic reduction played a relatively small role in the site's activities, and maintenance activities are represented by only a moderate amount of associated tools, which include burins, scrapers, borers and notches. Non-local stone raw material, from distances greater than 10km, make up approximately 50 percent of the artifact assemblage, suggesting that considerable material was brought to the site. Animal bone is relatively abundant and densely distributed, with a low diversity of species, including only red deer and boar among the identified species and otherwise containing mostly unidentifiable remains of large and medium-large mammals. A total of 74 percent of the identifiable body parts are fragments of long bones. Despite the abundance of red deer, no antler remains were found. This site appears to have been a small, brief occupation concentrated largely on the focused hunting and butchering of a few species of large game. Limb bones appear to have been processed for marrow and the remains left behind. The absence of antler may reflect the season of occupation, a concentration on kills of female animals, or simply the fact that antler was apparently little used as a raw material during the Late Paleolithic.

KAPPEL

Kappel is another Late Paleolithic site situated on a sand and gravel ridge jutting out into the former lake, but it shows dramatic differences from Henauhof West (Jochim et al. 2015). This site was discovered in 2002 and 224 square meters were excavated from 2003 to 2007. The artifacts, mostly lithics, were found primarily in a sand and gravel layer, which was formed during the Younger Dryas Period and lies beneath the topsoil. Some artifacts were found in peat and clay layers surrounding

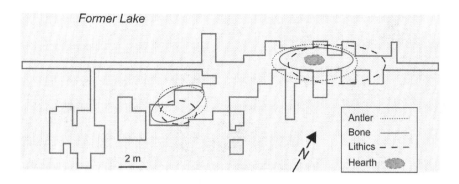

Figure 2.4. Henauhof NW2

the ridge, and a number of artifacts, including ceramics, were redeposited with sand and peaty sand to form a southeast extension of the ridge. The artifacts in this area showed clear evidence of mixing, with Neolithic ceramics underlying Late Paleolithic stone artifacts. This discussion focuses on the main, apparently undisturbed central portion of the ridge. Based on stratigraphic information, the majority of the artifacts date to the Younger Dryas Period, but some dates on bones found in the clay layers indicate that occupation of the location occurred as early as the Meiendorf Interstadial before 14,000 cal BP. Apart from the erosional episode that reconfigured the east and southeast sections of the present ridge, no evidence of major post-depositional disturbance is evident.

The few bones were found primarily in the peat and clay along the edge of the ridge and mostly predate the Younger Dryas. Identified species include elk, horse, red deer, aurochs and fish, mainly pike. The relatively large lithic assemblage, primarily found in the sand, has an overall average density of 20.1 per square meter. Kappel appears to represent a location that was repeatedly occupied during the Late Paleolithic, resulting in a comparatively large number of artifacts distributed throughout the surface of the ridge, particularly concentrated in the Younger Dryas sand.

HENAUHOF NORTHWEST 2

Henauhof Northwest 2 is a well-dated Late Mesolithic site located on the former shore of the Federsee. It was discovered by test units and excavated in 1991 (Jochim 1998). Patterns in the stratigraphic deposits suggest little postdepositional disturbance. The lithic density is 1.9 per square meter, similar to that of Henauhof West, but the bone density is much lower, at 2.2 per square meter. Significantly, this much

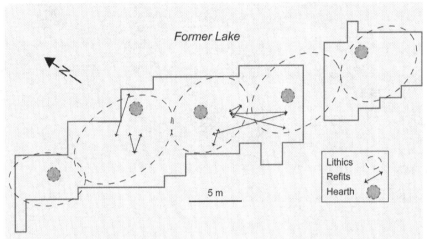

Figure 2.5. Henauhof Nord (after Kind 1997).

smaller bone assemblage of 156 has a higher species diversity, with identified fragments of red deer, roe deer, boar, aurochs and beaver, as well as 20 fish bones. This
difference, together with the abundance of deer antler and a more balanced tool
assemblage, suggests that this site is functionally different from Henauhof West. It
appears to be a small residential site less focused on targeted species and containing more evidence for maintenance activities and manufacturing, particularly with
antler as a raw material. Notably, no finished antler tools were found at the site, but
such tools are abundant at a nearby, roughly contemporary Late Mesolithic site,
suggesting that finished antler tools may have been taken away to another site.

HENAUHOF NORD II

Henauhof Nord II is a Late Mesolithic site also located on the former shore of the
lake. It was discovered in 1988 and excavated in 1989 (Kind 1997). A total of 281
square meters were excavated and revealed a site that presents yet another different
archaeological picture. According to the excavator, the only stratigraphic evidence of
significant postdepositional disturbance was apparent in the northeastern periphery
of the excavated area. The lithics have a low average density of 1.6 per square meter.

Functionally, this site has been interpreted as a short-term logistical camp ultimately tied to a residential camp elsewhere. The assemblage is dominated by blade
fragments with a length ranging between 1 and 3 cm. These form over 65 percent
of the assemblage and are all manufactured from Jurassic chert originating 30–50
kilometers or farther away. No evidence of their local manufacture is present in the

assemblage, suggesting that these blades were brought in ready-made. The only core and scant reduction debris at the site, on the other hand, are of a different, local raw material. Supporting this interpretation are the relatively few lithic refits that have been found. Due to the almost complete absence of faunal material, it is difficult to specify the activities that occurred at the site, but it is likely that the blade fragments were associated largely with hunting and butchering.

THE ROLE OF POSTDEPOSITIONAL PROCESSES

Before an examination of intra-site patterns can proceed in order to reconstruct behavioral interpretations, the role of natural processes must be assessed (Mackie et al., chapter 5; Dello-Russo et al., chapter 6; Huckell et al., chapter 7; Bement et al., chapter 8; Bamforth, chapter 9). All four sites are situated on the lakeshore and thus may have been affected by wave action and/or lake transgressions (Terry et al., chapter 3). The literature on postdepositional factors in archaeology is large, but a number of generalizations can be drawn. For example, according to Dibble et al. (1997), evidence of postdepositional disturbance may be reflected by (1) broad vertical distribution of artifacts (Mackie et al., chapter 5), (2) patterns in the strike and dip of artifacts, (3) aspects of artifact composition, and (4) absence of refits (Huckell et al., chapter 7; Bement et al., chapter 8; Bamforth, chapter 9). To this may be added, especially in the case of water transport, size-sorting of materials, irrespective of their type and function (Ismail-Meyer et al. 2013) (Huckell et al., chapter 7; Bamforth, chapter 9).

The water level of the Federsee in the Late Paleolithic fluctuated between 579.5 and 581.7 meters above sea level (Zimmermann 1961:272). The vertical distribution of artifacts in the two Late Paleolithic sites is 581.0 to 581.5 m for Kappel and 582.5 to 582.7 m for Henauhof West. Thus, the site of Kappel would clearly have been in jeopardy of disturbance from waves and transgressions, whereas Henauhof West was less so. During the Late Mesolithic, the water level was higher, reaching to 582.5 meters (Kind 1997:36). The artifact distributions in both Late Mesolithic sites lie just above this elevation, from 582.55 to 582.65 m for Henauhof Nord II and from 582.55 to 582.84 for Henauhof Northwest 2. It is thus appropriate to examine these sites for patterns of natural disturbance.

The artifacts in all four sites demonstrate relatively clear vertical distributions: roughly 10 cm thick for HN II, 19 cm for HW, and 20 cm for HNW2. In Kappel, the overall absolute elevational distribution on the main ridge varies with the curvature of the ridge, and in any one square meter the vertical range is 15 cm. Plotting of artifacts of different size categories for all four sites indicate no patterns of different distributions of artifacts by size. In three of the sites, (HN II, HW, HNW2) there are intact hearths with artifacts clustered around them. In two sites (HW, HNW2) clusters of bone or antler occur within the overall scatter of lithic artifacts. Lithic refitting was carried out for three sites (KP, HW, HN II) and shows a number of linkages within the overall artifact distribution for each site. Unfortunately, strike and dip of artifacts were not measured for the four sites. Based on this evidence, however, it appears that postdepositional disturbance has been relatively insignificant in creating the observed distributional patterns in the four sites.

SPATIAL PATTERNS

Ethnoarchaeological research documents considerable variability among living hunter-gatherers in the kinds of artifact patterning they create in their campsites (Bartram et al. 1991; Fisher and Strickland 1989, 1991; O'Connell 1987; O'Connell et al. 1991; Yellen 1977). The patterns of bone refuse among and within sites can vary depending upon prey size, transport decisions and labor availability, among other factors. The type of activities, the redundancy of their placement (Mackie et al., chapter 5; Bamforth, chapter 9), the length of site occupation and the degree of sweeping and dumping (Mackie et al., chapter 5) can all influence the clustering of artifacts. A clear lesson to be learned from such research is that there is no one-to-one relationship between artifact patterns and behavior, no clear, single "signature" of different activities or site functions in the archaeological record (Bamforth, chapter 9). Such variability can create much uncertainty in any interpretation of intra-site patterns. By viewing these patterns within the context of what else is known about the sites, however, interpretations may be strengthened.

Henauhof West

Clear spatial patterning of the artifacts in this site supports the interpretation of a brief, single occupation (figure 2.2). At one edge of the excavated area was an informal hearth, roughly 70 cm in diameter, with a nearby upright stone, probably an anvil. Artifacts formed clear concentrations. Two clusters of bone were found, one adjacent to the hearth and the other 3 meters away. Bones in the near-hearth area are smaller, with a median weight of 0.55 g, compared to the median of 1.09 g in the other area. In both areas, well over 95 percent of identifiable fragments are from large and medium-large mammals. The hearth area is dominated by long bone, cranial and rib fragments, whereas the non-hearth area, which has a greater range of body parts, is dominated by long bone and vertebral fragments. The near-hearth concentration appears to represent a general processing area, with marrow extraction dominant, whereas the second concentration may be a small area of discard.

Lithic artifacts also show concentrations, in this case in three areas, one of which overlapped the near-hearth area (Area 1) and the others approximately 6 m (Area 2) and 11 m (Area 3) from the hearth. Each of the three lithic concentrations is dominated by a single, different stone raw material, suggesting separate episodes of reduction and deposition (Huckell et al., chapter 7). Area 1 contains 84 percent non-local Jurassic chert, the best quality material; Area 2 is dominated by the local tan chert and radiolarite, and Area 3 contains predominantly local radiolarite, which is generally the poorest of the primary material used in the area. Area 1 is dominated by broken blades and flakes and shows a median weight of 0.45 g. Area 2 has a much larger median weight (1.36 g) and is dominated by larger flakes and whole blades. Area 3 consists largely of small flakes and chips and has an average weight of 0.10 g. Many of the artifacts in Area 1 near the hearth were fire-altered, and lithic refits were found only within this area (Puckett and Graf, chapter 4). Area 1 appears to reflect initial reduction activities using the non-local material brought to the site; the frequent broken blades and flakes may be the result of intensive trampling in this area, which, given the overlap with a concentration of bones, seems to represent generalized, hearth-centered activity. The other two lithic concentrations, each with a different proportion of mostly local raw materials, appear to represent separate and subsequent episodes of reduction.

Kappel

In this site no clear clusters of artifacts were observed (figure 2.3). The major detectable spatial pattern is an area of approximately 27 square meters in which the sand and gravel were packed into an extremely compact deposit that made simple troweling virtually useless. Elsewhere on the ridge the sand was very loose. Along the northern edge of this compact area is a line of rocks. Notably, the average artifact density in the compact area is 27.3 per square meter, significantly higher than the density of 16.1 per square meter that characterizes the rest of the ridge. Geological investigations found no natural causes for this compact area, so it is tempting to interpret it as the result of human activity. Specifically, because the compact area has, in comparison to the rest of the main ridge, a higher artifact density, as well as a significantly higher proportion of broken blades and virtually all of the lithic refits that were found, it may simply represent the portion of the ridge most heavily used and compacted by foot traffic. The line of rocks might even represent the remains of some kind of windbreak.

The lack of meaningful clusters of basic lithic forms or tool types or raw materials reflects the blurring of any single-occupation patterns by repeated use. A wide range of lithic artifact types may reflect either a palimpsest of different functionally specialized sites or the persistent use as a diversified residential site over time.

HENAUHOF NORTHWEST 2

A hearth, consisting of a shallow basin lined with clay, was found at one edge of the excavated area (figure 2.4). This site had two clear concentrations of red deer antler fragments, one around the hearth; the other lies about 6 m away. Bone is similarly concentrated in two areas overlapping those of antler. The hearth area has a smaller median bone weight and a greater range of body parts, including more of those with higher meat utility, whereas the other bone concentration contains only the identified remains of cranial and carpal fragments. Marrow extraction does not seem to have been important. Two areas of concentration of lithic artifacts also coincide with those of bone and antler. All stages of lithic reduction and a variety of different tool types are present in each, but the median weight of the lithics in the hearth area is significantly lower. In this site, as well as in the two sites previously discussed, a combination of local and non-local raw materials is represented in both the reduction debris and the retouched tools. The hearth concentration appears to represent a generalized activity area, including antler-working, butchering and lithic reduction. Based on the distinct spatial patterning and the relatively small lithic assemblage, this site also appears to represent a small, relatively brief occupation, but somewhat longer than that of Henauhof West. The more formal hearth and the diverse materials in two concentrations suggest two areas that supported a variety of domestic activities, one clearly hearth-centered. The second may reflect a generalized discard area containing somewhat larger material.

HENAUHOF NORD II

Five hearths were found spaced 5–9 meters apart and arranged in a rough line along the former shoreline (figure 2.5). A total of 454 lithic artifacts were recovered, but virtually no faunal materials were preserved except two antler axes. The artifacts are spread across the excavated surface in close proximity to the line of hearths but show only hints of discrete concentrations in the form of somewhat denser areas around each hearth.

Using each hearth as a basis, the excavator estimated an area of materials and activities associated with each, forming five non-overlapping portions of the site. The composition of the lithic assemblages associated with each, in terms of basic forms and raw materials, is similar among all regions, but lithic refits are confined within one area or link two adjacent areas at most. Although a number of separate occupations is one possible interpretation of this site, the relatively even spacing of well-defined hearths and the uniformity of the lithic assemblages suggest that a single occupation is a more likely interpretation. Separate social units may have carried out a range of similar activities during a brief occupation of what appears to be a logistical camp.

TABLE 2.1. Artifact distribution of the four sites

	HW	Kappel	HNW2	HN II
Lithic density/sq. m	1.7	20.1	1.9	1.6
Bone density/sq. m	10.6		2.2	
Faunal diversity	Lower		Higher	
Antler			Much	
Non-local stone material	45%	2%	37%	92%
Lithics with cortex	31%	29%	44%	32%
Cortex/rejuvenation flakes	9%	1%	23%	4%
Maintenance tools/tools	41%	59%	56%	27%
Hearths	1		1	5

COMPARISON OF SITES

A general comparison of the four sites can be useful in indicating the nature of each site and its role in an overall settlement system (table 2.1). The relative density of lithic artifacts, for example, can provide a hint of variations among the sites in duration or frequency of occupation. Kappel stands out in this regard, with an average density of 20.1 per square meter, whereas the other three sites show densities between 1.6 and 1.9 per square meter. On this basis alone, Kappel might be presumed to have been occupied for a longer period or to have shown more occupations than the other sites.

Relative bone density might also be useful in inferring occupation history, but the conditions of bone preservation appear to vary widely among the sites. The sites of Kappel and Henauhof N II are largely lacking in bone remains, presumably because their surfaces lay exposed for longer periods before burial. Only Henauhof West and Henauhof NW2 show excellent preservation and produced substantial faunal collections, and these differ considerably from one another, despite the similarity between the two in lithic density. Henauhof NW2 has a bone artifact density of 2.2 per square meter, while Henauhof West has a density of 10.6, implying that the two sites differed substantially in activities. Furthermore, although the assemblages at both sites are dominated by red deer in terms of bone weight among the identified remains, they differ significantly in terms of the role of other species (Terry et al., chapter 3; Bement et al., chapter 8). As mentioned earlier, despite its much smaller assemblage (156, compared to 883 for Henauhof West), Henauhof NW2 has more species of identified mammal and a higher proportion of birds and fish. Henauhof West, with its larger and denser faunal collection, appears to be more focused on large game, primarily red deer. Finally, the proportion of antler, primarily of red deer, differs greatly between the two sites with good preservation. Henauhof West contains no antler, despite the abundance of red deer remains, whereas Henauhof NW2 contains more antler than bones, based on weight, including a number of pieces with obvious cut marks.

All four sites contain the same array of stone raw materials, but in different proportions, which reflect differences in overall mobility and organization of the settlement systems. Local materials from within a 10 km radius, including a brown chert and red and green radiolarites, are dominant at the site of Kappel, forming over 90 percent of the assemblage. By contrast, these materials comprise only 12 percent of the assemblage of Henauhof Nord II, which is dominated by 82 percent Jurassic chert from sources 30–50 km away. This latter material constitutes only 1 percent of the Kappel assemblage. These two categories of material are more balanced in the assemblages at the other two sites. In addition, all four sites contain small amounts of a banded chert derived from sources 175 km away.

The relative importance of primary lithic reduction among the sites is suggested by the proportion of artifacts with cortex remaining. Henauhof NW2 stands out in this respect, with 44 percent of the artifacts having cortex (of which 70% occurs on local materials). By comparison, the other three sites have between 29 to 32 percent of artifacts with cortex in their assemblages. Obviously some primary reduction occurred at all sites, but it appears to have been more important at HNW2. This inference is supported by a calculation of the proportion of cortex flakes and cortex blades together with core rejuvenation flakes in each assemblage. At HNW2 this figure is 23 percent, whereas the other sites show percentages of 1–9 percent.

Another aspect of the lithic assemblages that can be informative about site function and activities is the proportion among retouched tools of so-called "maintenance" tools—that is, those not associated directly with food procurement but with activities of manufacturing and repair. In these four sites, such tools include scrapers, burins, borers and notches. Henauhof Nord II has by far the fewest, with these tools representing only 27 percent of the assemblage, followed by Henauhof West with 38 percent, Henauhof NW2 with 56 percent, and Kappel with 59 percent.

A last point of comparison is the presence and nature of hearth features at the sites. Kappel has no obvious hearths, although traces of charcoal are scattered across the excavated surface. Both Henauhof West and Henauhof Nord II have simple hearths consisting of oval concentrations of charcoal; Henauhof West has one of these, whereas Henauhof Nord II has five, spaced 5–9 meters apart and arranged in a rough line parallel to the former lakeshore. Henauhof NW2 has one hearth, but it is somewhat more substantial, consisting of an oval basin lined with clay containing charcoal and ashy soil, suggesting a slightly greater investment of energy into its construction (Terry et al., chapter 3; Bamforth, chapter 9).

In a wide-ranging examination of Upper Paleolithic sites of Europe, Kind (1984) found considerable variation among the sites, but underlined the importance and virtual ubiquity of the *hearth area*, a feature consisting of hearth plus associated artifacts within a rather small radius, as a significant component of the sites. This feature has been clearly recognized ethnographically (e.g., Yellen 1977). The size of hearth areas varies, with examples of 6 square meters among the !Kung (Yellen 1977), 12 square meters among the Alyawara (O'Connell 1987) and 25 square meters among the Kua (Bartram et al. 1991). Among the four archaeological sites discussed here, three have preserved hearths, with hearth areas of approximately 19 square meters (HW), 20 square meters (HNW2) and 40 square meters (HN II). This variation may reflect slight differences in the length of occupation, number of inhabitants, and/or type and intensity of activities.

For two of the sites, HW and HNW2, a distinction may be made in the distribution of artifacts between hearth areas and outlying concentrations. In both cases, the hearth area appears to represent a diversity of activities including lithic reduction, butchering, marrow extraction (HW) and antler working (HNW2). The outlying areas may represent discard of bone and stones and, in the case of HW, a brief episode of lithic reduction. Although HN II shows only diffuse areas of concentration around each hearth, these areas, like the more discrete hearth areas of the other two sites, contain a diversity of lithic artifacts types, suggesting a diversity of activities focused on the hearths. These patterns are similar to those found ethnographically by Yellen (1977) among the !Kung, in which the hearth constituted the focus of multiple activities.

DISCUSSION

These four sites show considerable variation in terms of:

Their location on a sand spit or solid shoreline

The presence and nature of hearths

The density of lithic artifacts

The relative importance of lithic reduction

The relative importance of different tool categories

The composition and proportion of different stone raw materials

The density of bone artifacts

The diversity of faunal species represented

The importance of antler as a raw material

The major determining factors of this variability certainly include site function and degree of reoccupation. The sites are separated in time, however, by approximately 5,000 years, and some of the differences among them reflect this. The Late Mesolithic differs from earlier periods by lithic technological changes that include a greater emphasis on the production of well-made, regular blades, apparently reflecting increased anticipatory production of tools in a changed environment. In addition, this period in general witnessed a clearly greater use of antler as a raw material.

The specific spatial patterns of these sites vary along three major dimensions: the degree of artifact clustering, the spacing of different clusters, and the resulting area of occupied space. One important factor that appears to affect this variation is the duration of occupation and how it influences discard behavior. It may be hypothesized that the longer the occupation, the greater the tendency to remove debris from heavily used areas (Bamforth, chapter 9). This would result in a greater tendency to create separate discard areas with an increasing distance from the habitation area.

None of these sites appears to have been occupied for a substantial period of time. Based on several features, including the somewhat more formal hearth, the diversity of prey, the important role of primary lithic reduction and of maintenance tools, and the evidence of focused antler-working, Henauhof NW2 appears to show the relatively longest occupation duration of the four sites. This site not only has a clear discard area containing bone, antler and lithics, but this area is quite far—6 meters—from the hearth area. As a result, the occupation area is approximately 93 square meters.

The site of Henauhof West, by contrast, has a more informal hearth, relatively much more bone but a much less diverse faunal assemblage, less evidence of primary lithic reduction and maintenance activities, and a more dispersed distribution of artifact concentrations, including two lithic areas away from the hearth that contain different stone raw materials and appear to be separate work areas. The site appears to be a residential camp, but one more focused on hunting and butchering, with less investment in site layout, less evidence of focused manufacturing, and probably a briefer occupation period. This site does have an apparent discard area, but it is only 3 meters from the hearth area and the overall occupation area is roughly 83 square meters.

The site of Henauhof Nord II presents yet another different picture, one suggesting an even briefer occupation by several social units or individuals. These occupants invested very little in site organization beyond the construction of simple hearths and carried out few lithic reduction or maintenance activities. No significant artifact concentrations and no obvious discard areas are evident. The average area of occupation around each hearth is approximately 40 square meters.

Finally, Kappel, with its diffuse and dense distribution of artifacts, appears to represent a repeatedly occupied location that witnessed a significant amount of lithic reduction and maintenance activities, blurring most evidence of site organization except perhaps a concentration of activities in a small, central area of the sand ridge.

CONCLUSION

Intra-site patterns have the potential to provide much information about site activities and their spatial organization. When this information is combined with other data, including artifact density, raw material sources, relative tool proportions and nature of features, it can make a significant contribution to our understanding of site function and more general settlement organization and land use. For European research, at least, this implies that significantly more attention needs to be given to the discovery and excavation of open-air sites where such data are not limited by the constraints of caves and rock shelters.

REFERENCES

Jochim, Michael. 1998. *A Hunter-Gatherer Landscape*. New York: Plenum.

Jochim, Michael, et al. 2015. "Eine Spätpaläolithische Fundstelle am Ufer des Federsees: Bad Buchau-Kappel, Flurstück Gemeidebeunden." *Fundberichte aus Baden-Württemberg* 35: 37–134. Stuttgart, Germany.

Kind, Claus-Joachim. 1997. *Die Letzten Wildbeuter*. Materialhefte zur Archäologie 39. Stuttgart: Konrad Theis Verlag.

Reinerth, Hans. 1929. *Das Federseemoor als Siedlungsland des Vorzeitmenschen*. Führer zur Urgeschichte 9. Augsburg.

Schlichtherle, Helmuth. 1980. "Sondierungen in Jungsteinzeitlichen Moorsiedlungen des Federsees." *Archäologische Ausgrabungen in Baden-Württemberg 1979*: 3–34.

3

Organization of Living Space at Late Pleistocene Campsites of the Studenoe Site, Transbaikal Region, Siberia

KARISA TERRY, ALEKSANDER V. KONSTANTINOV, AND IAN BUVIT

Late Pleistocene settlement systems in the Transbaikal Region of Siberia were established by 21,000 cal years BP, and underwent changes as climates ameliorated into the Holocene by around 12,000 cal BP. During this time the area was characterized by construction of stone-outlined circular structures, or dwelling features, with activities situated around central, stone-outlined hearths in riparian environments of major waterways. We explore the developmental variability of these unique structures along the Chikoi River in the southwestern Transbaikal during the Early and Terminal Late Glacial. We focus on changes in the way foragers organized their interior and exterior living spaces, highlighting (1) dwelling and occupational surface sizes; (2) quantity, size and location of hearths; and (3) indoor and outdoor activities. Our data indicate that dwelling construction probably reflects waxing and waning of group size and probable social distance of occupants. During the Last Glacial Maximum occupation (21,000 cal BP), Early Late Glacial foragers constructed larger, multi-hearth dwellings around small, aggregated family groups who shared indoor space. After 17,000 cal BP, as climates began ameliorating, smaller dispersed family groups inhabited smaller, more isolated tents, even though total habitational area, including indoor and outdoor spaces and use, were similar.

https://doi.org/10.5876/9781646422265.c003

INTRODUCTION

Studies of past hunting and gathering societies' organization of living spaces, especially those alive during the Paleolithic period, typically revolve around seasonal or organizational movements on the landscape or activity areas within the sites themselves (e.g., Binford 1983; Blades 1999). Paleolithic dwellings, and ethnographic hunter-gatherer habitations for that matter, typically appear as ephemeral, poorly delineated spaces that are further compounded by post-depositional processes, which inhibits comparisons of built human spaces. Some exceptions include Gravettian mammoth bone dwellings on the Central Eurasian Plains (i.e., Gavrilov 2015; Iakovleva 2015; Soffer and Preslov 1993), brush huts from Jordan (e.g., Nadel and Werker 1999), and seasonal site structures at the Bull Creek Site in the south-central United States (Bement et al., chapter 8). The Studenoe site in the Transbaikal region of Siberia contains unusual preservation of multiple well-preserved dwellings within clearly stratified layers, providing a rare opportunity to add to these studies.

Here, we focus on the scale of the habitational site itself to reveal social dynamics of its occupants, including how they managed and utilized indoor domestic areas (in our case dwellings) and outdoor habitational space. Attention is focused on how changes in community configuration affect the role and structure of the built indoor and outdoor spaces. We use housing features and artifact activity areas to make sense of what this patterning may reveal about the social composition of campsites.

In this paper, we explore changes in habitational sites in the Transbaikal Region of Siberia as climates ameliorated from the end of Marine Isotope Stage (MIS) 3 60,000–24,000 cal BP to the end of MIS 2, roughly 23,000–12,000 cal BP. Specifically, we examine variability of dwelling construction and site use during the Late Upper Paleolithic contrasting Early Late Upper Paleolithic (Early Late Glacial) with Terminal Late Upper Paleolithic (Terminal Late Glacial) occupations at the Studenoe Site. We focus on changes in the way foragers built and used their domestic space, including (1) dwelling and occupational surface sizes; (2) quantity, size, location, and spacing of hearths; and (3) indoor and outdoor activities based on artifact and stone tool assemblage composition.

BACKGROUND

STUDY AREA AND LATE PLEISTOCENE ENVIRONMENTS

The Transbaikal region is located in southern Siberia, stretching east from the eastern shores of Lake Baikal to the Shilka and Amur Rivers, and south to Russia's border with Mongolia and China (figure 3.1). The Studenoe site consists of two multicomponent occupations of the first and second terraces of the Chikoi River in southern

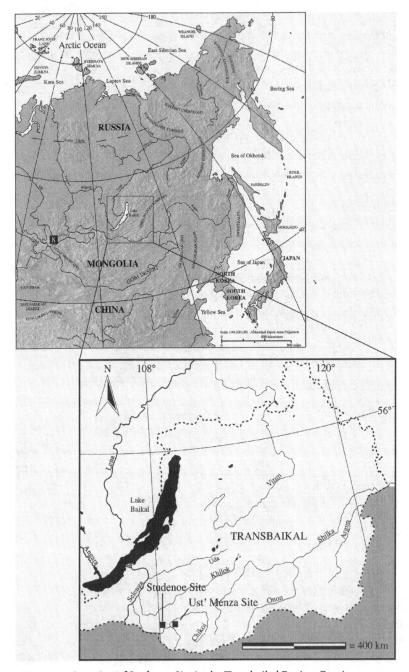

Figure 3.1. Location of Studenoe Site in the Transbaikal Region, Russia.

Transbaikal. Because of its unique position in the contact zone between North and Central Asia, several environmental zones were present in the Transbaikal region during the Pleistocene.

During MIS 3 (60,000–24,000 cal BP) the climate was relatively warm and humid in the Transbaikal (Chlachula 2001a; Frenzel et al. 1992a; Goebel 1999; Kind 1974; Maloletko 1998), but cooling and drying conditions ensued at the onset of MIS 2 (24,000–12,000 cal BP; Kind 1974; Tarasov et al. 1999; Velichko 1984; figure 3.2). Subsequently, during the LGM, generally dated to roughly 23,000–19,000 cal BP (~19,500–16,100 ^{14}C years BP; Mix et al. 2001), as temperatures reached their lowest point, aridity increased, forests disappeared, and permafrost expanded to its southernmost extent (Chlachula 2001a, 2001b; Frenzel et al. 1992b; Maloletko 1998; Velichko 1984). Mountain-tundra dominated alpine regions while valleys and basins were covered with cold-steppe grasses (*Gramineae*) and *Artemisia* (Maloletko 1998; figure 3.2). Pollen studies from the western Transbaikal indicate cold and arid steppe environments increased while tree species, such as pine (*Pinus silvestris, Pinus sibirica*) and birch (*Betula sp.*) decreased (Lbova 2000). The LGM roughly correlates to the Early Late Upper Paleolithic Period (Early Late Pleistocene; figure 3.2).

By 20,000 cal BP (17,000 ^{14}C years BP; Chlachula 2001b) climatic warming began, as mean annual temperatures increased to 2–4°C cooler than present, and precipitation to 25–50 mm less than present (Chlachula 2001a; Klimanov 1997; Maloletko 1998; figure 3.2). Paleoenvironmental studies by Chlachula (2001b) within north-central Asia, including the Transbaikal region, indicate a cool period existed during the Younger Dryas, roughly 12,850–11,500 cal BP (11,000–10,000 ^{14}C BP). During this time cold tundra-steppe vegetation covered river valleys, with small shrubs occupying areas adjacent to rivers (Chlachula 2001b). With generally increasing temperatures and precipitation, the landscape gradually transitioned from tundra-steppe during the LGM, to meadow-steppe, and to forest-steppe at the Terminal Pleistocene roughly 11,500 cal BP (10,000 ^{14}C years BP; Chlachula 2001b; figure 3.2).

Steppe and taiga animal species are characteristic of the Transbaikal during the entire late Pleistocene and into the Holocene, indicative of the mosaic environment of the region (Chlachula 2001b; figure 3.2). Tundra-steppe and forest-steppe fauna coexisted in the Transbaikal during this time, including moose (*Alces alces*), reindeer (*Rangifer tarandus*), red deer (*Cervus elaphus*), bison (*Bison priscus*), horse (*Equus caballus*), roe deer (*Capreolus capreolus*), Mongolian gazelle (*Procapra guttourosa*), Asian wild ass (*Equus hemionus*), saiga (*Saiga tartarica*), wolf (*Canis lupus*), and brown bear (*Ursus arctos*; Chlachula 2001b; Vereshchagin and Kuz'mina 1984; figure 3.2).

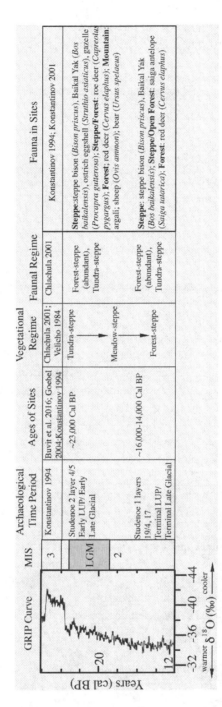

GRIP Curve	MIS	Archaeological Time Period (Konstantinov 1994)	Ages of Sites (Buvit et al. 2016; Goebel 2004; Konstantinov 1994)	Vegetational Regime (Chlachula 2001; Velicho 1984)	Faunal Regime (Chlachula 2001)	Fauna in Sites (Konstantinov 1994; Konstantinov 2001)
	3	Studenoe 2 layer 4/5 / Early LUP/ Early Late Glacial	~23,000 Cal BP	Tundra-steppe → Meadow-steppe → Forest-steppe	Forest-steppe (abundant), Tundra-steppe	**Steppe**:steppe bison (*Bison priscus*), Baikal Yak (*Bos baikalensis*), ostrich eggshell (*Struthio asiaticus*), gazelle (*Procapra gutterosa*); **Steppe/Forest**: roe deer (*Capreolus pygargus*); **Forest**: red deer (*Cervus elaphus*); **Mountain**: argali; sheep (*Ovis ammon*); bear (*Ursus spelaeus*)
	LGM					
	2	Studenoe 1 layers 19/4, 17 Terminal LUP/ Terminal Late Glacial	~16,000–14,000 Cal BP	Forest-steppe	Forest-steppe (abundant), Tundra-steppe	**Steppe**: steppe bison (*Bison priscus*), Baikal Yak (*Bos baikalensis*); **Steppe/Open Forest**: saiga antelope (*Saiga tatarica*); **Forest**: red deer (*Cervus elaphus*)

Figure 3.2. Climatic, environmental, and archaeological time periods of the Transbaikal region and Studenoe Site.

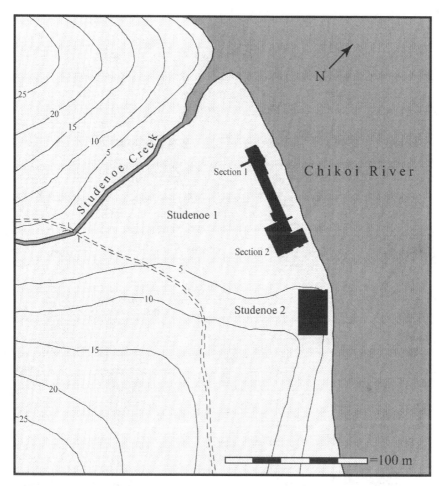

Figure 3.3. Topographic map of the Studenoe site showing excavation locations (after Konstantinov 2001: Konstantinov 1994).

STUDENOE SITE

The Studenoe site consists of two multilayered loci situated adjacent to the Chikoi River (figure 3.3). The younger Studenoe 1 occupation is located on the lower first terrace, while Studenoe 2 is located on the higher second terrace (figure 3.3). Numerous stratified Late Upper Paleolithic occupational surfaces from both loci contain multiple dwelling and hearth features with associated cultural material. Excavations began in 1970 by Chita State Pedagogical University archaeologist I. I. Kirillov. Then, M. V. Konstantinov and A. V. Konstantinov directed nearly yearly excavations between

1980 and 2004 (Konstantinov 1994; Konstantinov 2001; Konstantinov et al. 2003). Cultural layers of both loci are situated within 2 cm bands of sand and silt deposited by frequent low-energy overbank flooding of the Chikoi River. Following site abandonment, these fluvial deposits rapidly buried occupational surfaces, leaving the original context relatively undisturbed (figures 3.4 and 3.6; Buvit 2000, 2008; Buvit and Terry; Goebel et al. 2000; Razgilde'eva 2003).

STUDENOE 2: EARLY LATE GLACIAL (EARLY LATE UPPER PALEOLITHIC)

The Early Late Glacial occupation is found at Studenoe 2, situated on the higher 9–10 m terrace of the Chikoi River (see figure 3.4). This locus contains twelve Late Upper Paleolithic cultural layers (3, 4/1, 4/2, 4/3, 4/4, 4/5, 4/6, 5, 6, 7/1, 7/2, and 8) situated within sediments comprised of rapidly accruing sand and silt beds (Buvit 2008, 2000; Buvit et al. 2003). Based on charcoal and bone samples collected from dwellings and hearths, the oldest cultural layers at Studenoe 2 (4/5 through 8) formed between about 21,000–24,000 cal BP (18,000 and 21,000 ^{14}C BP; figure 3.4; Buvit 2008; Buvit et al. 2016). Cultural layers 4/4 (12,200±2600 BP AA-67843; Buvit 2008) through 3 most likely formed after 20,000 cal BP (17,000 ^{14}C BP). Dwelling features with central hearths, along with stone and bone tools and faunal remains, characterize most of these layers.

Within the Late Glacial aged layers, one stone-outlined dwelling was found in cultural layers 8, 5, and 4/5, with central hearths only in layers 5 and 4/5. Other cultural layers contained hearths and charcoal smears with artifacts and bone fragments (cultural layer 4/4), or no features and fewer than 10 artifacts (cultural layers 7/2, 7/1, 6, 4/6, 4/3, 4/2; Konstantinov 2001; Konstantinov et al. 2003).

In cultural layer 8, very few stone and bone tools were present with a possible dwelling feature on a gravel bar (Konstantinov et al. 2003), therefore it was not included in this study. A large, (7 × 10 m) partially disturbed, rock-outlined dwelling with three central hearths was uncovered in cultural layer 5 along with two charcoal smears, 908 artifacts, and 283 bone fragments (Konstantinov 2001). Unfortunately, this dwelling was also not included in our data because of the level of disturbance. Therefore, cultural layer 4/5 is the only layer represented in the Early LUP sample.

The large, rock-outlined, multi-hearth dwelling feature in cultural layer 4/5 formed during a brief time period of rapid alluvial sedimentation 21,600–21,800 cal years BP (18,600–18,800 ^{14}C years BP; figure 3.5; Buvit 2000, 2008; Buvit et al. 2003; Goebel et al. 2000; Konstantinov 2001; Kuzmin et al. 2004; Razgilde'eva 2003). Radiocarbon dates on charcoal are inconsistent at this particular site, displaying several reversals in all cultural layers. Therefore, we consider the three bottom dates on the profile (figure 3.4) extracted from animal bones to be the most reliable because these dates all range within two standard errors of each other. Also,

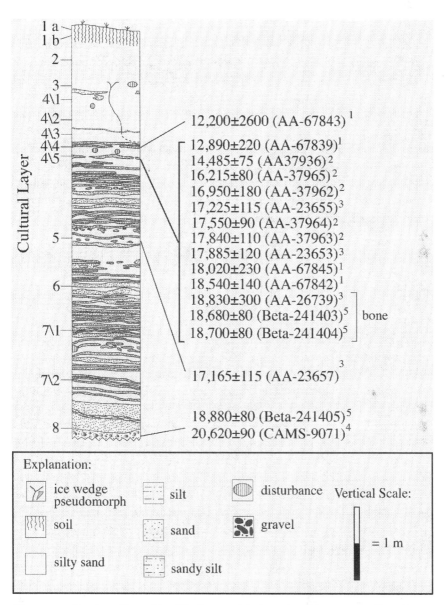

Figure 3.4. Stratigraphic profile of Studenoe 2 showing cultural layers and radiocarbon ages from Paleolithic layers (after Buvit et al. 2005). Radiocarbon age references: (1) Buvit 2008; (2) Konstantinov 2001; (3) Goebel et al. 2000; (4) Buvit et al. 2005; (5) Buvit et al. 2016.

radiocarbon ages from other sites in the region on animal bones do not show reversals like charcoal dates. Razgilde'eva (2003) concludes that the six central hearths within the dwelling were built at different times as the radiocarbon ages are not succinct and use is not uniform. This problem with the radiocarbon dates may be inherent with dating charcoal in the southern Transbaikal region. A. Konstantinov (2001) concludes that this is a single integrated dwelling based on the following observations: (1) the outer wall construction is identical around each individual hearth foci; (2) the outlining cobbles are continuous with no evidence of rebuilding or repositioning; (3) the extent of hearth fill is likely a function of not needing to maintain a fire in specific hearths during periods of occupation, not the result of dwelling abandonment. Furthermore, there is no evidence of micro-disturbances within the 2-cm stratified layers of alternating sand and silt (Buvit 2008).

The dwelling is outlined by 157 river cobbles (18.5 m by 5 m) with entrances (1 m) between hearths 1 and 2, 3 and 4, 4 and 5, and 5 and 6 (figure 3.5). Entrances were identified based on gaps in the outlining stones that also contained concentrations of cultural material extending up to 50 cm outside the structure (Konstantinov 2001). A. Konstantinov (2001) describes the possible construction of the dwelling as follows: Two forked poles were located at either end of the long axis of the structure, with several additional poles along the center of this axis. At least three poles were lashed together to form a single ridge-pole that was set on top of the foundation poles. Additional poles were leaned against this ridge-pole, forming smaller semi-conical units around two hearths. These four semi-conical units were unified into one large structure (Konstantinov 2001).

Artifacts (N = 1059) consisting of tools, microblades, microblade cores, flakes, blades, retouched flakes and blades, and 2,100 pieces of faunal remains were found concentrated around hearths and charcoal smears within the dwelling (Konstantinov 2001). Stone borers, micro-scrapers, micro-notches, points, chisels, burins, scrapers, choppers, and bone needles make up the tool inventory (Konstantinov 2001). Small ostrich shell and rhyolite beads, ochre, as well as quartzite river cobbles with polished edges were also found in the dwelling (Konstantinov 2001). The presence of microblades and micro-debitage (less than 2 cm in size) further indicate that disturbance of cultural materials within sites was minimal. Faunal remains were extremely fragmented, however a bear (*Ursus spelaeus*) tooth, noble deer (*Cervus elaphus*) teeth, roe deer (*Capreolus pygargus*), argali sheep (*Ovis ammon*) vertebrae, and ostrich eggshell (*Struthio asiaticus*), were identified as well as gazelle (*Procapra gutterosa*), steppe bison (*Bison priscus*), or Baikal Yak (*Bos baikalensis*) long bones (Konstantinov 1994; Konstantinov 2001). These species live in a wide range of habitats that were present in the region during this time period, including steppe grasslands, wooded areas, and mountain slopes (figure 3.2).

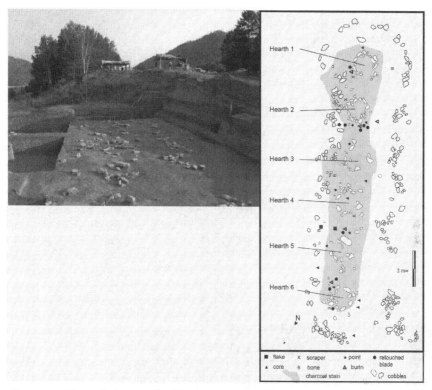

Figure 3.5. Map and photograph of Studenoe 2 cultural layer 4/5 showing dwelling, hearths and artifacts (after Buvit 2008; Konstantinov 2001).

STUDENOE 1: TERMINAL LATE GLACIAL
(TERMINAL LATE UPPER PALEOLITHIC)

Studenoe 1 is located on the lower 5–6 m terrace of the Chikoi River (figure 3.3). Terminal Late Glacial (Terminal Late Upper Paleolithic) cultural layers 14 through 19/4 are again situated within rapidly accruing, low-energy sand and silt layers of the Chikoi River (figure 3.6; Buvit et al. 2003; Buvit 2008). Radiocarbon ages from late Upper Paleolithic cultural layers date from 15,800–13,800 cal years BP (12,800–10,800 ^{14}C BP; figure 3.6; Buvit 2000; Konstantinov 1994; Konstantinov et al. 2003).

One or two stone-outlined dwellings, ranging in size from 1.7 × 2.6 m to 4.4 × 5.1 m (Konstantinov 2001), with 1–2 central hearths were discovered in cultural layers 19/4, 19/3, 18/2, 18/1, 17, and 16, along with stone and bone artifacts and bone fragments. Features in cultural layers 19/1, 15, and 14 include unlined hearths with stone and bone tools and bone fragments dispersed around them (Konstantinov 1994;

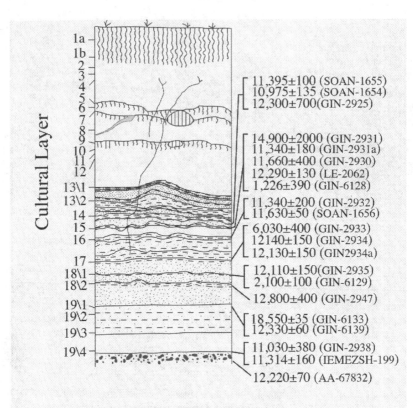

Cultural Layer

1a
1b
2
3 — 11,395±100 (SOAN-1655)
4 — 10,975±135 (SOAN-1654)
5 — 12,300±700 (GIN-2925)
6
7
8
9 — 14,900±2000 (GIN-2931)
10 — 11,340±180 (GIN-2931a)
11 — 11,660±400 (GIN-2930)
12 — 12,290±130 (LE-2062)
13\1 — 1,226±390 (GIN-6128)
13\2
14 — 11,340±200 (GIN-2932)
—— 11,630±50 (SOAN-1656)
15 — 6,030±400 (GIN-2933)
16 — 12140±150 (GIN-2934)
—— 12,130±150 (GIN2934a)
17
18\1 — 12,110±150 (GIN-2935)
18\2 — 2,100±100 (GIN-6129)
—— 12,800±400 (GIN-2947)
19\1
19\2 — 18,550±35 (GIN-6133)
19\3 — 12,330±60 (GIN-6139)
19\4 — 11,030±380 (GIN-2938)
—— 11,314±160 (IEMEZSH-199)
—— 12,220±70 (AA-67832)

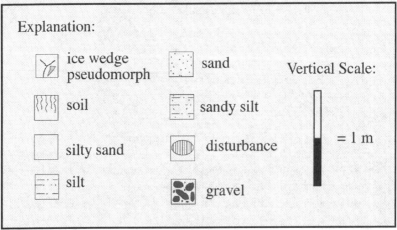

Explanation:

ice wedge pseudomorph

soil

silty sand

silt

sand

sandy silt

disturbance

gravel

Vertical Scale: = 1 m

Figure 3.6. Stratigraphic profile of Studenoe 1 showing cultural, layers and radiocarbon ages from Paleolithic layers (after Buvit 2000). Radiocarbon ages from Konstantinov 1994.

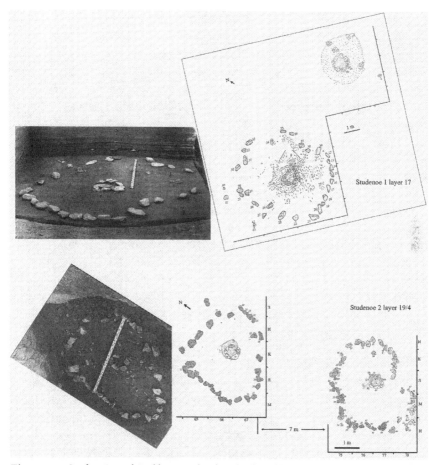

Figure 3.7. Studenoe 1 cultural layer 17 (top) and cultural layer 19/4 (bottom) showing dwellings (large cobbles or dashed lines), hearths (large cobbles and stipples) and artifacts (triangles, vertical lines, Xs, Hs, and Zs) (after Konstantinov 2001).

Konstantinov 2001; Konstantinov et al. 2003), thought to represent the remains of disturbed dwellings. Stone artifacts include tools, microblades, microblade cores, flakes, blades, and retouched flakes and blades, with incised bone and antler points and knives (Konstantinov 1994; Konstantinov 2001; Konstantinov et al. 2003). Again, the presence of microblades and micro-debitage (less than 2 cm in size) further indicates that disturbance of cultural materials within sites was minimal. Dwellings were built on top of the remains of older constructions, typically with 10 cm of sterile sediment between them (Konstantinov 2001). Dwelling construction includes a circular outline of river cobbles, with a roughly 1 m entrance gap that typically contained cultural material extending up to roughly 0.5 m outside of the feature (figure 3.7). A. Konstantinov (2001) interprets these features as conical in shape with a center pole onto which lateral leaning poles were lashed. Usually, one stone-outlined hearth was placed in the dwelling center.

This study only includes layers 19/4 and 17 because they exhibit the best preservation with clearly demarcated, stone-outlined dwellings and hearths. Two stone-outlined dwellings, each with one hearth, were found in cultural layer 19/4 (figure 3.7). Scrapers, a borer, flakes, bone fragments, and pieces of ochre were scattered around the hearths (Konstantinov 1994; Konstantinov 2001). Fauna recovered from cultural layer 19/4 include Baikal Yak (*Bos baikalensis*) and steppe bison (*Bison priscus*; figure 3.2; Konstantinov 1994; Konstantinov 2001).

In cultural layer 17 two dwellings were uncovered, each with one stone-outlined hearth, a charcoal smear, and bone and stone tools inside and around the hearths (figure 3.7; Konstantinov 1994). More than 1,600 artifacts were recovered, including microblade cores, scrapers, burins, microblades, blades, flakes, and choppers, a bone awl and needle, and antler needles and worked pieces (Konstantinov 1994; Konstantinov 2001). Fauna recovered from cultural layer 17 included noble deer (*Cervus elaphus*) and saiga antelope (*Saiga tatarica*; figure 3.2; Konstantinov 1994).

ORGANIZATION OF LIVING SPACE: COMPARISONS OF EARLY AND TERMINAL LATE GLACIAL OCCUPATIONS

Variability of Dwelling and Living Area Construction and Use

Several comparisons allow a general assessment of variability in the manner in which foragers at the Studenoe site constructed and used both their built environment and indoor and outdoor spaces. We focus on basic comparisons, including general dimensions of dwelling features and occupational surfaces, quantity and spatial relationships between features, and comparisons of cultural material and tool assemblages based on find locations.

DWELLING AND OCCUPATIONAL SURFACE DIMENSIONS

Comparisons of dwellings and occupational surfaces are presented in table 3.1. Obviously, the Early Late Glacial (Early Late Upper Paleolithic) layer contained only one dwelling, while Terminal Late Glacial Layers (Terminal Late Upper Paleolithic) had two. This is a pattern we see in other Early and Terminal Late Upper Paleolithic layers at both loci at Studenoe (Konstantinov 2001). Dwelling size was measured based on either a cobble outline or the combination of cobbles and an abrupt boundary of cultural material density. If we accept the interpretation that Studenoe 2 cultural layer 4/5 was a single occupation, then it is clear that this one Early Late Glacial

TABLE 3.1. Dwelling size data comparing Early and Terminal Late Glacial occupations from the Studenoe Site (Konstantinov 2001)

Time	Cultural Layer	Dwelling N	Dwelling Area m²	Occupational Area m²	Ratio of Dwelling to Occupational Area
Terminal Late Glacial	Studenoe 1 19/4	2	11.52 15.91	90	3.28
	Studenoe I 17	2	8.68 22.44	128	4.11
Terminal Late Glacial mean			14.6	109	
Early Late Glacial	Studenoe 2 4/5	1	92.5	101	1.09
			Early LUP vs. Late LUP t = 4.5101; df = 2; p < 0.001	Early LUP vs. Late LUP t = 1.96; df = 2; p > 0.05	

dwelling is significantly larger, roughly six times larger, than the Terminal Late Glacial dwellings (table 3.1). However, in terms of occupational surfaces—the total surface area over which cultural material was found at the site—Early and Terminal Late Glacial layers are similar, ranging from 101–109 m² (table 3.1). The manner in which this occupational surface was used for interior and exterior living was quite different, however. Habitation of dwellings was restricted to one large structure with less outdoor occupational space, in terms of the ratio between the two, in the Early Late Glacial. However, this space was divided into two smaller isolated dwellings with more outdoor space during the Terminal Late Glacial (table 3.1).

HEARTH QUANTITY, LOCATION, AREA, AND FILL DEPTH

Within the Early Late Glacial dwelling, six relatively large hearths were closely situated to each other (table 3.2). Mean distances between hearths are significantly less than those between Terminal Late Glacial hearths (table 3.2). These hearths are also significantly larger, more than twice as large, as Terminal Late Glacial hearths (table 3.2). Terminal Late Glacial hearths, on the other hand, are significantly smaller and spaced far apart, separated by an average of 6 m, and found both within and outside of dwellings (table 3.2). Assuming depositional rates were similar, Early Late Glacial hearths may also have been utilized longer or more often than those found within Terminal Late Glacial layers. Mean hearth fill depths are significantly deeper, nearly

TABLE 3.2. Hearth data comparing Early and Terminal Late Glacial occupations from the Studenoe Site (Konstantinov 2001)

Time	Cultural Layer	Hearth within Dwelling N	Hearth area m²	Hearth fill cm	Distance Between Hearths m
Terminal Late Glacial	Studenoe 1 19/4	2	0.4225	2	8
			0.25	1	
	Studenoe 1 17	2	1	2	4
			0.87	0.8	
Terminal Late Glacial mean			0.6	1.6	6
Early Late Glacial	Studenoe 2 4/5	6	2.32	3	2
			1.89	5	1.5
			1.68	2	1
			2.1	3	1
			1.89	2	1.5
			1.43	3	
Early Late Glacial mean			1.9	3	1.4
			t = 5.88; df = 8; p < 0.001	t = 2.526; df = 8; p < 0.001	t = 5.28; df = 8; p < 0.001

twice as thick, in the Early Late Glacial than the Terminal Late Glacial (table 3.2). This is provisional data, however, that needs more investigation. In summary, hearth data may indicate that possibly larger groups with less isolated, interior dwelling space, or less defined from other members, occupied the Early Late Glacial dwelling. Relatively large, multiple hearths may have been more intensively used or reused, while smaller groups with clearly demarcated boundaries between interior dwelling spaces occupied each Terminal Late Glacial dwelling. Smaller hearths were used less intensively or for a shorter time period.

INTERIOR VS. EXTERIOR ACTIVITIES
CULTURAL MATERIAL AND FAUNAL REMAINS

Although geomorphic depositional processes indicate that low-energy flood-ing inundated site surfaces post-habitation, there remains a chance that cultural material that might have been left on surfaces outside of stone-outlined dwellings could have been impacted to a greater degree than those protected by the stones encircling interior dwelling material. Nevertheless, we feel comparisons of interior and exterior remains are reliable based on the presence of microblades and micro-debitage in both contexts.

Interior activities were emphasized during both time periods. The majority of cultural material (92%) found in the Early Late Glacial is confined to the dwelling interior (Konstantinov 2001). Again, this material consists of microblade technology, various tools made on large blades and flakes including scrapers, projectile points, notches, burins, chisels, gravers, wedges, choppers, retouched flakes and blades, bone tools, including a carved handle and needles, ostrich egg shell and rhyolite beads, and ochre.

Faunal remains from the Early Late Glacial were also concentrated within the interior of the dwelling, but were highly fragmented or represented by teeth. The few large bones found were located outside of the dwelling (Konstantinov 2001). This may indicate the late stages of processing and/or consuming of animal bones within the structure, or some other unidentified taphonomic process. Faunal remains include bear (*Ursus spelaeus*), noble deer (*Cervus elaphus*), roe deer (*Capreolus pygargus*), argali sheep (*Ovis ammon*), ostrich eggshell (*Struthio asiaticus*), gazelle (*Procapra gutterosa*), steppe bison (*Bison priscus*), and Baikal Yak (*Bos baikalensis*) (Konstantinov 1994; Konstantinov 2001). These fauna are quite diverse and represent several environmental habitats (figure 3.2).

In the Terminal Late Glacial layers, the majority of finds (72%) were concentrated inside dwellings (Konstantinov 2001); however, a higher percentage was located outside than in the Early Late Glacial. Similar to Studenoe 2, artifacts include microblade technology with associated incised bone and antler points and knives, scrapers, chisels, gravers, wedges, choppers, retouched flakes and blades, bone and antler tools, including mauls, needles and various worked pieces, and ochre.

Again, most faunal remains from both Terminal Late Glacial layers were found inside the dwellings, but were highly fragmented. Fauna include species that inhabit open forest and steppe environments like those of the Early Late Glacial (figure 3.2). However, only two types were exploited during the same occupation, including Baikal Yak (*Bos baikalensis*) and steppe bison (*Bison priscus*) in cultural layers 19/4 and noble deer (*Cervus elaphus*) and saiga antelope (*Saiga tatarica*) in cultural layer 17 (Konstantinov 2001; figure 3.2). This may be an indication of either shorter duration of site occupation during the Terminal Late Glacial, or fewer people occupying the site. This is a pattern found in other Terminal Late Glacial occupational layers not included in this study, and at Terminal Late Glacial layers at the Ust' Menza site upriver from Studenoe.

INTERIOR/EXTERIOR ACTIVITIES COMPARING
STONE TOOL ASSEMBLAGES

Finally, comparisons of stone tools found inside and outside of dwellings provide information about types of activities carried out in each space. Not surprisingly, the majority of stone tools were found in interior spaces of dwellings regardless of time period (table 3.3). The exception includes only five presumably woodworking tools, consisting of notches in the Early Late Glacial, and gouges and a wedge during the Terminal Late Glacial. These were the only tools found outside of dwellings; however, numerous flakes or microblades were also found outside of dwellings (table 3.3). Woodworking and flintknapping activities may have taken place outdoors regardless of time period. All other activities may have been confined mostly to indoor spaces (table 3.3).

REORGANIZATION OF SOCIAL STRUCTURE:
GROUP AGGREGATION AND DISPERSAL

Although our data indicate that interior dwelling space served as the focal point for activities throughout the Late Glacial and those activities were similar, the construction of that space changed over time.

Early Late Glacial settlements may have been inhabited by larger, communal, or extended families who shared more sizable indoor habitational space but occupied a more restricted outdoor area. Assuming that each hearth was occupied by a nuclear family based on ethnographic data (Gould and Yellen 1987; Yellen 1977), potentially up to six nuclear families could have shared the dwelling at one time. However, based on evidence that one hearth may have been vacant at least part of the time, this number could be only five. This estimate, however, might be too high. Nuclear families may have maintained semi-autonomous hearth areas that were united under a single structural ceiling, indicating that ties outside of the nuclear family itself may have been intimate enough to integrate such close domestic arrangements with more distant relations. Thus, space was delineated by areas around nuclear family hearths as more intimate, and outside of this area as more distant. Hearth fill data indicates it is possible the dwelling was occupied over a fairly long time period, exhibiting either a longer habitation duration or reoccupation. A wide array of exploited game may be indicative of either this long duration, reoccupation, or availability of certain game during site occupation. Thus, aggregation of extended families could have been seasonally driven as they are for the Ju'hoansi during the dry season (Yellen 1977). Ethnographic studies of the Ju'hoansi (Yellen 1977) have also shown these aggregation periods are times of ritual ceremonies, although we

TABLE 3.3. Find location (interior/exterior) of lithic artifacts comparing Early (Studenoe 2 cultural layer 4/5) and Terminal Late Glacial (Studenoe 1 cultural layers 19/4 and 17) occupations from the Studenoe Site (Konstantinov 2001; Terry 2010)

	Terminal Late Glacial			Early Late Glacial		
	EXTERIOR	INTERIOR		EXTERIOR	INTERIOR	
cores	0	7	interior	0	7	interior
scrapers	1	8	interior	0	7	interior
burins	0	4	interior	0	5	interior
chisel/gouge	2	0	exterior	0	5	interior
borer/graver	0	0		0	6	interior
chopper	0	5	interior			
notch (spokeshave)	0	0		3	0	exterior
projectile point	0	0		0	3	interior
retouched flakes	0	3	interior	0	25	interior
microwedge	1	0	exterior			
retouched microblades	0	0		0	2	interior
retouched blades and fragments	0	0		0	11	interior
microblades and fragments	0	104	interior	100	143	both
blades and blade fragments	0	5	interior	0	40	interior
flakes and flake fragments	702	833	both	0	822	interior
Total N Lithic Artifacts	706	969	1675	103	1076	1179
	42%	58%		9%	91%	
Total N Lithic Tools	5	27		3	60	
	16%	84%		5%	95%	

have not presented any compelling evidence from Studenoe 2 to support this idea at the site. These attributes are only found during the Early Late Glacial at Studenoe 2 in cultural layer 4/5, but the fairly large dwelling (70 m²) with three central hearths in cultural layer 5 may be indicative of this type of pattern.

By the Terminal Late Glacial, habitational spaces might have been constructed around smaller family units, possibly nuclear organization, that maintained isolated dwelling habitational spaces. Several cultural layers at Studenoe 1 exhibited one or two small dwellings with one central hearth. Again, assuming that each nuclear family occupies one hearth, each dwelling only accommodated one nuclear family. Indoor dwelling area was more restricted, but the larger outdoor living area possibly accommodated interactions of more distant relations. Thus, there were more barriers, walls and open air between intimate spaces and more public space between families who occupied the camp. Ethnographic data suggests these nuclear families could have been close or distant blood or marriage relatives, or maintained a relationship based on friendship (Yellen 1977). There is no evidence here of larger dwellings with multiple hearths like Studenoe 2. As such, there is no evidence of large group aggregation during the Terminal Late Glacial.

Although there is evidence of a reorganization between the Early and Terminal Late Glacial occupations in terms of social structure and organization of habitational space, there is not a clear shift in stone tool technologies or economic activities that were focused around hunting large and small steppe- and forest-dwelling animal species. Climatic and environmental differences before and after the LGM may be driving the patterns at Studenoe. Foragers may have needed to aggregate either seasonally or permanently during the extremely cold and dry environments of the 23,000–20,000 cal years BP Early Late Glacial occupations at Studenoe 2. They may have needed to opportunistically exploit a wide array of game available in the area, or provide more opportunities to share resources. By the end of the LGM after 17,000 cal years BP, climates began warming and the constraints of extreme cold and scarce resources may have lifted to some degree. Faunal communities may also have reorganized themselves either seasonally or geographically on the landscape. Communities of extended families may have begun the seasonal or permanent disaggregation of extended families into small, more isolated nuclear family units to target specific types of game at certain times.

Although these are fairly clear patterns in our data, they elicit further questions and more detailed analyses. Faunal seasonality data and stone tool economy comparisons will provide more details to hopefully expose more subtle patterns related to length and seasonality of occupation and levels of campsite mobility. Finally, these studies should extend to the Ust' Menza site, with similar occupational time periods, preservation, and site structure, to provide more evidence of the patterns found at Studenoe.

REFERENCES

Binford, L. 1980. "Willow Smoke and Dog's Tails: Hunter-Gatherer Settlement Systems and Archaeological Site Formation." *American Antiquity* 45: 4–20.

Binford, L. 1983. *In Pursuit of the Past: Decoding the Archaeological Record.* London: Thames and Hudson.

Blades, B. 1999. "Aurignacian Lithic Economy and Early Modern Human Mobility: New Perspectives from Classic Sites in the Vézère Valley of France." *Journal of Human Evolution* 37: 91–120.

Buvit, I. 2000. "The Geoarchaeology and Archaeology of Studon'oye." Master's thesis, Texas A&M University, College Station.

Buvit, I. 2008. "Geoarchaeological Investigations in the Southwestern Transbaikal Region, Russia." PhD dissertation, Washington State University, Pullman.

Buvit, I., M. Waters, M. V. Konstantinov, and A. V. Konstantinov. 2003. "Geoarchaeological Investigations at Studenoe, an Upper Paleolithic Site in Siberia." *Geoarchaeology* 18: 649–673.

Buvit, I., and K. Terry. 2011. "Current Topics in Siberian Paleolithic Prehistory: Land Use, Mobility, and Technological Organization in the Transbaiakal." In *Handaxes in the Imjin Basin: Diversity and Variability in the East Asian Paleolithic*, edited by Seonbok Yi, 219–254. Seoul: Seoul National University Press.

Buvit, I., K. Terry, and M. V. Konstantinov. 2016. "Radiocarbon Dates, Microblades and Late Pleistocene Human Migrations in the Transbaikal, Russia and the Paleo-Sakhalin-Hokkaido-Kuril Peninsula." *Quaternary International* 425: 100–119.

Chlachula, J. 2001a. "Pleistocene Climate Change, Natural Environments and Palaeolithic Occupation of the Upper Yenisei Area, South-Central Siberia." *Quaternary International* 80–81: 101–130.

Chlachula, J. 2001b "Pleistocene Climate Change, Natural Environments and Palaeolithic Occupation of the Angara-Baikal Area, East Central Siberia." *Quaternary International* 80–81: 69–92.

Frenzel, B., H. Beug, K. Brunnacker, D. Busche, P. Frankenberg, P. Fritz, M. Geyh, H. Hagedorn, J. Hovermann, A. Kessler, W. Konigswald, K. Krumsiek, W. Lauer, H. Mensching, H. Moser, K. Munnich, Chr. Sonntag, and R. Vinken. 1992a. "Climates during the Last Interglacial." In *Atlas of Paleoclimates and Paleoenvironments of the Northern Hemisphere: Late Pleistocene-Holocene*, edited by B. Frenzel, M. Pecsi, and A. Velichko, 90–92. Budapest: Geographical Research Institute, Hungarian Academy of Sciences.

Frenzel, B., H. Beug, K. Brunnacker, D. Busche, P. Frankenberg, P. Fritz, M. Geyh, H. Hagedorn, J. Hovermann, A. Kessler, W. Konigswald, K. Krumsiek, W. Lauer, H. Mensching, H. Moser, K. Munnich, Chr. Sonntag, and R. Vinken. 1992b. "Climates during the Last Glacial Maximum." In *Atlas of Paleoclimates and Paleoenvironments of the Northern Hemisphere: Late Pleistocene-Holocene*, edited by B. Frenzel, M. Pecsi, and A. Velichko, 97–100. Budapest: Geographical Research Institute, Hungarian Academy of Sciences.

Gavrilov, K., E. V. Voskresenskaya, E. N. Maschenko, and K. Douka. 2015. "East Gravettian Khotylevo 2 Site: Stratigraphy, Archeozoology, and Spatial Organization of the Cultural Layer at the Newly Explored Area of the Site." *Quaternary International* 359–369: 335–346.

Goebel, T. 1999. "Pleistocene Human Colonization of Siberia and Peopling of the Americas: An Ecological Approach." *Evolutionary Anthropology* 8 (6): 208–227.

Goebel, T., M. Waters, I. Buvit, M. Konstantinov, and A. Konstantinov. 2000. "Studenoe-2 and the Origins of Microblade Technologies in the Transbaikal, Siberia." *Antiquity* 74: 567–575.

Gould, R. A., and J. Yellen. 1987. "Man the Hunted: Determinants of Household Spacing in Desert and Tropical Foraging Societies." *Journal of Anthropological Archaeology* 6 (1): 77–103.

Iakovleva, L. 2015. "The Architecture of Mammoth Bone Circular Dwellings of the Upper Palaeolithic Settlements in Central and Eastern Europe and Their Socio-Symbolic Meanings." *Quaternary International* 359–360: 324–334.

Kind, N. V. 1974. "Geochronology of the Late Anthropogene from Isotope Data." Trudy 257, Nauka, Moscow (in Russian).

Klimanov, V. 1997. "Late Glacial Climate in Northern Eurasia: The Last Climatic Cycle." *Quaternary International* 41/42: 141–152.

Konstantinov, A. V. 2001. *Ancient Dwellings of the Transbaikal*. Nauka, Novosibirsk, Russia (in Russian).

Konstantinov, M. 1994. *The Stone Age of the Eastern Part of Baikal Asia*. Chita, Russia: Chita State Pedagogical Institute (in Russian).

Konstantinov, Mikhail V., Aleksander V. Konstantinov, Sergei G. Vasiliev, Larisa V. Ekimova, and Irina I. Razgil'deeva. 2003. *Under Protection of the Great Shaman*. Chita, Russia: Chita State Pedagogical University and Chita Institute of Natural Resources (in Russian).

Kuzmin, Y., A. J. T. Jull, and I. Razgil'deeva. 2004. "Chronology of the Upper-Paleolithic Site Studenoe 2 (Transbaikal, Siberia): Case Study of the Multi-Hearth Dwelling in Horizon 4/5." *Current Research in the Pleistocene* 21: 3–5.

Lbova, L. 2000. *Paleolithic of the Northern Zone of the Western Transbaikal* (in Russian). Ulan-Ude: Publication of the Buryat Science Center.

Maloletko, A. 1998. "The Quaternary Palaeogeography of North Asia." In *The Paleolithic of Siberia: New Discoveries and Interpretations*, edited by A. P. Derevianko, D. B. Shimkin and W. R. Powers, 14–22. Urbana: University of Illinois Press.

Mix, A., E. Bard, and R. Schneider. 2001. "Environmental Processes of the Ice Age: Land, Oceans, Glaciers (EPILOG)." *Quaternary Science Reviews* 20: 627–657.

Nadel, E., and E. Werker. 1999. "The Oldest Ever Brush Hut Plant Remains from Ohalo II, Jordan Valley, Israel (19,000 BP)." *Nature* 73 (842): 755–764.

Razgil'deeva, I. 2003. "Planigraphs of the Paleolithic Dwellings of the Studenoe Archaeological Complex (Western Transbaikal)." Unpublished PhD dissertation in Archaeology, Zabaikal State Pedagogica University, Chita, Russia (in Russian).

Soffer, O., and N. D. Preslov. 1993. *From Kostenki to Clovis. Upper Paleolithic-Palaeoindian Adaptations*. New York: Plenum Press.

Tarasov, P., O. Peyron, J. Guiot, S. Brewer, V. Bolkova, L. Bezusko, N. Dorofeyuk, E. Kvavadze, I. Osipova, and N. Panova. 1999. "Last Glacial Maximum Climate of the former Soviet Union and Mongolia Reconstructed from Pollen and Plant Macrofossil Data." *Climate Dynamics* 15: 227–240.

Terry, K. 2010. "Extreme Measures: Upper Paleolithic Raw Material Provisioning Strategies and Settlement of the Transbaikal Region, Siberia." PhD dissertation, Washington State University.

Velichko, A. 1984. "Introduction." In *Late Quaternary Environments of the Soviet Union*, edited by A. Velichko, xxiii–xxvii. Minneapolis: University of Minnesota Press.

Vershchagin, N., and I. Kuz'mina. 1984. "Late Pleistocene Mammal Fauna of Siberia." In *Late Quaternary Environments of the Soviet Union*, edited by A. Velichko, 219–226. Minneapolis: University of Minnesota Press.

Yellen, J. 1977. *Archaeological Approaches to the Present: Models for Reconstructing the Past*. New York: Academic Press.

4

Understanding Space at Owl Ridge, Central Alaska

Identifying Activities and Camp Use

NEIL N. PUCKETT AND KELLY E. GRAF

As the studies in this volume demonstrate, spatial analysis is a powerful tool for researching and interpreting human behavior at the site level. Such work allows archaeologists to pinpoint activity areas, identify associated artifacts, interpret past behavior, study economic and ecological approaches, and understand factors impacting artifact deposition (Bamforth and Becker 2007; Keeler 2007; Kintigh 1990; Krasinski and Yesner 2008; Marean and Bertino 1994; Lancelotti et al. 2017; Surovell and Waguespack 2007; Taylor et al. 2017). To successfully analyze archaeological sites, researchers rely on the preserved record and data collected during excavation. On many sites, simple spatial relationships are easily identified during field work and observed as a result of visual pattern recognition and relationships between artifacts and features (e.g., Krasinski and Yesner 2008; Surovell and Waguespack 2007). However, not all sites provide such clear contextual clues. Even when artifact associations are apparent, researchers must be careful that these reflect behavioral rather than taphonomic processes (see Huckell et al., chapter 7; Schiffer 1996).

The Owl Ridge site in central Alaska's Teklanika river valley is an example where spatial artifact distribution does not present obvious patterns or behavioral explanations. Fortunately, by combining a suite of spatial statistics, interpretations about the artifact assemblage can move beyond classification, and questions about behavior and activities at Owl Ridge can be addressed. In this chapter, we build on past assemblage studies by applying spatial statistics to test the hypothesized presence of use areas. We delve further into the artifact assemblage's provenience data to

https://doi.org/10.5876/9781646422265.c004

determine if statistically significant spatial relationships exist within or between particular tool classes and materials. We also preliminarily investigate raw materials in the context of spatial relationships between tool classes. The results demonstrate different behaviors for each of the three archaeological components. We argue that the way inhabitants used the site changed through time, suggesting inhabitants had unique approaches to the landscape that were associated with distinct paleoenvironmental conditions, supporting Gore and Graf (2018). Owl Ridge is an example of a place persistently used by humans during the late Pleistocene.

CONTEXTUALIZING OWL RIDGE

Late Pleistocene Paleoenvironments of Central Alaska

The terminal Pleistocene intervals—Older Dryas, Allerød, Younger Dryas, and Holocene Thermal Maximum—encompass the periods when people camped at Owl Ridge and inhabited central Alaska (Bigelow and Edwards 2001; Bigelow and Powers 2001; Graf and Bigelow 2011; Kaufman et al. 2004; Kokorowski et al. 2008).

Late glacial environments prior to 14,000 cal BP generally consisted of an herb-tundra biome dominated by grasses, sedges, and *Artemisia* sp. (Anderson et al. 2004; Bigelow and Powers 2001). Mammoth, horse, bison, wapiti, and moose roamed this open landscape along with smaller mammals (Guthrie 2017, 2006; Meiri et al. 2014). Warming, increased humidity, and rising lake levels during the Allerød, around 14,000–13,000 cal BP, allowed birch and willow to spread into the region, forming a shrub-tundra landscape (Anderson et al. 2004; Bigelow and Powers 2001; Brubaker et al. 2005). Mammoth and horse went extinct by 13,500 cal BP, but grazers who also browse and browsers (e.g., bison, wapiti, and moose) continued to occupy the region (Guthrie 2006). Waterfowl in the Broken Mammoth faunal assemblage indicate these species became more common on the landscape at this time (Yesner 2007).

During the Younger Dryas interval (12,800–11,700 cal BP), dryer and colder conditions, especially north of the Alaska Range, dominated the interior. A biome shift brought increases in *Artemesia* sp., lower lake levels, and rapid deposition of eolian sands and silts (Abbott et al. 2000; Bigelow and Edwards 2001; Bigelow and Powers 2001; Bigelow et al. 1990; Hu et al. 1993). Bison and wapiti continue throughout the Younger Dryas, but there is a drop in moose populations combined with the appearance of caribou in the archaeological record (Bowers and Reuther 2008; Guthrie 2006; Yesner 2001, 2007). By 11,000 cal BP, the Holocene Thermal Maximum resulted in the expansion of *Populus* from its earlier scarce presence (Anderson and Brubaker 1994). Conversely, lake levels continued to be low, indicating a warm but relatively dry climate. After 10,000 cal BP an environmental shift allowed *Picea* to spread into central Alaska and lake levels to increase. This shift resulted in warmer, wetter conditions and the emergence of boreal forests similar to present-day Alaska (Abbot et al. 2000; Barber and Finney 2000; Bigelow and Powers 2001; Lloyd et al. 2006). Wapiti went extinct during this time, but bison, moose, and caribou remain in the record (Guthrie 2006).

THE LATE PLEISTOCENE ARCHAEOLOGY OF CENTRAL ALASKA

While potential evidence exists for an earlier human presence in eastern Beringia (Bourgeon et al. 2017; Moreno-Mayar et al. 2018; Vachula et al. 2018), the earliest unequivocal evidence for humans comes from the Swan Point site. It is located in the Tanana valley, ~100 km southeast of Fairbanks, Alaska, and dates to 14,100 calendar years before present (cal BP). Its lowest component (CZ4b) contains wedge-shaped microblade cores and microblades similar to those found at eastern Siberian late Upper Paleolithic sites (Gómez Coutouly 2011, 2012; Holmes 2011). People continued to live in central Alaska as technologies changed. For nearly 1000 years following the earliest occupation at Swan Point, site assemblages represent an industry referred to by Powers and Hoffecker (1989) as the Nenana techno-complex. Its toolkit contains end scrapers, side scrapers, gravers, wedges, retouched flakes and blades, cobble tools, bifaces, and diagnostic Chindadn-type, teardrop-shaped and triangular, bifacial points (Goebel 2011; Goebel et al. 1991; Gore and Graf 2018; Graf and Goebel 2009; Graf and Bigelow 2011; Graf et al. 2015; Hoffecker 2001; Hoffecker et al. 1993; Powers and Hoffecker 1989; Yesner 1996, 2001; Younie and Gillispie 2016).

A second techno-complex in central Alaska, dating from 12,500 to at least 10,000 cal BP is the Denali complex (West 1967). These assemblages are associated with lanceolate and concave-based bifacial points, microblade cores, microblades, burins, side scrapers, and retouched flakes (Goebel and Bigelow 1996; Graf and Bigelow 2011; Graf et al. 2015; Pearson 1999; Powers et al. 2017). While some unifacial tool types, such as side scrapers and retouched flakes, are found in both Nenana and Denali techno-complexes, only Denali complex assemblages contain microblades, burins, and lanceolate point technologies. Nenana complex assemblages contain diagnostic Chindadn points and unifacial tools manufactured on blades (Goebel et al. 1991). Despite claims that the CZ3b assemblage at Swan Point contains both Chindadn-type points and microblades (Holmes 2001, 2011), Hirasawa and Holmes (2017) report that microblade technology cannot confidently be associated with CZ3b. Additionally, the original association between microblade technology and Chindadn points reported at Healy Lake Village was found to be the result of mixing from post-depositional processes and a coarse-grained excavation technique (Erlandson et al. 1991).

Researchers debate the behavioral adaptations resulting from this terminal Pleistocene lithic variability in eastern Beringia (Goebel and Buvit 2011). Some suggest the different techno-complexes represent different human populations (Hoffecker and Elias 2007), while others consider each to represent a unique human response to rapid climate and biome change, especially given the techno-complexes are chronologically patterned (Graf and Bigelow 2011). This pattern is also seen in western Beringia (Goebel et al. 2003, 2010; Pitulko 2011; Pitulko et al. 2017). At least three sites in the Nenana valley (Owl Ridge, Dry Creek, and Moose Creek) contain both techno-complexes with clear spatial and temporal separation between a stratigraphically lower and older Nenana component and stratigraphically higher and younger Denali components (Gore and Graf 2018; Graf and Bigelow 2011; Graf et al. 2015; Pearson 1999; Powers et al. 2017). Similarly, at Swan Point the earliest component is associated with the pre-Allerød herb tundra, Nenana tool-kits date to the Allerød warming event, and the latter half of the Younger Dryas stage is associated with the appearance of the Denali complex (Graf and Bigelow 2011). In contrast, some argue the Nenana and Denali complexes are part of a single, 4,000-year-long Beringian Tradition (Holmes 2001, 2011; Potter et al. 2014) based on the early presence of microblades at Swan Point and persistence of Chindadn points through ~11,250 cal BP at two sites in the Tanana valley (Broken Mammoth and Swan Point) (Potter et al. 2014). Rather than reflecting adaptations to major paleoenvironmental shifts during the late Pleistocene, this position posits that different technological assemblages in the region reflect situational adaptations. Thus, the lithic variability observed represents different choices made by a single population when facing varying conditions, such as seasonal change, proximity to toolstone, upland/lowland resources extraction, or game choice (e.g., Dall sheep vs. wapiti) (Gal 2002; Holmes 2001; Potter 2005; Wygal 2009, 2011).

Challenges exist for each of the above models attempting to explain the Late Pleistocene archaeological complexes in central Alaska. The single tradition model lacks compelling evidence that both Nenana and Denali complexes are found together in the same spatio-temporal context. If they are indeed part of the same overall adaptive strategy used by a single group, then we expect to find them together at some sites as part of the "Beringian Tradition" system. For example, at a residential site we expect to find components of both Nenana and Denali tool-kits in the same component, same stratum, or same geoarchaeological context; however, we have yet to observe this (Goebel 2011). The primary challenge to the multi-tradition/multi-population model has been the persistence of possible Chindadn points in the Tanana valley, while the Denali industry is present in other regions of central Alaska (Potter et al. 2014:94). Perhaps, however, these points represent continuation of the technological-organization strategy used during the previous interval, because a similar faunal composition continued in this lowland setting until boreal forests emerged (Graf and Bigelow 2011). Without details of the rest of the lithic industry from these late Chindadn sites, we cannot rule out the explanation that their continued presence results from human response to resource distributions. We also cannot rule out the possibility that these components represent palimpsests or even cases of early artifacts being curated by later populations, though the latter seems unlikely given that microblade technology is not clearly present alongside the Chindadn points.

We argue the debate between these two models can be informed by spatial statistics. If different, stratigraphically-separated components at the same site illustrate unique artifact distribution patterns and therefore unique activity areas, then this provides evidence for shifts in behavioral adaptations through time. If populations varied their behaviors at a given site over time, their changes should result in alterations to spatial distribution of materials and artifacts at that location. Below, we demonstrate changes in landscape use between the three different technological components at the Owl Ridge site (see Gore and Graf 2018) by showing statistically significant spatial differences between tools and toolstone material distributions over time.

Climatic shifts provide a foundation from which spatial distributions at Owl Ridge may be interpreted. If site use and spatial patterning remain the same despite clear shifts in the climate, it would confirm the null hypothesis and refute the climatic-adaptive model explaining central Alaskan technological complexes. If, however, there are unique spatial relationships and artifact distributions across the site's different temporal components *and* these differences correlate with paleoenvironmental changes, then the null hypothesis can be rejected. In this case the paleoenvironmental model for central Alaskan archaeological variability is maintained. We will use our results to develop interpretations for the spatial patterns observed and what they represent with respect to technology, culture, and paleoecological adaptations at Owl Ridge.

SPATIAL STATISTICAL STUDIES IN LATE PLEISTOCENE ALASKA

Few publications focus on intrasite spatial statistics at open-air Paleoindian sites in Alaska. At Dry Creek, Thorson (2006) studied components 1 and 2 to determine if they had overlapping spatial distributions. He argued that the components were mixed with poor spatial integrity, contradicting Hoffecker's (2017) reports on the site. Additional excavations by a Texas A&M University team in 2011 confirmed Hoffecker's initial reports of spatial integrity across the site and within each component, refuting Thorson's (2006) conclusions (Graf et al. 2015). Refit studies at the Walker Road site in central Alaska indicate that the three artifact concentrations from the Nenana component are spatially discrete, with almost all refits isolated within each individual concentration (Higgs 1992). Since some refits did cross concentrations, it appears likely the concentrations represented a contemporaneous occupation, but Higgs (1992) notes seasonal occupations could be possible. Studies at the Mesa site in northern Alaska used the combination of refit studies, raw material analysis, and spatial analysis to show the microblade occupation was separate from the Paleoindian Mesa Complex occupation. The spatial analysis showed that, overall, the two occupations were spatially separated, but some microblades did occur with Mesa Complex artifacts. The refit studies showed this co-occurrence was the result of downslope artifact movement in which Mesa Complex artifacts and some microblades were mixed. The fact that raw materials used in microblade production were absent in the Mesa Complex assemblage illustrates the use of different raw material sources and confirms separate occupations (Bever 2006; Kunz et al. 2003). At the Gerstle River Quarry site in central Alaska, Potter (2005, 2007) identified spatially unique faunal clusters resulting from different yet contemporaneous processing areas. He further demonstrated that the specific butchering and processing activities performed at the site differed by location. Krasinski and Yesner (2008) used K-means clustering to identify statistically significant clusters of faunal and toolstone materials in CZ3 and CZ4 at Broken Mammoth. Isolating the clusters and then comparing the ratios and density of materials allowed them to identify particular areas tied to different processing or production activities. They argued that activities intensified from CZ4 to CZ3, possibly indicating increased populations or a shift from a faunal processing camp to a cache or semi-permanent base camp (Krasinski and Yesner 2008).

These studies represent a wide range of approaches and goals for intrasite spatial analyses at open-air sites. The narrowest studies from Dry Creek and Walker Road primarily sought to investigate site integrity and substantiate or refute already established interpretations of artifact distributions and temporal relationships (Higgs 1992; Hoffecker 2017). The most intensive spatial analyses at the Gerstle River Site and Broken Mammoth used the variety of materials resulting from site preservation to answer important questions about specific behaviors and resource economies (Krasinski and Yesner 2008; Potter 2005, 2007). The research at Mesa has the most similarity to the Owl Ridge analyses discussed below. In addition to addressing component integrity with both spatial analysis and refit studies, the researchers used raw material to demonstrate different occupations and raw material sources (Bever 2006; Kunz et al. 2003). Here, we consider both raw material and artifact distributions, but with a focus on identifying and comparing the relationships between artifact classes within each component. Raw material provides guidance on interpretations related to site clustering and spatial integrity.

UNDERSTANDING OWL RIDGE SITE USE AND ACTIVITY AREAS

The Site

Owl Ridge is located west of the Nenana valley, north of Denali National Park, on a small ridgeline above the Teklanika River (figure 4.1). Local sediments consist of interbedded loess, cliff-head sand, and colluvial deposits covering the Teklanika glacial outwash terrace (Graf et al. 2019). The site overlooks the Teklanika River valley and would have provided a clear view of game during Late Pleistocene shrub-tundra conditions. Its location, 61 m above First Creek, provides a source of fresh water, and the site's proximity to fluvial deposits provides a local source of toolstone material (Gore and Graf 2018). Minimal erosion on this landform allowed for the discovery of surface artifacts during initial survey (Plasket 1976). After the site's discovery, University of Alaska archaeologists performed preliminary test excavations in 1977 and recorded the site's stratigraphy in 1978. They returned to the site in 1982 and 1984 to complete systematic, grid-based test excavations across the site with the goal of finding archaeology in dateable contexts. This work allowed Phippen (1988) to identify three archaeological components and date two of them: component 1 to 11,340–9,060 ^{14}C BP and component 2 to 9,325–7,230 ^{14}C BP. In 2007 and 2009–2010, one of us (Graf) revisited the site to conduct block excavations. We added a total of 53 m^2 to the approximately 27 m^2 already excavated in the vicinity of the blocks by the University of Alaska Fairbanks (figure 4.2).

The 2007–2010 work found that Owl Ridge cultural deposits are ~125 cm thick. The stratigraphy consists of three sandy loams, representing three separate loess deposition events. These are separated by two sand layers. The lower sand, sand 1, is a thin eolian deposit probably resulting from cliff-head sand deposition. The upper sand, sand 2, is a thick series of colluvial deposits (figure 4.3) (DiPietro et al. 2019; Gore and Graf 2018; Graf et al. 2019). Three cultural components were isolated and dated within these individual strata. Component 1 was in the top 5 cm of loess 1, associated with a weak paleosol, and consisted of a clear Nenana complex tool assemblage (Phippen 1988). Two dates from this stratum provide a range of 13,300–12,775 cal BP (all ^{14}C dates in this chapter were calibrated using the Intcal13 curve in the online version of OxCal 4.3 [Ramsey 2019; Reimer et al. 2013]) (Gore and Graf 2018; Graf and Bigelow 2011; Graf et al. 2019; Phippen 1988). Within loess 2, a buried paleosol contained component 2. Loess 2 was affected by minor cryoturbation (solifluction) that minimally displaced some artifacts within the stratum (Graf et al. 2019). A series of 13 radiocarbon samples from this paleosol date the component to 12,560–11,396 cal BP (Gore and Graf 2018; Graf and Bigelow 2011; Graf et al. 2019). Component 3 was found near the contact between sand 2 and loess 3. The vast majority of its artifacts were in the upper 5 cm of sand 2, with a few exceptions located in

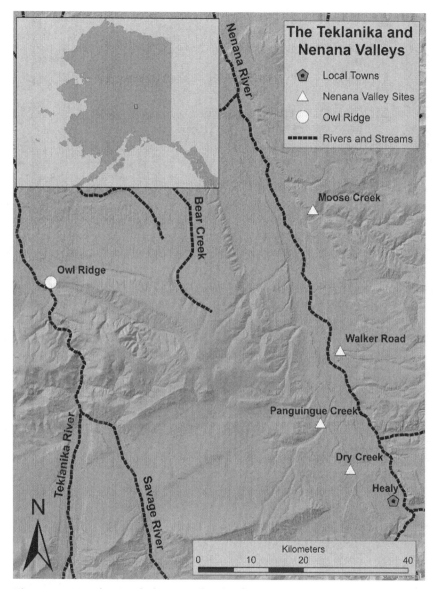

Figure 4.1. Map showing the location of Owl Ridge in central Alaska

the bottom of the overlying loess 3 (Melton 2015). A possible component-3 hearth is dated to 11,390–11,170 cal BP (Graf et al. 2019). Components 2 and 3 consist of tool assemblages Graf et al. (2019) assign to the Denali complex.

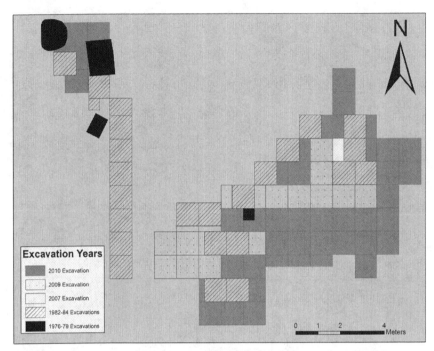

Figure 4.2. Map of the full excavation area for Owl Ridge showing the excavation year for each block. Note that the 1980s units excavated along the northwestern edge of the primary block area were not originally completed due to the presence of permafrost. The lower, previously frozen deposits were excavated in 2007.

Date ranges for the three components at Owl Ridge demonstrate temporally distinct ages between the Nenana and Denali complexes. The ages themselves align with the separate paleoenvironmental events discussed above. Component 1 falls near the end of the Allerød warming period, immediately prior to the onset of the Younger Dryas. Component 2 materials lie on a paleosol indicative of a stable environment post-dating an early Younger Dryas event, which formed sand 1 during cold, dry, and windy conditions. Component 3 immediately predates the Holocene Thermal Maximum but post-dates the Younger Dryas. People at Owl Ridge during component 3 took advantage of the continued warming and milder climate in Alaska during the lead up to modern conditions (Gore and Graf 2018). Based on findings from the excavations, Owl Ridge is an example of a site with temporally discrete tool complexes in stratigraphic components aligning with different paleoenvironmental conditions. This observation allows us to test whether the different occupational events have unique spatial relationships between artifacts

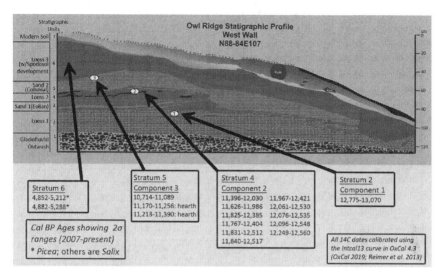

Figure 4.3. Stratigraphy of the west wall showing labeled sediment packages and associated radiocarbon dates.

reflecting different approaches to landscape use, technological adaptations, and/or site organization.

A total of 4,104 flaked lithic artifacts were recovered during all excavations at Owl Ridge (Gore and Graf 2018). Materials such as charcoal and hammer stones that have the potential to reveal useful information about the spatial relationships at Owl Ridge were also collected. However, many of these artifacts and materials lack specific point provenience data. Artifacts recovered in the screen have only general provenience data. Additionally, piece-plotting systems changed between the 1980s and the 2000s. To avoid errors and focus on specific spatial relationships, only materials that were mapped using a total station and three-dimensional piece plotting from 2007–2010 are included in this analysis. This includes 1,591 artifacts and ecofacts: 433 from component 1,275 from component 2, and 883 from component 3. Of the 1,591 piece-plotted objects, 1,517 lithic artifacts were pulled from Gore and Graf's (2018) raw material database to study and compare raw material distributions.

PREVIOUS ASSEMBLAGE RESEARCH

An artifact refit study completed on all flaked-stone artifacts with three-point provenience from all components excavated between 2007–2010 found a total of 119 refits (Melton 2015). Of these, only two refits were from different components. All others were between artifacts in their respective component. One cross-component refit was found between components 1 and 2 in a compressed stratigraphic context near the edge of the terrace where component designations were difficult to determine in the field. Given this, Melton (2015) argued this cross-component refit resulted from component misidentification for one of the artifacts. The second cross-component refit was between an artifact from component 2 in the excavation and a surface artifact where a 1980s backdirt pile was located, suggesting it was missed by screeners. With the remaining 117 refits, Melton (2015) demonstrated component integrity across the site.

Thirty-three component 1 refits were observed, suggesting the presence of 3 discrete activity areas. Component 2 contained seventeen refits in two discrete artifact clusters or activity areas. Finally, component 3 contained sixty-nine refits; however, these were distributed across the site as well as between the two densest concentrations of artifacts. There were no discrete component 3 refit clusters and refits showed movement of artifacts between the two dense artifact concentrations. Melton (2015) classified most of the site refits as breaks; only 24 percent resulted from sequential reduction, and these sequential breaks mostly represent primary reduction activities. Component 3 contained the highest number of refits resulting from uniface production, likely reflecting a distinct technological focus for this assemblage (Melton 2015). These results are echoed in Gore and Graf's (2018) artifact analysis discussed below.

To better understand technological organization through time at Owl Ridge, Gore and Graf (2018) compared several toolstone-related variables among the three components. Because none of the lithic artifacts from the site were manufactured on obsidian, they used the presence and type of stone cortex to determine which raw materials in each component were local and which were non-local. They determined that through time, the lithic assemblages became more dominated by local toolstones. The first inhabitants were bringing more non-local sources to the site, whereas the last inhabitants were almost exclusively using the local toolstone. Another interesting pattern is that, over time, site visitors increasingly performed more varied tasks. During the component 1 occupation they performed more secondary reduction activities, such as reshaping and resharpening finished hunting tools, especially on non-local toolstones. During the component 2 occupation they were performing primary and secondary reduction activities, making and resharpening both hunting and processing tools made on both local and non-local toolstones. Finally, during the component 3 occupation site, inhabitants performed more primary reduction of the local toolstone and manufacturing of more processing tools than before. Gore and Graf's (2018) data provide evidence of a gradual shift toward familiarity with the local Owl Ridge and Teklanika river landscape.

These studies provide a good starting point for spatial analysis. Melton's (2015) work demonstrates the components are spatially discrete, and there is evidence for at least three activity areas in component 1 and two activity areas in component 2. We use spatial statistics to assess whether these areas are as spatially discrete as the refit analysis suggests. We also assess whether the two mapped artifact concentrations in component 3 preserve evidence of different or similar activities to explain the movement of these artifacts within the component. Gore and Graf's (2018) work provides a lithic technological foundation for interpreting any spatial differences that are observed within and between the three components. Ultimately, Gore and Graf's (2018) work informs our research by demonstrating differences in technology and landscape use that must be considered when interpreting any spatial differences or similarities found within and between the three components.

METHODOLOGY

THEORETICAL FOUNDATIONS

Any interpretation of the spatial relationships at Owl Ridge or any other open-air site representing forager behaviors must consider ethnographic and ethnoarchaeological records of similar cultural adaptations. Studies demonstrate that material use, discard, and natural taphonomic impacts affect the distribution of artifacts at any site (Murray 1980; Schiffer 1996; South 1979). Binford's (1983) ethnoarchaeological studies of mobile foragers and pastoralists provide useful descriptions for activity areas centered around hearths. Generally speaking, individuals working around hearths drop small objects and debris around the "drop zone" next to the hearth and toss larger objects beyond the hearth or behind the drop zone. This creates a doughnut-shaped distribution of materials around the hearth area (Binford 1983). Binford (1983) observed this pattern among the Kalahari San, Nunamiut, and Navajo and it has been documented in numerous Upper Paleolithic archaeological contexts (Cahen et al. 1979; Carr 1991; Simek 1987; Simek and Larick 1983; Whallon 1973). Anderson (1988) demonstrated that materials associated with hearth-centered activities tended to be limited to a 2-meter diameter at Onion Portage. He argued that this diameter would gradually increase as more people worked around a single hearth. Surovell and Waguespack (2007) noted two additional patterns associated with hearths: higher artifact densities in the hearth-adjacent area and a steep increase in artifact density as the distance from the hearth center increases to ~35cm.

Activities not centered around hearths, however, often create different patterns of dispersal. For instance, butchering activities require individuals to continuously move around a site area and are generally not centered on hearths. Artifact distribution for these activities is expected to be more diffuse than those associated with tool production or other hearth-based behaviors (Binford 1978a, 1978b). Traffic around a site may also change artifact distribution as materials are kicked, moved, or size-sorted (Binford 1983; Stevenson 1991). Hearth and site cleaning are additional factors that may result in clustered distributions of materials across a site. Cleaning activities often result in dump zones where dense concentrations of artifacts may be misinterpreted as activity areas (Bamforth and Becker 2007). South (1979) notes that in addition to the size-related drop zones that Binford (1978a) observed, artifact size is likely to have a direct effect on whether an object is "cleaned" or left in place; the smaller an artifact is, the more likely it will stay where it was dropped. This is a pattern true of both prehistoric and historic sites (McKeller 1973; South 1979).

These models for forager artifact dispersal provide an interpretive framework for understanding clusters and artifact distributions across a site. Hearths, faunal material, and artifact size are useful for interpreting the spatial organization of sites. Unfortunately, Owl Ridge presents a challenge in that only one possible hearth was observed, no faunal remains are preserved, and artifact size has not yet been systematically documented. Nonetheless, cluster areas are useful in the context of Anderson's (1988) observations. Noting the relationship between artifact types within a cluster and identifying the distribution of toolstone materials within statistically significant clusters will also allow for site use interpretations within and between components at Owl Ridge.

Assemblage Organization and Statistical Tests

Prior to statistical analysis, it was crucial to establish whether site artifacts underwent significant post-depositional movement. As discussed above, studies of site stratigraphy, chronology, artifact refitting, and technological organization have shown the three components maintain vertical integrity. Likewise, these studies provide strong evidence of horizontal integrity, with separation between perceived artifact clusters and with the location of refits within components 1 and 2 forming identifiable refit clusters. In component 3, while some refits are cross-concentration, the vast majority are found within them. These data suggest minimal post-depositional artifact movement and relative integrity of flake stone reduction activity areas. As such, it is likely the relative spatial associations resulting from the final cultural disposal of each artifact have been preserved. By combining the spatial analysis and statistics discussed below, we seek to identify the nature of site organization at the time of abandonment and burial (Schiffer 1996).

We selected materials for our analysis from a master database for Owl Ridge that identifies all of the artifacts collected since 1976. Initial selection excluded all excavated materials without a known or discrete Northing, Easting, and elevation measurement. We also removed materials excavated prior to 2007 to avoid any unintended error in spatial provenience. The remaining 1,597 pieces were separated by component and imported into ArcMap 10.3 for mapping and statistical analyses. We also imported the lithic-artifact dataset from Gore and Graf (2018) into ArcMap, allowing us to associate raw material with tool classes. The imported datasets were used to create a set of shapefiles, the standard file type used by ArcMap to store and display spatial information. These shapefiles allowed us to perform spatial comparisons between artifact types and raw materials.

The shapefiles created from the datasets were separated by component and by artifact type within each component. Each component's artifact type shapefiles were isolated or combined as they related to activities or behavioral relationships. Table 4.1 provides an exhaustive list of all the shapefiles created for analysis. Once created, each shapefile, except those identifying raw material type, were subject to a series of statistical analyses using ArcToolbox. We summarize these statistical tests below.

TABLE 4.1. All shapefiles created for statistical spatial analysis

Shapefile Name	Description
Component_1	All component 1 artifacts and materials
Component_1_Bifaces	Bifaces
Component_1_BifacesBTF	Bifaces and biface thinning flakes (BTFs)
Component_1_BifPnt_BTFRet	Bifaces, points, BTFs, and retouch chips
Component_1_BifPnts	Bifaces and points
Component_1_BTF	BTFs
Component_1_Char_NoCoreTools	Charcoal, bifaces, points, retouched flakes, and unifaces
Component_1_CharBif	Charcoal and bifaces
Component_1_CharBifPnt	Charcoal, bifaces, and points
Component_1_CharTools	Charcoal and all tools, including cores and tested cobbles
Component_1_Charcoal	Charcoal
Component_1_CharRet	Charcoal and retouch chips
Component_1_CorticalCobFlk	Cortical flakes, cores, and tested cobbles
Component_1_CorticalFlk	Cortical flakes
Component_1_Flakes	Unclassified flakes and flake fragments
Component_1_Points	Points
Component_1_RetBTF	Retouch chips and BTFs

continued on next page

TABLE 4.1.—*continued*

Shapefile Name	Description
Component_1_RetFlk	Retouch chips
Component_1_RetTools	Unifacial tools and retouched flakes
Component_1_RetToolsFlk	Unifacial tools, retouched flakes, and retouch chips
Component_1_Toolsall	Bifaces, points, retouched flakes, unifaces, cores, and tested cobbles
Component_1_ToolsNoCor	Bifaces, points, retouched flakes, and unifaces
Component_2	All component 2 artifacts and materials
Component_2_biface	Bifaces
Component_2_bifaceBTF	Bifaces and BTFs
Component_2_bifpnt	Bifaces and points
Component_2_bifpoint_BTFret	Bifaces, points, BTFs, and retouch chips
Component_2_BTF	BTFs
Component_2_Char_NoCoreTools	Charcoal samples and tools, but no cores or tested cobbles
Component_2_Charcoal	Charcoal
Component_2_CharcoalTools	Charcoal, bifaces, points, retouched flakes, unifaces, cores and tested cobbles
Component_2_CharCores	Charcoal, cores, and tested cobbles
Component_2_CharRet	Charcoal, retouched flakes, and unifaces
Component_2_cores	Cores and tested cobles
Component_2_CoresCortical	Cores, tested cobbles, and cortical flakes
Component_2_coresFormal	Cores
Component_2_CorticalFlk	Cortical flakes
Component_2_Flakes	All debitage
Component_2_NocoreTools	Bifaces, points, retouched flakes, and unifaces
Component_2_points	Points
Component_2_points_ret	Points and retouch chips
Component_2_RetBTF	Retouch chips and BTFs
Component_2_Retouch	Retouch chips
Component_2_RetTools	Retouched flakes and unifaces
Component_2_RetToolsFlk	Retouched flakes, unifaces, and retouch chips
Component_2_TestedCob	Tested cobbles
Component_2_Tools	Bifaces, points, retouched flakes, unifaces, cores, and tested cobbles

continued on next page

TABLE 4.1.—*continued*

Shapefile Name	Description
Component_2_ToolsFlakes	Bifaces, points, retouched flakes, unifaces, cores, tested cobbles, BTFs, and retouch chips
Component_3	All component 3 artifacts and materials
Component_3_Bifaces	Bifaces
Component_3_BifacesBTF	Bifaces and BTFs
Component_3_BTF	BTFs
Component_3_Char_NoCoreTools	Charcoal samples and tools, but no cores or tested cobbles
Component_3_Charcoal	Charcoal
Component_3_CharCores	Charcoal, cores, and tested cobbles
Component_3_CharTools	Charcoal, bifaces, retouched flakes, unifaces, cores, and tested cobbles
Component_3_Cores	Cores and tested cobbles
Component_3_CorticalFlk	Cortical flakes
Component_3_CorticalTools	Cortical flakes, cores and tested cobbles
Component_3_Flakes	All debitage
Component_3_FormalCores	Cores
Component_3_NoCoreTools	Bifaces, retouched flakes, and unifaces
Component_3_NoCoreTools_NoScrap	Bifaces, retouched flakes, and unifaces; Removed outlying endscraper
Component_3_NoCoreTools_RetBif	Bifaces, retouched flakes, unifaces, retouch chips, and BTFs
Component_3_RetouchChp	Retouch chips
Component_3_RetouchTools	Retouched flakes and unifaces
Component_3_RetouchTools_NoScrap	Retouched flakes and unifaces; Removed outlying endscraper
Component_3_RetouchToolFlks	Retouched flakes, unifaces, and retouch chips
Component_3_TestedCob	Tested cobbles
Component_3_Tools	Bifaces, retouched flakes, unifaces, cores, and tested cobbles
Component_3_Tools_NoScrap	Bifaces, retouched flakes, unifaces, cores, and tested cobbles; Removed outlying endscraper
Component_3_ToolsFlakes	Bifaces, retouched flakes, unifaces, cores, and tested cobbles
Comp1_Mats	Component 1 flaked stone artifacts' raw material types

continued on next page

TABLE 4.1.—*continued*

Shapefile Name	Description
Comp1_RM01	Component 1 CCS artifacts
Comp1_RM02	Component 1 quartzite artifacts
Comp1_RM04	Component 1 basalt artifacts
Comp1_RM07	Component 1 MCS artifacts
Comp1_RM10	Component 1 andesite artifacts
Comp2_Mats	Component 2 flaked stone artifacts' raw material types
Comp2_RM01	Component 2 CCS artifacts
Comp2_RM02	Component 2 quartzite artifacts
Comp2_RM04	Component 2 basalt artifacts
Comp2_RM07	Component 2 MCS artifacts
Comp2_RM10	Component 2 andesite artifacts
Comp3_Mats	Component 3 flaked stone artifacts' raw material types
Comp3_RM01	Component 3 CCS artifacts
Comp3_RM02	Component 3 quartzite artifacts
Comp3_RM04	Component 3 basalt artifacts
Comp3_RM07	Component 3 MCS artifacts
Comp3_RM10	Component 3 andesite artifacts
Comp3_RM14	Component 3 rhyolite artifacts
Comp3_RM17	Component 3 grano-diorite artifacts

AVERAGE NEAREST NEIGHBOR ANALYSIS

The average nearest neighbor (ANN) test measures the distance between each artifact in the feature class and its closest neighboring artifact. These measurements
are averaged and then compared to a theoretical average based on a random distribution within a predetermined area. A smaller actual average than the theoretical average indicates clustering, whereas a larger actual average indicates an evenly
distributed dispersal. These results are reported as z-scores with negative values
indicating clustering and positive values indicating dispersal; significant p-values
indicate spatial distributions are statistically different from a randomly generated
distribution. For the purposes of this research, clustering, randomness, and even
distributions are all meaningful.

Since the random distribution is based on a previously defined total area, adjust-
ments to this area have the potential to impact the statistical significance of the results.
Specifically, larger areas increase the randomly generated average distance, allowing

clustering results across a wider range of average nearest neighbor values and dispersed results across a narrower range. A smaller total area will have the opposite effect on the results (ESRI 2017a; Mitchell 2005). To control for site area, two different area values were used and compared during the nearest neighbor tests. We used the area of the main excavation block, 62.5 m², as the control reflecting the maximum known site area. While this area includes ~12.5 m² excavated in the 1980s that contained artifacts not included in these analyses, we used the entire main block area to represent the site's total known primary occupation space. Since this approach had the potential to artificially decrease the p-values for each test, we also used a smaller, component-based area reflecting the minimum area in which artifacts from each component were found: 44.5 m² for component 1, 52.5 m² for component 2, and 55.5 m² for component 3. This allowed us to better test the soundness of our results. The smaller areas were only used in cases where the p > 0.001; below this p-value, the smaller areas always maintained statistical significance (Kintigh 1990; Pinder et al. 1979; Whallon 1974).

RIPLEY'S K ANALYSIS

The Ripley's K test in ArcToolbox uses the "Multi-Distance Spatial Cluster Analysis" tool and determines the clustering or dispersal of a dataset across multiple distances. It uses the Ripley's K function to show how spatial clustering changes relative to changes in the size of the neighborhood being measured (ESRI 2017d; Mitchell 2005). We used the Ripley's K edge correction formula as a second statistical test to check the robustness of our ANN results. Kintigh (1990) pointed out that ANN has the potential to show artificial clustering near the edge of excavations or as a result of excavating a limited space. While using two different area values for each test in the ANN helped determine if the maximum or minimum use area has an impact on the results, Ripley's K allowed us to confirm the significance of results near p = 0.05. It also let us test whether a site area larger than the primary excavation block was likely to impact the results. The Ripley's K edge correction formula gives additional weight to neighbors that are further from the edge of the study area, so tests where artifacts are common near the boundaries may be artificially weakened. Unfortunately, this test only works well if more than 30 individual entries exist within a shapefile (ESRI 2017d; Mitchell 2005). For this reason, shapefiles with very low numbers of artifacts were not tested. Finally, to successfully test if the excavation area impacted the ANN results, Ripley's K requires the sampling area be defined. We created a shapefile of the primary excavation block and used it to accurately run the Ripley's K test.

K-MEANS CLUSTERING

K-Means Clustering in ArcMap produces statistically related clusters based on a predicted number of groups. The algorithm partitions the points into groups wherein differences between individual points are minimized. K-Means can minimize differences between spatial data alone, or the user can identify features that K-Means uses to relate objects by a factor other than just distances (ESRI 2017b; Kintigh 1990; Mitchell 2005;). For this study we only use spatial relationships to create clusters so that our preconceived ideas about artifact relationships had minimal impact on cluster formation. K-Means is easiest when a seed feature is provided for each group and the exact number of groups to be tested is known (ESRI 2017b; Krasinski and Yesner 2008; Mitchell 2005). However, the Owl Ridge site does not have distinct features around which clustering is expected. Further, while the number of activity areas is predicted from Melton's (2015) refit analysis, the number of potential clusters may change depending on the type of artifact relationships we examine. Identifying work areas is one useful approach, but for some components, it may be useful to look for particular tool reduction events or other behaviors resulting in spatially associated artifacts. Since our goal was to identify the number of clusters illustrating the strongest spatial relationships in each component, we tested multiple numbers of clusters. We also used random seeds so the results would better reflect spatial relationships between the artifacts rather than our assumptions as to where clusters should be located (Kintigh 1990). We used ArcMap to produce an F-Statistic predicting the optimal number of groupings based on the spatial data provided (ESRI 2017b; Mitchell 2005). This was a useful starting point; however, we tested numbers of clusters besides those identified by the F-statistic until the most meaningful spatial relationships were identified. We only ran K-Means clustering for each component as a whole; K-Means was not used to look for clusters associated with individual or combined artifact classes. We tested both two-dimensional (2D) (Northing and Easting) and three-dimensional (3-D) (Northing, Easting, and Elevation) spatial data to determine which provided more meaningful clusters.

KERNEL DENSITY MAPS

Kernel Density calculates the density of objects to create a heat map that shows where the object density is highest. In ArcMap, these maps can be adjusted to show a range of densities with more or less resolution (ESRI 2017c; Mitchell 2005). While resolution control is useful for clearly showing how fast artifact numbers drop, it is most useful when considering an artifact class with low numbers. In these cases, the heat map may give the illusion of high density despite there being only a handful of artifacts across the site. For these classes, we lowered the measured density as much as possible while doing our best to maintain a visualization of meaningful hotspots. We use Kernel Density maps for all artifact and material classes in each component. This allowed for quick visual comparisons of artifact distributions across and between each component. The results are useful for predicting particular activity locations associated with artifact types and to determine if the K-Means clusters are related to particular artifact or material classes across the site.

RESULTS

AVERAGE NEAREST NEIGHBOR ANALYSIS

At Owl Ridge, most of the ANN tests show clustering for the different artifact classes. Table 4.2 lists the ANN results for each class and combined class test. The results observed are not surprising since, as discussed above, human activities are often associated with particular locations and should result in clustered materials. To effectively compare how artifacts were used within and between each component at Owl Ridge, this discussion focuses on the results that show exceptions to statistically significant clustering. The general distribution of artifacts for each component is illustrated in figures 4.4–4.6.

Within component 1 (figure 4.4), bifaces cluster across the main excavation area (62.5 m^2), but not in the smaller component specific area (44.5 m^2). Points also cluster across the main excavation area, but at a significance of p < 0.10. Within the component area, this class is randomly distributed. When bifaces and points are combined into a single shapefile, they demonstrate clustering at both 62.5 m^2 and 44.5 m^2. Both artifact classes also have low numbers (Bifaces n = 6; Points n = 5), a factor that reduces the opportunities for clustering to occur. The fact that combining these classes results in clustering, even though their numbers remain low (n = 11), strongly supports a behavioral relationship. Bifaces and points both cluster with associated flake types, biface thinning flakes (BTFs) and retouch chips, as expected. The retouched tools class (i.e., retouched flakes and unifaces) demonstrate a strong random distribution in both areas tested, but this class clusters with all other tools and with retouch chips. Charcoal demonstrates a random distribution, a result again likely to relate to its low numbers (n = 4). However, when combined with any artifact class, including retouched tools, charcoal demonstrates spatial clustering.

Component 2 (figure 4.5) shows slightly different spatial patterns across the tested classes. Bifaces cluster across the main block area (p < 0.05), but the smaller component 2 area (52.5 m^2) results in a slightly higher p-value (p = 0.0502). While the increased value implies that the clustering results are weak, they are much stronger than in component 1. An additional difference is that points always cluster in component 2. Retouched tools demonstrate significant dispersal in this component, one of only two tool classes demonstrating this spatial pattern in the entire study. Surprisingly, retouched tools are not spatially associated with retouch chips; combining these classes results in a random distribution. This is unexpected, since retouch chips are debitage removed during the manufacture and resharpening of

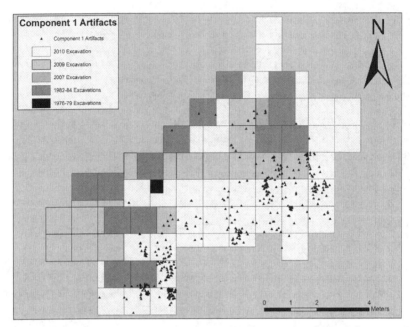

Figure 4.4. General distribution of artifacts and materials in component 1.

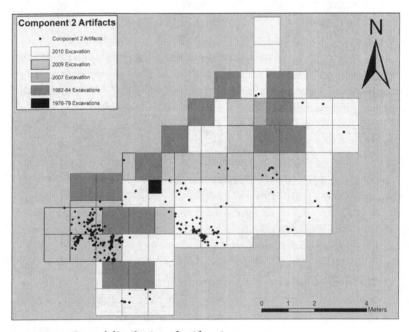

Figure 4.5. General distribution of artifacts in component 2.

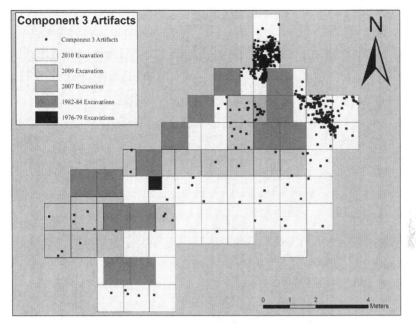

Figure 4.6. Map of the general artifact distribution for component 3.

tools. Similarly, ANN does not result in clustering between retouched tools and bifaces, points, and/or cores. Charcoal is the only class that clusters with retouched tools. Cores (i.e., both cores and tested cobbles) have a random distribution, but cluster with both cortical flakes and charcoal. Overall, the component shows strong spatial clustering between formal tools and formal tool byproducts (e.g., BTFs and retouch chips), strong associations between charcoal and all cultural materials, but little-to-no clusters associating expedient tools and any other cultural materials.

Despite the fact that component 3 contains the densest concentrations of artifacts for all three components (figure 4.6), the ANN tests resulted in the most cases of randomness. Bifaces, retouched tools, and all tools (both with and without cores) produce random distributions when tested using both the main block and component (55.5 m^2) areas. BTFs show slight clustering (p = 0.045540) across the main excavation area, but a random distribution at 55.5 m^2. Combining bifaces and BTFs results in significant clustering (p < 0.05) at 62.5 m^2, but again, the clustering weakens for the 55.5 m^2 area (p = 0.07606). In three different classes (all tools, tools without cores, and retouched tools) a single end scraper was located in the furthest southwestern corner of the excavation block. It appeared to be a visual outlier (figure 4.7), and when we removed it from the analysis, all three artifact classes demonstrate statistically

TABLE 4.2. All ANN results for tool classes and combined classes

Shapefile	Component	Area (m2)	Spatial Relationship	z-score	p-value
Component_1	1	62.5	Clustered	−20.111851	< 0.001
Component_1_Toolsall	1	62.5	Clustered	−3.224276	< 0.01
Component_1_Toolsall	1	44.5	Clustered	−2.318664	< 0.05
Component_1_ ToolsNoCor	1	62.5	Clustered	−3.347265	< 0.001
Component_1_Bifaces	1	62.5	Clustered	−2.110140	< 0.05
Component_1_Bifaces	1	44.5	Random	−1.633305	0.102405
Component_1_ BifacesBTF	1	62.5	Clustered	−5.887996	< 0.001
Component_1_BifPnts	1	62.5	Clustered	−3.270131	< 0.01
Component_1_BifPnts	1	44.5	Clustered	−2.700943	< 0.01
Component_1_BifPnt_ BTFRet	1	62.5	Clustered	−9.080976	< 0.001
Component_1_BTF	1	62.5	Clustered	−5.308113	< 0.001
Component_1_Charcoal	1	62.5	Random	−0.252210	0.800879
Component_1_Charcoal	1	44.5	Random	0.409373	0.682266
Component_1_ CharTools	1	62.5	Clustered	−3.494355	< 0.001
Component_1_ CharTools	1	44.5	Clustered	−2.638739	< 0.01
Component_1_Char_ NoCoreTools	1	62.5	Clustered	−3.617344	< 0.001
Component_1_CharBif	1	62.5	Clustered	−3.073285	< 0.01
Component_1_CharBif	1	44.5	Clustered	−2.522318	< 0.05
Component_1_CharRet	1	62.5	Clustered	−3.583377	< 0.001
Component_1_CharRet	1	44.5	Clustered	−3.126834	< 0.01
Component_1_ CharBifPnt	1	62.5	Clustered	−3.308068	< 0.001
Component_1_ CharBifPnt	1	44.5	Clustered	−2.548876	< 0.05
Component_1_ CorticalFlk	1	62.5	Clustered	−6.564358	< 0.001
Component_1_ CorticalCobFlk	1	62.5	Clustered	−6.440739	< 0.001

continued on next page

TABLE 4.2.—*continued*

Shapefile	Component	Area (m2)	Spatial Relationship	z-score	p-value
Component_1_Flakes	1	62.5	Clustered	−19.830613	< 0.001
Component_1_Points	1	62.5	Clustered	−1.689250	0.091172
Component_1_Points	1	44.5	Random	−1.210082	0.226247
Component_1_RetFlk	1	62.5	Clustered	−5.655598	< 0.001
Component_1_RetBTF	1	62.5	Clustered	−7.995736	< 0.001
Component_1_RetTools	1	62.5	Random	−1.073295	0.283139
Component_1_RetTools	1	44.5	Random	−0.404526	0.685826
Component_1_RetToolsFlk	1	62.5	Clustered	−4.191337	< 0.001
Component_1_RetToolsFlk	1	44.5	Clustered	−2.755636	< 0.01
Component_2	2	62.5	Clustered	−17.992922	< 0.001
Component_2_Tools	2	62.5	Random	−1.102703	0.270156
Component_2_Tools	2	52.5	Random	−0.385793	0.69965
Component_2_ToolsFlakes	2	62.5	Clustered	−7.157211	< 0.001
Component_2_NocoreTools	2	62.5	Random	−1.323426	0.185694
Component_2_NocoreTools	2	52.5	Random	−0.725482	0.468156
Component_2_biface	2	62.5	Clustered	−2.151799	< 0.05
Component_2_biface	2	52.5	Clustered	−1.958147	0.050213
Component_2_bifaceBTF	2	62.5	Clustered	−7.631355	< 0.001
Component_2_bifpnt	2	62.5	Clustered	−3.471511	< 0.001
Component_2_bifpnt	2	52.5	Clustered	−3.236669	< 0.01
Component_2_bifpoint_BTFret	2	62.5	Clustered	−8.929452	< 0.001
Component_2_BTF	2	62.5	Clustered	−7.955653	< 0.001
Component_2_Charcoal	2	62.5	Clustered	−5.893825	< 0.001
Component_2_CharcoalTools	2	62.5	Clustered	−4.248594	< 0.001
Component_2_Char_NoCoreTools	2	62.5	Clustered	−3.909303	< 0.001

continued on next page

TABLE 4.2.—*continued*

Shapefile	Component	Area (m2)	Spatial Relationship	z-score	p-value
Component_2_CharCores	2	62.5	Clustered	−6.485071	< 0.001
Component_2_CharRet	2	62.5	Clustered	−3.262181	< 0.01
Component_2_CharRet	2	52.5	Clustered	−2.528392	< 0.05
Component_2_cores	2	62.5	Random	−0.537063	0.591224
Component_2_cores	2	52.5	Random	−0.196326	0.844355
Component_2_CoresCortical	2	62.5	Clustered	−5.215052	< 0.001
Component_2_CorticalFlk	2	62.5	Clustered	−5.014264	< 0.001
Component_2_Flakes	2	62.5	Clustered	−16.705881	< 0.001
Component_2_points	2	62.5	Clustered	−2.571243	< 0.05
Component_2_points	2	52.5	Clustered	−2.415797	< 0.05
Component_2_points_ret	2	62.5	Clustered	−4.940601	< 0.001
Component_2_Retouch	2	62.5	Clustered	−4.185665	< 0.001
Component_2_RetBTF	2	62.5	Clustered	−8.915888	< 0.001
Component_2_RetTools	2	62.5	Dispersed	2.105216	< 0.05
Component_2_RetTools	2	52.5	Dispersed	2.723828	< 0.01
Component_2_RetToolsFlk	2	62.5	Random	−0.801709	0.422721
Component_2_RetToolsFlk	2	52.5	Random	−0.09542	0.923981
Component_3	3	62.5	Clustered	−31.671863	< 0.001
Component_3_Tools	3	62.5	Random	−0.347783	0.728003
Component_3_Tools	3	55.5	Random	0.113597	0.909557
Component_3_NoCoreTools	3	62.5	Random	−0.051144	0.959211
Component_3_Tools_NoScrap	3	62.5	Clustered	−4.325008	< 0.001
Component_3_ToolsFlakes	3	62.5	Clustered	−7.568812	< 0.001
Component_3_Bifaces	3	62.5	Random	0.139760	0.888850
Component_3_Bifaces	3	55.5	Random	0.382437	0.702138

continued on next page

TABLE 4.2.—*continued*

Shapefile	Component	Area (m2)	Spatial Relationship	z-score	p-value
Component_3_ BifacesBTF	3	62.5	Clustered	−2.411715	< 0.05
Component_3_ BifacesBTF	3	55.5	Clustered	−1.774011	0.076061
Component_3_BTF	3	62.5	Clustered	−1.999628	0.045540
Component_3_BTF	3	55.5	Random	−1.372422	0.169932
Component_3_Charcoal	3	62.5	Clustered	−6.005062	< 0.001
Component_3_ CharTools	3	62.5	Clustered	−4.936775	< 0.001
Component_3_Char_ NoCoreTools	3	62.5	Clustered	−2.547441	< 0.05
Component_3_ NoCoreTools_RetBif	3	62.5	Clustered	−7.940146	< 0.001
Component_3_ CharCores	3	62.5	Random	−0.721239	0.470762
Component_3_Cores	3	62.5	Dispersed	3.323371	< 0.001
Component_3_ CorticalFlk	3	62.5	Clustered	−15.093410	< 0.001
Component_3_ CorticalTools	3	62.5	Clustered	−14.170562	< 0.001
Component_3_Flakes	3	62.5	Clustered	−32.005204	< 0.001
Component_3_ FormalCores	3	62.5	Random	0.415140	0.678039
Component_3_ RetouchChp	3	62.5	Clustered	−5.603494	< 0.001
Component_3_ RetouchTools	3	62.5	Random	0.850282	0.395168
Component_3_ RetouchTools	3	55.5	Random	1.253499	0.210024
Component_3_ RetouchToolFlks	3	62.5	Clustered	−6.125453	< 0.001
Component_3_ RetouchTools_NoScrap	3	62.5	Clustered	−3.357499	< 0.001
Component_3_ TestedCob	3	62.5	Dispersed	3.674211	< 0.001
Component_3_ NoCoreTools_NoScrap	3	62.5	Clustered	−3.993275	< 0.001

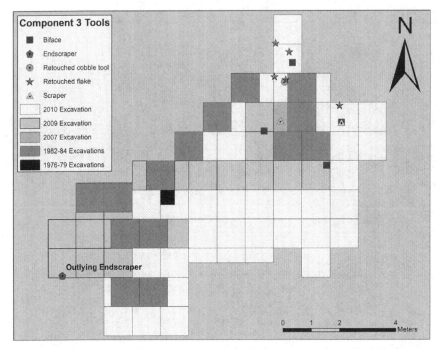

Figure 4.7. Distribution of component 3 tools (excluding cores and tested cobbles). Outlier end scraper is highlighted.

significant clustering (p < 0.01). Tested cobbles and cores demonstrate strong dispersal results (p < 0.001). Cores cluster with cortical flakes largely due to flakes' strong clustering (p = 0, z = −15.09341). It should be noted that charcoal strongly clusters by itself and combines with all artifact classes to cluster. The only exception to this pattern is the core class, which combines with charcoal to result in a random distribution.

RIPLEY'S K

The results showed that for every shapefile where the ANN test resulted in a p-value approaching zero, Ripley's K always provided a matching statistically significant result (figure 4.8). Similarly, most artifact shapefiles with both random (p-value > 0.05) and significant (p-value < 0.05) ANN distributions resulted in correlated Ripley's K results. We did note a few exceptions to this observation, discussed below. Note that any tool class where n < 25 was not tested using Ripley's K.

The all-tools class from component 1, which is svtrongly clustered using ANN, only clusters for the lower and middle neighbor distances with Ripley's K. Farther

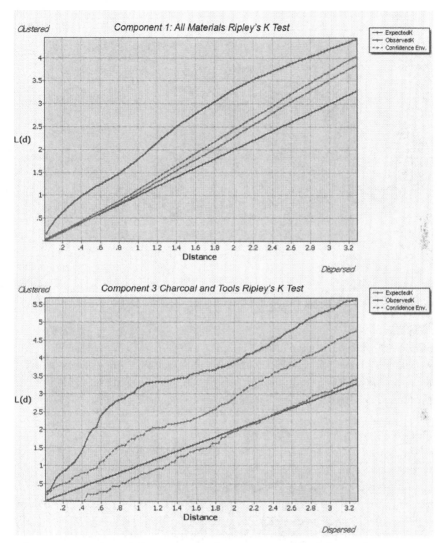

Figure 4.8. Sample Ripley's K test results for component 1: all artifacts and component 3: charcoal and tools, illustrating that significance does not change for these tool classes.

distances and those between the low and mid distances indicate a random distribution. This tool class did have fewer than 30 points (n = 27) so the results are not robust. The combined biface and BTF class in component 1 demonstrates randomness at the extreme neighbor distances (closest and farthest). The combination of

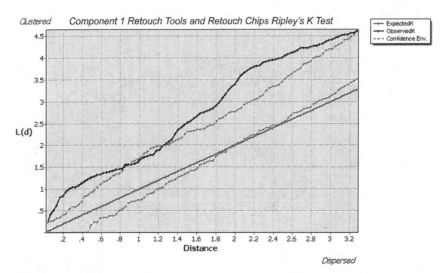

Figure 4.9. Ripley's K results for component 1 Retouch tools and retouch chips showing potential issues with the statistical clustering demonstrated by ANN.

retouch chips and retouched tools for component 1 results in randomness at the middle neighbor distances. The component 2 classes combining charcoal with all tools, tools without cores, and retouched tools each show random distributions at the farther neighbor distances. Finally, for component 3, two classes (BTFs as well as BTFs and bifaces) result in reversals of the ANN tests. Ripley's K strongly demonstrates significant clustering for both of these.

The general consistency between the ANN results and the Ripley's K edge correction tests suggest that the ANN tests are not demonstrably impacted by the excavation area or sampling. The exceptions identified above usually demonstrate that as distance between neighbors increases, so too does their statistical randomness. This is to be expected since objects far apart are less likely to be clustered and are more likely to be behaviorally unassociated. We do note the results for retouch chips and retouched tools in component 1 may illustrate some sampling issues. The retouch tools and retouch chips < 25 cm from the southern and southeastern excavation edges may be skewing the ANN results. The number of these artifacts near the excavation boundary make up a higher relative proportion of the total retouch chips and retouch tools than the proportion of near-boundary artifacts in any other component 1 artifact class. As such, these artifacts may present an example of artificial clustering discussed by Kintigh (1990). Additional excavation in these areas would clarify if the clustering is the result of sampling errors (figures 4.9 and 4.10).

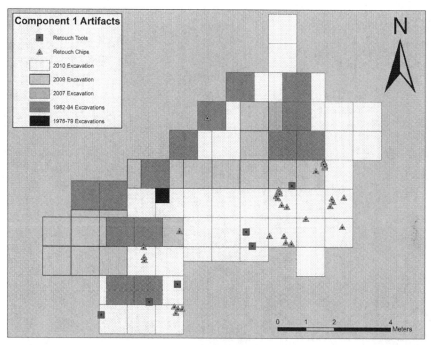

Figure 4.10. Map showing the distribution of retouch chips and retouch tools from component 1. Note their proximity to the edge of the excavation area.

K-MEANS CLUSTERING

The different clusters created by K-Means for component 1 appear random in all but two cases. Three clusters were created using both 2-D and 3-D tests that strongly correlate to the activity areas Melton (2015) identified in her refit analysis (figure 4.11). 3-D tests also resulted in a set of 11 clusters that visually correlate with particular artifact type classes. Cortical flakes correlate with clusters in the center of the site and the northernmost cluster in the southwestern activity area. Retouch chips are associated with two clusters in the northeastern activity area, and BTFs overlap a group between the clusters associated with retouch chips. Raw materials also show strong correlation with these clusters. The chert (CCS) Kernel Density map correlates with clusters in the southwestern and northeastern activity areas. Basalt has a near perfect correlation with a cluster at the eastern edge of the component. A cluster present at the southwestern edge of the component exactly overlaps a concentration of microcrystalline silicate (MCS). MCS also overlaps a second cluster found in the northeastern activity area. Andesite has a strong correlation with a cluster at the eastern edge of the southwestern activity area as well as the central cluster.

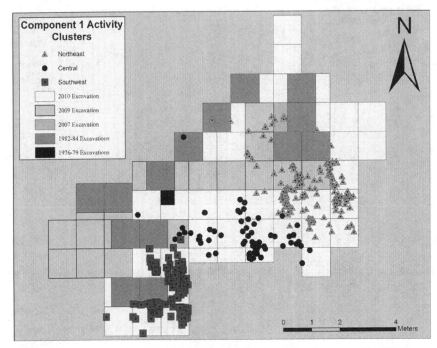

Figure 4.11. Component 1 K-means clusters overlapping the activity areas identified during refit analysis. Note that two plotted artifacts appear in two 1980s squares. Phippen (1988) encountered permafrost in these units, so the remaining stratum 2 sediments were excavated in 2007.

These results suggest that material type correlates far stronger with the component 1 clusters produced by K-means than do artifact classes. When combined, andesite and core reduction flakes directly correlate with the same cluster in the central and southwestern activity areas. Basalt and retouch chips correlate strongly with a single cluster at the eastern edge of the component. CCS and MCS combine with BTFs to correlate with clusters in both the northeastern and southwestern activity areas.

Component 2 K-means tests using 2-D spatial data produced visually appealing sets of 3 and 4 groups. Upon further inspection, random spatial overlap between the clusters' points suggests they are not associated with behaviors or artifact types. Conversely, the 3-D test showed a clear cluster of 2 groups that, again, strongly correlate with the activity areas proposed in the refit analysis (figure 4.12) (Melton 2015). It also produced a set of 4 groups that resulted in more discrete spatial relationships. There may be some association between tool classes and the 4 3-D groups, as revealed by the Kernel Density maps. All artifact types are found in the southwestern activity area, but cortical flakes are associated with a small cluster in the

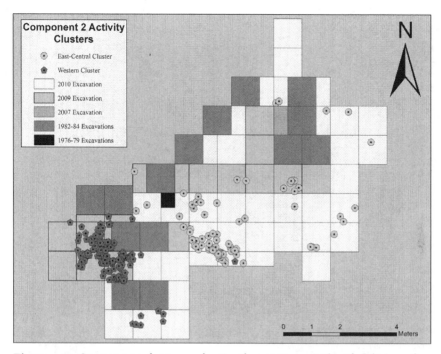

Figure 4.12. Component 2 clusters overlapping the activity areas identified during refit analysis.

northeastern corner of the component. Retouch chips and tools also correlate with a cluster in the center of the eastern activity area. A set of eight groups created using 3-D K-Means correlates with both artifact and materials types. BTFs overlap two clusters at the southwestern edge of the component. Relationships were also observed between the CCS Kernel Density map and clusters at both the south-western edge of the site and at the component's south center. MCS correlates with a pair of clusters at the western edge of the site and north of the activity areas. Other raw material classes have too few artifacts to identify any meaningful correlations. When artifacts and material types are combined, BTFs correlate with both CCS and MCS and, similar to above, cluster to the west. Cortical flakes only correlate with MCS. This means they are primarily concentrated in the western activity area, but also occur in the same small eastern cluster where MCS is found.

Component 3 was the most difficult to test since K-Means clusters appeared to arbitrarily group artifacts across the site. This difficulty resulted from the presence of two to three dense artifact concentrations in the northeastern corner of the component combined with a generally diffuse artifact scatter to the south and west.

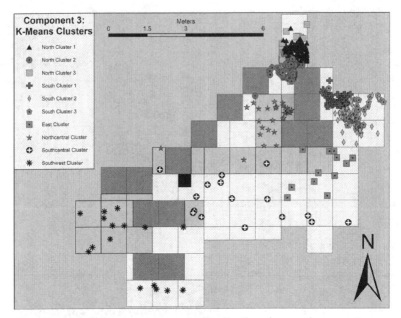

Figure 4.13. Set of 10 component 3 clusters distributed across the excavation area.

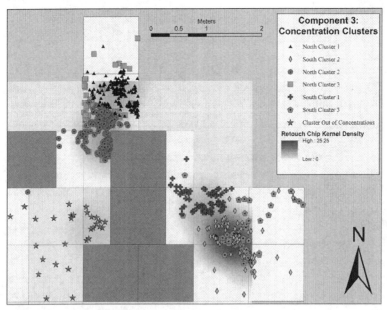

Figure 4.14. K-Means and Kernel Density correlations between retouch chips and clusters in the component 3 concentrations.

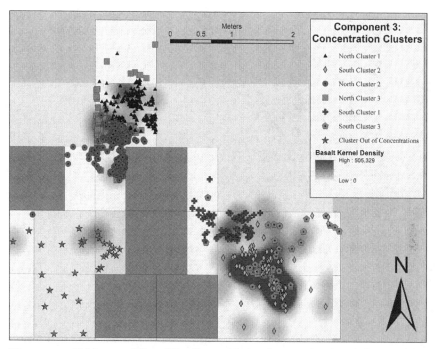

Figure 4.15. K-Means and Kernel Density correlations between basalt and clusters in the component 3 concentrations.

For all numbers of groups, the 2-D results appeared particularly random. The 3-D tests produced a set of 10 clusters (figure 4.13) that correlates with Kernel Density maps for BTFs, cortical flakes, and retouch chips (figure 4.14). These 10 clusters also correlate with raw materials concentrations. Quartzite, which is densest in the northwestern concentration, is the only raw material that correlates with a cluster between the two primary component 3 concentrations. Basalt directly correlates with one of two clusters found at the southern margin of the southeastern concentration (figure 4.15). Andesite has a near perfect association with two separate clusters in the northwestern concentration (figure 4.16) while rhyolite is the only raw material to correlate with a cluster just south and west of the artifact concentrations. Finally, Granodiorite, like andesite, is associated with the northwestern concentration but only in its southern cluster. We note that the southwestern cluster, southcentral, and eastern clusters represent a generally diffuse scatter of artifacts across the southern half of the excavation area (figure 4.13). While the K-means test has created distinct clusters, the diffuse scatter suggests that these clusters are not necessarily spatially discrete or indicative of differential behaviors.

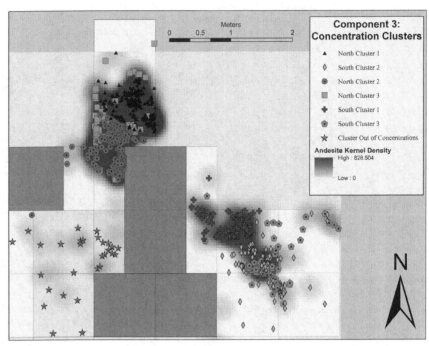

Figure 4.16. K-Means and Kernel Density correlations between andesite and clusters in the component 3 concentrations.

While these results comparing K-means clusters and kernel density maps in both concentrations closely align with particular material types and artifacts, there is a distinct difference between the northwestern and southeastern concentrations. In the southeastern concentration andesite and basalt show distinct spatial relationships, with the former dominant to the north and the latter dominant in the south. Additionally, CCS is only found in the northern portion of this concentration while MCS is only found in the south (figure 4.17). Flake types also have distinct patterns: cortical flakes are common throughout the concentration, whereas retouch chips are only common near the southern end and BTFs are sparsely distributed (figure 4.18). Conversely, all of these materials and artifact types overlap in the northwestern concentration with little to no spatial separation. Andesite is clearly the dominant material type, but it is consistently spatially associated with all other material types. The only raw material that appears to have a spatially distinct pattern are the five CCS artifacts in the concentration's northwestern quadrant (figure 4.19). This pattern holds true for cortical flakes and BTFs as well. Retouch chips show some spatial patterning in that these nine artifacts are centrally distributed north

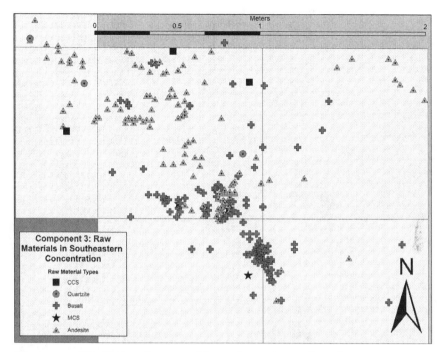

Figure 4.17. Distribution of raw material types in component 3's southeastern concentration.

to south through the concentration (figure 4.20). These observations indicate that while the kernel density maps show correlation between particular K-means clusters and artifact or material types, it is only in the southeastern concentration that artifact types and materials have unique spatial patterning. Conversely, the only strong correlation between K-means clusters and material type (andesite) in the northwestern concentration almost certainly results from the fact that andesite is the overwhelmingly dominant raw material in this area.

DISCUSSION

These results demonstrate variability in the spatial relationships between all three components with respect to where artifacts are found, the spatial relationships between different artifact classes and materials, and the discreteness of clusters and spatial associations. The observed differences provide additional support for the arguments made by Gore and Graf (2018) regarding differential landscape use between the components. The results indicate that the individuals occupying Owl

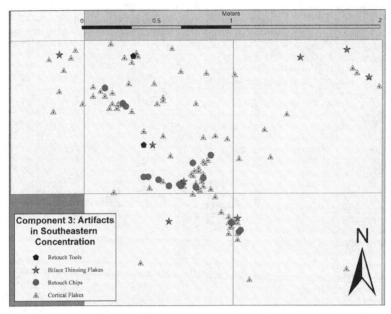

Figure 4.18. Distribution of flake types in component 3's southeastern concentration.

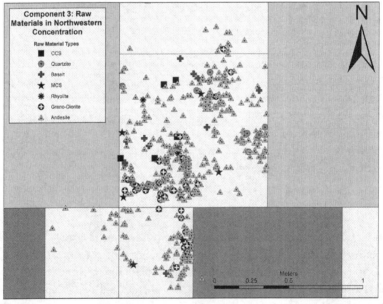

Figure 4.19. Distribution of raw material types in component 3's northwestern concentration.

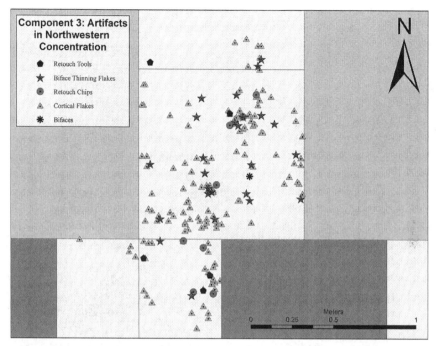

Figure 4.20. Distribution of flake types in component 3's northwestern concentration.

Ridge at different times left unique archaeological footprints representing different behavioral approaches. Taken together, the above spatial results allow us to propose a more detailed summary of site use for each component.

COMPONENT 1: HUNTING AND RE-TOOLING

The close association and clustering of points and bifaces observed in the ANN results indicate that retooling, tool retouch, and formal tool use was an important activity during this earliest occupation. Core reduction also occurred, but the small number of cores and tested cobbles in component 1 (n = 2) indicate core testing was not the primary focus. Gore and Graf (2018) suggest that materials reduced in this component were transported off the site. Based on the association between formal tools, retouch, and BTFs, one interpretation may be that the core reduction at component 1 was intended to resupply materials used during the retooling evinced by abandoned points and bifaces. The random distribution of expedient tools and unifaces indicates that the associated activities were not concentrated or that the tools were randomly discarded. We suggest, however, that the spatial association between charcoal and expedient tools shows a relationship between use areas and these informal tools.

The strong correlation between clusters found in the refit analysis and 3-D K-Means clustering show three separate activity areas in component 1. These lie at the main excavation block's southwestern corner, south-center, and northeastern edge. Within each activity area, spatial relationships point to a distinct set of behaviors. The strong association between the eleven clusters identified using K-Means, raw material kernel density maps, and artifact types help us to interpret particular behaviors in each activity area. In particular, the spatial associations suggest that both the northeastern and southwestern activity areas were dominated by tool production and retouch on CCS, MCS, and basalt. The central area saw more core reduction and expedient tool use/manufacture primarily using andesite.

The distinct shapes of each cluster also point to the organization of the activities undertaken. The southwestern cluster shows a semi-circular shape with an artifact void near the center. The semi-circle is roughly 2–2.5 meters in diameter with the densest artifact concentrations to the south and southeast. Only a single retouch tool was found in these concentrations. Conversely, most of the tools are found to the northeast with one point to the north. Just west and northwest of this cluster are two 1 × 2-meter test units excavated in 1982. While spatial provenience was not collected for the artifacts excavated in these units, Phippin (1988) identified 95 component 1 artifacts from the southern unit and 27 component 1 artifacts from the northern unit. All the artifacts collected from the southern unit were flakes, and 26 flakes and a single point were collected from the northern unit. We note that the 95 lithic artifacts identified in the southern pit increase the total artifacts in this cluster by ~55 percent and are associated with the western/open side of the semi-circle surrounding the central artifact void. We also point out that the artifact void observed borders the eastern edge of the southern 1982 test unit (figure 4.21). Taken together, the evidence points to the southwestern cluster being an activity area surrounding a central hearth. The size (2–3-meter diameter), presence of a central artifact void, and generally circular shape align with criteria for identifying hearth-based activities (Anderson 1988; Binford 1983; Surovell and Waguespack 2007). Biface and tool production occurred to the north and northeast of the hearth, overlooking the lower valley with waste material being deposited to the south and southeast.

The central cluster has a less distinct shape, consisting of two separate areas. The high concentration of artifacts to the east contains nearly all the refits in this cluster save one. This concentration also contains nearly all andesite and has a small cluster of tools to the south. There is also some indication of an artifact void just northeast of the densest artifact cluster (figure 4.21). The less dense artifact concentration to the west has a mix of materials and contains a single refit that extends into the southwestern cluster. No tools were found here, so it is potentially an area of secondary deposition of materials from both the southwestern and central clusters. These observations point to the central cluster being a tool workstation associated with andesite. Materials appear to have been disposed to the west and northwest with the western area grading into debitage disposal from the southwestern cluster. These activities may have been associated with a hearth to the northeast, but the shape is too ephemeral to be certain a hearth was present.

The northeastern cluster is the largest and has a dispersed artifact distribution. The highest artifact concentrations are found in the southern half of this cluster, where high artifact densities to the west and east surround a relative dearth of artifacts. This area forms a 2.5 to 3-meter diameter circular area. A more diffuse scatter of artifacts extends north from the southern area of higher artifact densities (figure 4.21). These observations point to a similar interpretation for the northeastern cluster's southern half as that discussed for the southwestern cluster: it is possible that a hearth is associated with the higher artifact densities, centrally located where artifact presence is low. The northern half of the northeastern cluster, however, requires more explanation. In addition to the diffuse artifact scatter, the northern end of the cluster contains three test units excavated in 1984 with no artifact or spatial information analyzed here (figure 4.11). Nonetheless, Phippen (1988) provides some information regarding the component 1 artifacts in these units. In particular, the number of artifacts found in them steadily decreases to the north. The southern-most test units contain 37 total artifacts, with an average of 18.5 artifacts per m². The unit just north of these contains eleven artifacts, and the northern-most unit contains just five artifacts. Nine tools were identified in the 1984 test units: two points, two scrapers, and a hammerstone in the southern units; a hammerstone, a core, and a scraper in the central unit; and a sidescraper in the northern unit. These artifacts lie just north of four artifacts piece-plotted in the northeastern cluster and included in our spatial analyses. When combined, these data suggest the northeastern cluster is a wide activity area associated with processing and tool use at the northern, more diffuse end, and tool production and reduction activities at the southern end. The density of materials, diameter, and somewhat circular shape of the southern half of the cluster may point to a hearth around which reduction activities took place.

Component 2: Core Reduction and Logistics

The two component 2 activity areas identified by Melton (2015) and the K-Means clusters are clearly distinct from the component 1 artifact distributions. The western cluster is about two meters northwest of the southernmost cluster in component 1. The eastern cluster is about one meter west of component 1's central cluster.

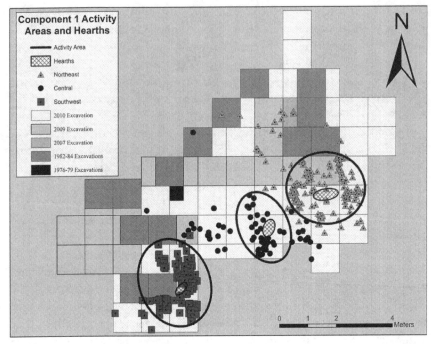

Figure 4.21. Component 1 clusters with high density artifact areas and potential hearths identified.

Both have a ~2-meter diameter/length, and artifact disposal appears more evenly dispersed than in component 1. The 1982 test units discussed above border the western cluster; however, Phippen (1988) identified no component 2 artifacts in the southern test unit and only one component 2 flake in the northern test unit. An additional test unit north of this cluster, excavated in 1984, contained no component 2 artifacts. Combined, these test units excavated in 1982 and 1984 provide no additional information to assist with the interpretation of component 2.

The difference in artifact distribution between the two clusters may be the result of secondary cultural activities resulting in redistribution, specifically dumping or hearth cleaning (Bamforth and Becker 2007; Sergant et al. 2006), differential behaviors such as butchering (Binford 1978a; 1978b; Potter 2005; 2007), or natural post-depositional movement. Dumping or hearth cleaning seems an untenable hypothesis. In particular, Sergant et al. (2006) point out that hearth dumps are small, dense concentrations of burnt materials (p. 1003). Bamforth and Becker (2007) defined dumps as having a small relative number of refits, overlapping artifact concentrations between components, refits between concentrations, and artifacts from different activities mixed within concentrations. None of these conditions are present in the component 2 activity areas. Conversely, it is possible that the cryoturbation associated with loess 2 and component 2 led to some post-depositional artifact movement, resulting in the dispersed pattern observed. This interpretation seems more likely to us, given that no hearth features were reported and cryoturbation features were present.

Spatial relationships and raw materials from the component 2 occupation help reveal the behaviors associated with the two activity areas. The component is associated with clustered points and bifaces. Retooling at the activity areas seems likely; however, unlike component 1, numerous cores and tested cobbles are also clustered in the two activity areas. It appears that more effort was put into logistical provisioning during the component 2 occupation. Gore and Graf (2018) provide additional evidence for this behavior, since component 2 has the lowest numbers of exotic toolstone. Nevertheless, provisioning appears to be directed toward producing formal tools, since these artifacts are still more common than expected. The dispersal of expedient tools may imply that, as with component 1, these tools were randomly discarded.

Kernel density results indicate CCS dominates the eastern activity area while MCS is more common in the western activity area and is associated with all flake reduction types. MCS is all but absent to the east. To the east, CCS dominated the few core-reduction related flaked-stone clusters. We note that the relatively poor correlation between spatial clusters, raw material, and tools as compared to component 1 add weight to our argument that these materials were subject to some movement after their primary use and disposal.

The spatial relationships present suggest the western activity area was where tool production and retooling efforts were focused. It contains the vast majority of BTFs, retouch chips, bifaces, and points, along with nearly all the MCS. It also contains the majority of charcoal samples and is about 2 meters in diameter. These details suggest it may have been a hearth-centered activity area in which the artifacts had been post-depositionally moved just enough to lose any diagnostic shape or evidence for the hearth's location. The more dispersed artifact clusters in the eastern half of the component is dominated by CCS, unifaces and expedient tools, contains less charcoal, and has a dearth of BTFs or retouch chips. This pattern may suggest that resource processing behaviors (e.g., butchering) were performed across the eastern half of the site. The western activity area, with its higher concentration of artifacts, may have been the hub from which processing behaviors extended eastward (Binford 1978a; Binford 1978b). Unfortunately, since faunal remains at Owl Ridge were not preserved, we cannot directly test this conjecture.

COMPONENT 3: EXPEDIENT TOOL USE, LOGISTICS, AND DUMPING

Component 3 shows unique spatial relationships relative to components 1 and 2. The two concentrations in component 3 are in the farthest northeastern corner of the excavation area, effectively 180 degrees from the densest activity areas in the other components. One of these concentrations lies farther northwest and the other slightly southeast. Component 3's concentrations are also far denser and contain more artifacts than the component 1 and 2 clusters. Melton (2015) noted that, unlike with components 1 and 2, component 3 artifact refits were found between the two concentrations, indicating movement between them. Additionally, the few bifaces present are not spatially associated with each other or exclusively related to the concentrations. While unifaces are associated with concentrations/activity areas in both component 2 and 3, they are much more tightly clustered in component 3 than in component 2 (excluding the outlying end scraper). Cores are found across the component and, unlike component 2, are not spatially clustered within the two concentrations. There are also more cores in component 3 than in the other two components combined. There are, however, interesting similarities between components 2 and 3. Both contain two artifact concentrations/activity areas, one of which contains tightly concentrated K-means clusters. Outside the concentration/ activity areas, both components have a diffuse pattern of artifacts dominated by dispersed cores and tested cobbles, two expedient tools, and no dense concentrations of flakes. Taken together, these similarities and differences help us identify unique aspects associated with component 3.

When comparing activities between the three components, the most obvious point of difference is that component 3's densest artifact concentrations moved away from the ridgeline, approximately 10 meters. As noted by Gore and Graf (2018), core reduction activities dominated the site at this time, and this is reflected by the dense concentrations of cortical flakes in both concentrations. It also appears that expedient tool use was more concentrated and focused within the primary use areas as opposed to the use of bifaces and cores. The dispersed distribution of cores and the random distribution between cores and charcoal are interesting, since core reduction activities clearly dominated lithic production. We would expect cores to be closely associated with activity areas and the core reduction debitage where they were reduced, but this is only true for three of the seven cores. This is the only component where core reduction debitage and andesite raw material dominate the artifact concentrations. It also has the only tight clusters of charcoal located within any concentrations/clusters along with the only possible hearth feature (Gore and Graf 2018; Graf et al. 2019).

Other spatial relationships observed in component 3 reflect the interpretations presented by Gore and Graf (2018). The presence of clustered unifaces in both concentrations suggests that these tools were used for more concentrated tasks and disposed of in a less haphazard fashion. The abundance of cores distributed across the site reflect the regular use and reduction of raw materials in order to supply the inhabitants' toolkits with expedient tools or any other necessary equipment. The sheer number of artifacts, so concentrated in the northeast, indicates a more intense occupation than occurred during the Allerød or Younger Dryas. This may reflect a higher population or an occupation focused not just on hunting but on accessing and processing numerous resources available in the area. Based on the existing evidence, however, we suggest that the greater amount of artifacts is the direct result of the more active and successful procurement of local toolstone relative to previous occupations. It is also possible that the high number of artifacts could reflect not a more intensive occupation but repeated site visits over an extended period. We argue that this is unlikely. First, the two concentrations containing most of the artifacts also contain the most refits, and specifically, the most sequential refits of any component (Melton 2015). The presence of so many sequential refits is more likely to reflect contemporaneous activity. We also note that this component is located on colluvial sands with no evidence of pedogenesis. Further, it is capped by a loess deposit that had undergone spodosol development, suggesting that only after component 3 was deposited did the landscape become more stable, and yet never again visited by humans. Combined, the presence of sequential refits and the site undergoing depositional change without soil formation indicate component 3 most likely represents a single, intensive occupation. If it does represent repeated visits, it was of the same group performing nearly identical tasks over a very short time period.

Concentration shape and spatial relationships also reveal information about component 3 behaviors. The southeastern concentration is about 2–2.5 meters across, and as discussed in the results, has stronger association between the K-means clusters and both artifact and raw material types. The densest artifact scatter is generally ovate, with the long axis running northwest/southeast. Across this concentration, the spatially distinct artifact and material clusters discussed in the results suggest that different reduction activities on different materials occurred in different sections. Andesite and CCS were primarily worked to the north while basalt and MCS were worked in the south. These spatial distributions likely reflect workstations around a central location. We also point out a reduced concentration of artifacts, roughly in the center of this ovoid, potentially indicating a hearth (figure 4.22) (Anderson 1988; Binford 1983; Surovell and Waguespack 2007)

The northwestern concentration is roughly 1–1.5 meters across and contains the most artifacts and the most charcoal. Unlike the southeastern concentration, this area has little spatial distinction between raw material and artifact types. Instead, this concentration has a high artifact density and a single hearth feature in the northwestern corner (figure 4.22). While the size of this concentration does not

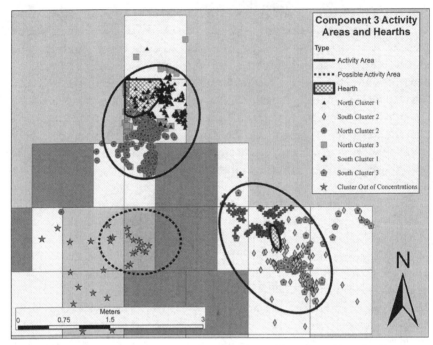

Figure 4.22. Component 3 concentrations with potential hearths and hearth adjacent materials identified.

match the expectations set by Anderson (1988), this concentration borders the limits of the excavation area to its east and west. As such, additional excavation is likely to expand its diameter, just as the maximum north/west extent of the concentration approaches 1.5–2 meters in length (figure 4.19).

Just south and west of the concentrations, units excavated in 1984 contain artifacts not considered in this spatial analysis (figures 4.6 and 4.13). While we refrained from considering the exact provenience of artifacts excavated in 1984, Phippen (1988) did identify 55 artifacts from component 3 across these four test units. Based on his discussion, most of these artifacts are associated with the two artifact concentrations discussed above or the diffuse scatter to the south. Additionally, the middle test unit contains a small group of artifacts associated with component 3's north-central cluster (figure 4.13). These additional artifacts suggest that the cluster may be another activity area.

An alternative behavioral explanation for these distributions could be Bamforth and Becker's (2007) dumping model recognized at the Allen site (see also Bamforth, chapter 9). In this context, the southeastern concentration could represent an activity area due to its size and the discrete spatial relationships between artifacts and raw materials, whereas the northwestern concentration may fit the pattern of a dumping location due to its density and variability of artifact and raw material types. Two characteristics of the component 3 concentrations could contribute to this interpretation. First, South (1979) and McKellar (1973) noted that artifacts subject to cleaning are likely to be size-sorted, the activity area should be made up of small objects, and dumping locations should have larger pieces. We do see a lot of retouch chips (the smallest debitage type) in the southeastern concentration; however, we also see many cortical spalls (often the largest debitage type) in this concentration. Second, the number of artifacts present in the northwestern concentration is far higher than any activity area or concentration anywhere else on the site, perhaps indicating component 3 visitors cleaned up across the site and dumped materials at the northwestern-concentration location (Bamforth and Becker 2007).

Despite possible correlations between the dumping model and component 3's northwestern concentration, we argue that each of the above observations can be equally explained by other factors observed within the component. First, the movement of artifacts between the two concentrations may be expected by their proximity. If two activity areas are so close, we should expect artifacts and/or people to move between them, especially as individuals collaborate on lithic reduction and toolstone procurement tasks (Binford and O'Connel 1984; McCall 2012; Milne 2012). Only 8 percent of the refits associated with component 3 are found between concentrations, whereas 90 percent of them come from within concentrations (the other 2 percent of refits are between the northwestern concentration and the southern sparse artifact scatter). To us, this pattern better reflects movement of people and raw materials between concentrations during lithic reduction rather than mass relocation of materials during site cleanup and dumping (Stout 2002). The raw material and artifact type variability within the northwestern concentration can be explained by intensive hearth-centric behavior where multiple individuals would have worked multiple tools in a small area. Indeed, a hearth feature was identified during excavation of this concentration (Graf et al. 2019). Further, the sequential refits discussed above align well with the lithic technology associated with this component: uniface production and core reduction. As such, the northwestern concentration appears to represent a workshop location where cores were reduced, unifaces produced, and some biface production took place. The potential size sorting between the northwestern and southeastern concentrations is just as likely to be the result of different activities being performed at the two concentration locations, especially given that both small and large debitage pieces are found in both concentrations. Owl Ridge is a logistical camp with only a few thousand artifacts deposited over a short period of time with discrete spatial separation. By comparison, the Allen site is a residential camp with thousands more artifacts with less discrete spatial separation that provides evidence of repeated episodes of dumping, which is to be expected at residential bases (Bamforth and Becker 2007). As discussed already, at Owl Ridge there is no evidence of repeated component 3 site occupations separated by extended periods, especially since the component lies in sediments that were undergoing active deposition.

The spatial distribution in the northwestern concentration of component 3 is most likely the result of a lithic workshop where extensive core reduction, most bifacial flake removal, and a small amount of unifacial production occurred, whereas the southeastern concentration is most similar to component 1's southwestern cluster: it is ~2 meters in diameter with spatially distinct concentrations containing different types of raw material and debitage. While the presence of a hearth is less definitive, the shape and artifact distribution does point to one being present. People working here appear to have focused their activities in particular areas, with andesite and CCS core reduction to the north and basalt and MCS retouch and tool sharpening to the south. The diffuse distribution of artifacts southwest of the concentrations has multiple possible explanations. The distribution of materials 1–3 meters southwest of the concentrations may represent the toss-zone outside the immediate drop zone next to the concentrations (Binford 1983). As discussed above, this area may also represent a less intensively used activity area that could be revealed with additional analyses. As with component 2, resource processing to the southwest may have resulted in the artifact distribution observed (Binford 1978a; 1978b). We also note the correlation between the outlying end scraper, a single core, and the component 1 and 2 concentrations in the southwestern excavation area. While it is apparent that those who occupied the site during component 3 focused their lithic reduction activities further from the edge of the ridge, there was still every reason to keep an eye out for animals in the Teklanika valley. It is possible that the end scraper, core, and some of the diffuse materials located in the southwestern-most area of component 3 represent a small, poorly preserved activity location where one or two individuals performed activities similar to those in the northeast while also watching the valley below.

CONCLUSION

This study has allowed us to investigate the distribution of artifacts across each of Owl Ridge's components, identify activity areas and associated artifact types, and ultimately help us interpret the behaviors that formed the site. Owl Ridge presents a challenge for spatial analysis because it is almost completely dominated by lithic material. The absence of discrete features, faunal material, or other organic remains means that we were not able to use organics or preserved activity features, such as hearths, to inform our interpretations and guide us in our research. Fortunately, by taking a statistical approach focused on spatial relationships, this study has demonstrated that archaeologists can uncover not just behavioral adaptations related to the site's space but organize these behaviors across the site. We can even present informed hypotheses about the location of past features, such as hearths, that have not survived.

The results presented provide additional support for the paleoenvironmental model explaining the presence of different toolkits in central Alaska. Owl Ridge was clearly an important place on the landscape across a wide range of time, exemplified by the three cultural components. Each component reflects a unique approach to landscape and toolstone use. During the Allerød and component 1, people used the site as a hunting camp, focusing on formal tools that were used in consistent spatial contexts across the site. They used local resources, but their local provisioning supplemented the resources they brought with them. The Allerød hunting camp had at least one hearth and perhaps as many as three. The occupants spent their time working around the hearth to the southwest, but also near possible hearths to the east and northeast. They reequipped the tools and restocked the materials they used while at the site and may have engaged in minimal processing in the northeastern activity area.

During the Younger Dryas and component 2, people came to the site with greater knowledge of the resources available and less equipment on hand. They again focused on producing formal tools around hearths, but more of these tools were made on site. The hunting camp may have been smaller, with only one or perhaps two hearths present, slightly closer to the edge of the ridge. There is also a chance that the occupants expanded their site activities to include resource processing using expedient tools and unifaces northeast of the ridgeline.

After the Younger Dryas, as climate began warming, Owl Ridge was occupied one last time. The component 3 occupation was more intense than earlier occupations, most likely due to the new focus on acquiring local toolstone resources. People came to the area knowing what toolstone resources were available and made extensive use of them when they got there. Like the Allerød occupants, they also had equipment on hand, perhaps reflecting greater landscape awareness and thus greater ability to efficiently acquire resources across a wider area. While at Owl Ridge, their toolstone use focused on reducing local raw materials to produce unifaces and other expedient tools in a workshop area centered around two hearths. They may have also engaged in processing activities across the rest of the site and used Owl Ridge as a base camp for forays into the Teklanika valley. Unlike previous inhabitants, the last occupants felt no need to have a hearthside view of the Teklanika valley while working local toolstones. But it is unlikely the valley was neglected, as the diffuse distribution of artifacts toward the ridgeline suggests occupants regularly deposited artifacts where they could see the valley below. Across these periods, Owl Ridge acted as a persistent place on the landscape where hunter-gatherers visited to take advantage of a commanding view and, until the growth of the Alaska's boreal forests, successfully pursued their lifeways.

Of course, the methods discussed in this paper are applicable to a wide range of archaeological questions and sites. While we focus here on the late Pleistocene in Alaska, intra-site spatial analyses are useful anywhere that archaeologists seek to clarify the relationships between artifacts at a site. We also reiterate that these methods are particularly useful for understanding site patterning and use when sites are limited in scope and preservation. For instance, these methods may be of particular interest in the southeastern United States, where organic materials and charcoal very rarely preserve. For this study, our interpretations are bound to be reconsidered as new data and new analyses are applied to Owl Ridge and other open-air sites across Alaska. Nonetheless, the results illustrate how culture and behavior are reflected in the type and distribution of artifacts across a given site. Spatial statistics provide powerful tools that allow for more nuanced analyses of sites, even when all but one or two material types—in this case lithics and charcoal—are preserved. At Owl Ridge, we will continue to look at variables such as tool size, raw material type, and paleoethnobotanical data, in conjunction with the recorded spatial data, to hone and refine our understanding of Alaska's first inhabitants.

REFERENCES

Abbot, M. B., B. P. Finney, M. D. Edwards, and K. R. Kelts. 2000. "Paleohydrology of Birch Lake, Central Alaska: A Multiproxy Approach to Lake-Level Records." *Quaternary Research* 53: 154–166.

Anderson, Douglas D. 1988. "Onion Portage: An Archaeological Site on the Kobuk River, Northwestern Alaska." *Anthropological Papers of the University of Alaska* 20: 27–48.

Anderson, Patricia M., and Linda B. Brubaker. 1994. "Vegetation History of Northcentral Alaska: A Mapped Summary of Late-Quaternary Pollen Data." *Quaternary Science Reviews* 13: 71–92.

Anderson, Patricia M., Mary E. Edwards, and Linda B. Brubaker. 2004. "Results and Paleoclimate Implications of 35 Years of Paleoecological Research in Alaska." In *The Quaternary Period in the United States*, edited by Alan R. Gillespie, Stephen C. Porter, and Brian F. Atwater, 427–440. Amsterdam: Elsevier.

Bamforth, Douglas B., and Mark Becker. 2007. "Spatial Structure and Refitting of the Allen Site Lithic Assemblage." In *The Allen Site*, edited by Douglas B. Bamforth, 123–147. Albuquerque: University of New Mexico Press.

Barber, Valerie A., and Bruce P. Finney. 2000. "Late Quaternary Paleoclimatic Reconstruction for Interior Alaska based on Paleolake-Level Data and Hydrologic Models." *Journal of Paleolimnology* 24: 29–41.

Bever, Michael R. 2006. "Rethinking the Putu Site: Results of the Spatial Analysis of a Fluted Point Site in Northern Alaska." *Arctic Anthropology* 43: 20–39.

Bigelow, Nancy H., Jim Begét, and W. Roger Powers. 1990. "Latest Pleistocene Increase in Wind Intensity Recorded in Eolian Sediments from Central Alaska." *Quaternary Research* 38: 160–168.

Bigelow, Nancy H., and Mary E. Edwards. 2001. "A 14,000 yr Paleoenvironmental Record from Windmill Lake, Central Alaska: Late Glacial and Holocene Vegetation in the Alaska Range." *Quaternary Science Reviews* 20: 203–215.

Bigelow, Nancy H., and W. Roger Powers. 2001. "Climate, Vegetation, and Archaeology 14,000–9,000 cal yr B.P. in Central Alaska." *Arctic Anthropology* 38: 171–195.

Binford, Lewis R. 1978a. "Dimensional Analysis of Behavior and Site Structure: Learning from the Eskimo Hunting Stand." *American Antiquity* 43: 330–361.

Binford, Lewis R. 1978b. *Nunamiut Ethnoarchaeology*. New York: Academic Press.

Binford, Lewis R. 1983. *In Pursuit of the Past: Decoding the Archaeological Record*. New York: Thames and Hudson.

Binford, Lewis R and James F. O'Connell. 1984. "An Alyawara Day: The Stone Quarry." *Journal of Anthropological Research* 40: 406–432.

Brubaker, Linda B., Patricia M. Anderson, Mary E. Edwards, and Anotoly V. Lozhkin. 2005. "Beringia as a Glacial Refugium for Boreal Trees and Shrubs: New Perspectives from Mapped Pollen Data." *Journal of Biogeography* 32: 833–348.

Bourgeon, Lauriane, Ariane Burke, and Thomas Higham. 2017. "Earliest Human Presence in North America Dated to the Last Glacial Maximum: New Radiocarbon Dates from Bluefish Caves, Canada." *PLOS One* 12: e0169486.

Bowers, P. M., and J. Reuther. 2008. "AMS Re-Dating of the Carlo Creek Site: Nenana Valley, Central Alaska." *Current Research in the Pleistocene* 25: 58–61.

Cahen, D., L. H. Kelly, and F. L. van Noten. 1979. "Stone Tools, Tool Kits, and Human Behavior in Prehistory." *Current Anthropology* 20: 661–672.

Carr, P. J. 1991. "Left in the Dust: Contextual Information in Model-Focused Archaeology." In *The Interpretation of Archaeological Spatial Patterning*, edited by E. M. Kroll and T. D. Price, 221–256. New York: Plenum Press.

Coffman, Sam C. 2011. "Archaeology at Teklanika West (HEA-001): An Upland Archaeological Site, Central Alaska." MA thesis, Department of Anthropology, University of Alaska, Fairbanks.

Cook, John P. 1996. "Healy Lake." In *American Beginnings: The Prehistory and Paleoecology of Beringia*, edited by Frederick H. West, 323–327. Chicago: University of Chicago Press.

DiPietro, Lyndsay M., Kelly E. Graf, Steve G. Driese, and Gary E. Stinchcomb. 2019. "Microstratigraphy of Owl Ridge: A Small-Scale Approach to Site Formation, Soil Development, and Paleoenvironment at a Pleistocene-Holocene Boundary Site in Central Alaska." *Quaternary International*, submitted October 21, 2018.

Erlandson, Jon, Rudy Walswer, Howard Maxwell, Nancy Bigelow, John Cook, Ralph Lively, Charles Adkins, Dave Dodson, Andrew Higgs, and Janett Wilber. 1991. "Two Early Sites of Eastern Beringia; Context and Chronology in Alaskan Interior Archaeology." *Radiocarbon* 33: 35–50.

ESRI. 2017a. "How Average Nearest Neighbor Works." Accessed December 15, 2017. http://pro.arcgis.com/en/pro-app/tool-reference/spatial-statistics/h-how-average -nearest-neighbor-distance-spatial-st.htm.

ESRI. 2017b. "How Grouping Analysis Works." Accessed December 15, 2017. http://pro .arcgis.com/en/pro-app/tool-reference/spatial-statistics/how-grouping-analysis-works .htm.

ESRI. 2017c. "How Kernel Density Works." Accessed December 15, 2017. http://pro.arcgis .com/en/pro-app/tool-reference/spatial-analyst/how-kernel-density-works.htm.

ESRI. 2017d. "How Multi-Distance Spatial Cluster Analysis (Ripley's K-function) Works." Accessed December 15, 2017. http://desktop.arcgis.com/en/arcmap/10.3/tools/spatial -statistics-toolbox/h-how-multi-distance-spatial-cluster-analysis-ripl.htm.

Gal, R. 2002. "Providence and Frugality: Tools for High Latitude Living." In *29th Annual Meeting of the Alaska Anthropological Association*. Alaska: Anchorage.

Goebel, Ted. 2011. "What Is the Nenana Complex? Raw Material Procurement and Technological Organization at Walker Road, Central Alaska." In *From the Yenisei to the Yukon: Interpreting Lithic Assemblage Variability in Late Pleistocene/Early Holocene Beringia*, edited by Ted Goebel and Ian Buvit, 199–214. College Station: Texas A&M University Press.

Goebel, Ted, and Nancy H. Bigelow. 1996. "Panguingue Creek." In *American Beginnings: The Prehistory and Palaeoecology of Beringia*, edited by Frederick H. West, 366–370. Chicago: University of Chicago Press.

Goebel, Ted, and Ian Buvit, eds. 2011. *From the Yenisei to the Yukon: Interpreting Lithic Assemblage Variability in Late Pleistocene/Early Holocene Beringia*. College Station: Texas A&M University Press.

Goebel, Ted, W. Roger Powers, and Nancy H. Bigelow. 1991. "The Nenana Complex of Alaska and Clovis Origins." In *Clovis Origins and Adaptations*, edited by Robert Bonnichsen and K. L. Turnmire, 49–79. Corvallis: The Center for the Study of the First Americans, Oregon State University.

Goebel, Ted, Sergei B. Slobodin, and Michael R. Waters. 2010. "New Dates from Ushki-1, Kamchatka, Confirm 13,000 cal BP Age for Earliest Paleolithic Occupation." *Journal of Archaeological Science* 37: 2640–2649.

Goebel, Ted, Michael R. Waters, Margarita Dikova. 2003. "The Archaeology of Ushki Lake, Kamchatka, and the Pleistocene Peopling of the Americas." *Science* 301: 501–505.

Gómez Coutouly, Y. A. 2011. "Identifying Pressure Flaking Modes at Diuktai Cave: A Case Study of the Siberian Upper Paleolithic Microblade Tradition." In *From the Yenisei to the Yukon: Interpreting Lithic Assemblage Variability in Late Pleistocene/Early Holocene Beringia*, edited by Ted Goebel and Ian Buvit, 75–90. College Station: Texas A&M University Press.

Gómez Coutouly, Y. A. 2012. "Pressure Microblade Industries in Pleistocene-Holocene Interior Alaska: Current Data and Discussions." In *Emergence of Pressure Blade Making: From Origins to Modern Experimentation*, edited by P. M. Desrosiers, 347–374. New York: Springer.

Gore, Angela K., and Kelly E. Graf. 2018. "Technology and Human Response to Environmental Change at the Pleistocene-Holocene Boundary in Eastern Beringia: A View from Owl Ridge, Central Alaska." In *Lithic Technological Organization and Paleoenvironmental Change: Global and Diachronic Perspectives*, edited by Erick Robinson and Frédéric Sellet, 203–234. New York: Springer.

Graf, Kelly E., and Nancy H. Bigelow. 2011. "Human Response to Climate during the Younger Dryas Chronozone in Central Alaska." *Quaternary International* 242: 434–451.

Graf, Kelly E., John Blong, and Ted Goebel. 2010. "A Concave-Based Projection from New Excavations at the Owl Ridge Site, Central Alaska." *Current Research in the Pleistocene* 27: 88–91.

Graf, Kelly E., Lyndsay M. DiPietro, Kathryn E. Krasinski, and Angela K. Gore. 2015. "Dry Creek Revisited: New Excavations, Radiocarbon Dates, and Site Formation Inform on the Peopling of Eastern Beringia." *American Antiquity* 80: 671–694.

Graf, Kelly E., and Ted Goebel. 2009. "Upper Paleolithic Toolstone Procurement and Selection across Beringia." In *Lithic Materials and Paleolithic Societies*, edited by Brooke Blades and Brian Adams, 55–77. London: Blackwell Publishers.

Graf, Kelly E., Angela K. Gore, J. Anne Melton, Tarah Marks, Lyndsay DiPietro, Ted Goebel, Michael R. Waters, and David Rhode. 2019. "Recent Excavations at Owl Ridge, Interior Alaska: Site Stratigraphy, Chronology, and Site Formation and Implications for Late Pleistocene Archaeology and Peopling of Eastern Beringia." *Geoarchaeology: An International Journal* (submitted February 15, 2019).

Guthrie, R. Dale. 2006. "New Carbon Dates Link Climatic Change with Human Colonization and Pleistocene Extinctions." *Nature* 441: 207–209.

Guthrie, R. Dale. 2017. "Paleoecology of the Site and its Implications for Early Hunters." In *Dry Creek: Archaeology and Paleoecology of a Late Pleistocene Alaskan Hunting Camp*, edited by W. Roger Powers, R. Dale Guthrie, Jon F. Hoffecker, and Ted Goebel, 153–192. College Station: Texas A&M University Press.

Hamilton, Thomas D., and Ted Goebel. 1999. "Late Pleistocene Peopling of Alaska." In *Ice Age Peoples of North America: Environments, Origins, and Adaptations*, edited by Robson Bonnichsen and Karen L. Turnmire, 156–199. Corvallis: Oregon State University Press.

Higgs, Andrew S. 1992. "Technological and Spatial Considerations of the Walker Road Site: Implications from a Lithic Refit Study." MA thesis, Department of Anthropology, University of Alaska, Fairbanks.

Hirasawa, Yu, and Charles E. Holmes. 2017. "The Relationship between Microblade Morphology and Production Technology in Alaska from the Perspective of the Swan Point Site." *Quaternary International* 442: 104–117.

Hodder, Ian. 1979. "Economic and Social Stress and Material Culture Patterning." *American Antiquity* 44: 446–454.

Hoffecker, John F. 2001. "Late Pleistocene and Early Holocene Sites in the Nenana River Valley, Central Alaska." *Arctic Anthropology* 38: 139–153.

Hoffecker, John F. 2017. "The Occupation Floors at the Dry Creek Site." In *Dry Creek: Archaeology and Paleoecology of a Late Pleistocene Alaskan Hunting Camp*, edited by Ted Goebel, 107–152. College Station: Texas A&M University Press.

Hoffecker, John F., and Scott A. Elias. 2007. *The Human Ecology of Beringia*. New York: Columbia University Press.

Hoffecker, John F., W. Roger Powers, and Ted Goebel. 1993. "The Colonization of Beringia and the Peopling of the New World." *Science* 259: 46–53.

Holmes, Charles E. 2001. "Tanana River Valley Archaeology Circa 14,000 to 9,000 BP." *Arctic Anthropology* 38: 154–170.

Holmes, Charles E. 2011. "The Beringian and Transitional Periods in Alaska." In *From the Yenisei to the Yukon: Interpreting Lithic Assemblage Variability in Late Pleistocene/Early Holocene Beringia*, edited by Ted Goebel and Ian Buvit, 179–191. College Station: Texas A&M University.

Hu, Feng Sheng, Linda B. Brubaker, and Patricia M. Anderson. 1993. "A 12,000-Year Record of Vegetation Change and Soil Development from Wein Lake, Central Alaska." *Canadian Journal of Botany* 71: 1133–1142.

Kaufman, D. S., T. A. Ager, N. J. Anderson, P. M. Anderson, J. T. Andrews, P. T. Bartlein, L. B. Brubaker, L. L. Coats, L. C. Cwynar, M. L. Duvall, A. S. Dyke, M. E. Edwards, W. R. Eisner, K. Gajewski, A. Geirsdóttir, F. S. Hu, A. E. Jennings, M. R. Kaplan, M. W. Kerwin, A. V. Lozhkin, G. M. MacDonald, G. H. Miller, C. J. Mock, W. W. Oswald, B. L. Otto-Bliesner, D. F. Porinchu, K. Rühland, J. P. Smol, E. J. Steig, and B. B. Wolfe.

2004. "Holocene Thermal Maximum in the Western Arctic (0–180°W)." *Quaternary Science Reviews* 23: 529–560.

Keeler, Dustin. 2007. "Intrasite Spatial Analysis of a Late Upper Paleolithic French Site Using Geographic Information Systems." *Journal of World Anthropology: Occasional Papers* 3 (1): 29–33.

Kintigh, Keith W. 1990. "Intrasite Spatial Analysis: A Commentary on Major Methods." In *Mathematics and Information Science in Archaeology: A Flexible Framework, Studies in Modern Archaeology*, edited by Albertus Vorrips, 165–200. Bonn, Germany: Holos.

Kokorowski, H. D., P. M. Anderson, C. J. Mock, and A. V. Lozhkin. 2008. "A Re-Evaluation and Spatial Analysis of Evidence for a Younger Dryas Climate Reversal in Beringia." *Quaternary Science Reviews* 27: 1710–1722.

Krasinski, Kathryn E., and David R. Yesner. 2008. "Late Pleistocene/Early Holocene Site Structure in Beringia: A Case Study from the Broken Mammoth Site, Interior Alaska." *Alaska Journal of Anthropology* 6: 27–41.

Kuhn, Steven L. 1995. *Mousterian Lithic Technology: An Ecological Perspective*. Princeton, NJ: Princeton University Press.

Kunz, Michael, Michaeol R. Bever, and Charles Adkins. 2003. "The Mesa Site: Paleoindians above the Arctic Circle." *Alaska Office, Open File Report No. 86.* Anchorage: US Bureau of Land Management.

Lancelotti, Carla, Joan Negre Pérez, Jonàs Alcaina-Mateos, and Fancesco Carrer. 2017. "Intra-Site Spatial Analysis in Ethnoarchaeology." *Environmental Archaeology* 22: 354–364.

Lloyd, Andrea H., Mary E. Edwards, Bruce P. Finney, Jason A. Lynch, Valerie Barber, and Nancy H. Bigelow. 2006. "Holocene Development of the Alaskan Boreal Forest." In *Alaska's Changing Boreal Forest*, edited by F. Stuart Chapin III, Mark W. Oswood, Keith Van Cleve, Leslie A. Viereck, and David L. Verbyla, 62–78. New York: Oxford University Press.

Marean, Curtis W., and Leanne Bertino. 1994. "Intrasite Spatial Analysis of Bone: Subtracting the Effect of Secondary Carnivore Consumers." *American Antiquity* 58: 748–768.

McCall, Grant S. 2012. "Ethnoarchaeology and the Organization of Lithic Technology." *Journal of Archaeological Research* 20: 157–203.

McKellar, Judith. 1973. "Correlations and the Explanation of Distributions." MS thesis, Arizona State Museum, Tucson.

Meiri, Meirav, Adrian M. Lister, Matthew J. Collins, Noreen Tuross, Ted Goebel, Simon Blockley, Grant D. Zazula, Nienke van Doorn, R. Dale Guthrie, Gennady G. Boeskorov, Gennady F. Baryshnikov, Andrei Sher, and Ian Barnes. 2014. "Faunal Record Identifies Bering Isthmus Conditions as Constraint to End-Pleistocene Migration to the New World." *Proceedings of the Royal Society B: Biological Sciences* 281: 20132167.

Melton, Judith A. 2015. "Pieces to a Puzzle: A Lithic Refit Study Evaluating Stratigraphic and Lithic Components of the Owl Ridge Site, Central Alaska." Senior undergraduate thesis, Department of Anthropology, Texas A&M University, College Station.

Milne, S. Brooke. 2012. "Lithic Raw Material Availability and Palaeo-Eskimo Novice Flintknapping." In *Archaeology and Apprenticeship: Body Knowledge, Identity, and Communities of Practice*, edited by Willeke Wendrich, 119–144. Tucson: University of Arizona Press.

Mitchell, Andy. 2005. *The ESRI Guide to GIS Analysis*, Volume 2. ESRI Press.

Moreno-Mayar, J. Víctor, Ben A. Potter, Lasse Vinner, Matthias Steinrücken, Simon Rasmussen, Jonathan Terhorst, John A. Kamm, Anders Albrechtsen, Anna-Sapfo Malaspinas, Martin Sikora, Joshua D. Reuther, Joel D. Irish, Ripan S. Malhi, Ludovic Orlando, Yun S. Song, Rasmus Nielsen, David J. Meltzer, and Eske Willerslev. 2018. "Terminal Pleistocene Alaskan Genome Reveals First Founding Population of Native Americans." *Nature* 553: 203–207.

Murray, P. 1980. "Discard Location: The Ethnographic Data." *American Antiquity* 45: 490–502.

Pearson, Georges A. 1999. "Early Occupations and Cultural Sequence at Moose Creek: A Late Pleistocene Site in Central Alaska." *Arctic* 52: 332–345.

Phippen, Peter G. 1988. "Archaeology at Owl Ridge: A Pleistocene-Holocene Boundary Age Site in Central Alaska." MA thesis, Department of Anthropology, University of Alaska, Fairbanks.

Pinder, David, Izumi Shimada, and David Gregory. 1979. "The Nearest-Neighbor Statistic: Archaeological Application and New Developments." *American Antiquity* 44: 430–445.

Pitulko, Vladimir V. 2011. "The Berelekh Quest: A Review of Forty Years of Research in the Mammoth Graveyard in Northeast Siberia." *Geoarchaeology* 26: 5–32.

Pitulko, Vladimir, Elena Pavlova, and Pavel Nikolskiy. 2017. "Revising the Archaeological Record of the Upper Pleistocene Arctic Siberia: Human Dispersal and Adaptations in MIS 3 and 2." *Quaternary Science Reviews* 165: 127–148.

Plasket, D. C. 1976. "Preliminary Report: A Cultural Resources Survey in an area of the Nenana and Teklanika Rivers of Central Alaska." Submitted to Alaska Division of Parks, Anchorage.

Potter, Ben A. 2005. "Site Structure and Organization in Central Alaska: Archaeological Investigations at Gerstle River." PhD dissertation, Department of Anthropology, University of Alaska, Fairbanks.

Potter, Ben A. 2007. "Models of Faunal Processing and Economy in Early Holocene Interior Alaska." *Environmental Archaeology* 12: 3–23.

Potter, Ben A., Charles E. Holmes, and David R. Yesner. 2014. "Technology and Economy among the Earliest Prehistoric Foragers in Interior Eastern Beringia." In *Paleoamerican

Odyssey, edited by Kelly E. Graf, Caroline V. Ketron, and Michael R. Waters, 81–103. College Station: Texas A&M University Press.

Powers, W. Roger, R. Dale Guthrie, and John F. Hoffecker. 2017. *Dry Creek: Archaeology and Paleoecology of a Late Pleistocene Alaskan Hunting Camp*, edited by Ted Goebel. College Station: Texas A&M University Press.

Powers, W. Roger, and John F. Hoffecker. 1989. "Late Pleistocene Settlement in the Nenana Valley, Central Alaska." *American Antiquity* 54: 263–287.

Ramsey, Christopher B. 2019. "OxCal 4.3." Accessed April 7, 2019. https://c14.arch.ox.ac .uk/oxcal/OxCal.html.

Reimer, P. J., E. Bard, A. Bayliss, J. W. Beck, P. G. Blackwell, C. Bronk Ramsey, C. E. Buck, H. Cheng, R. L. Edwards, M. Reidrich, P. M. Grootes, T. P. Guilderson, H. Haflidason, I. Hajdas, C. Hatté, T. J. Heaton, D. L. Hoffman, A. G. Hogg, K. A. Hughen, K. F. Kaiser, B. Kromer, S. W. Manning, M. Niu, R. W. Reimer, D. A. Richards, E. M. Scott, J. R. Southon, R. A. Staff, C. S. M. Turney, and J. van der Plicht. 2013. "Intcal13 and Marine13 Radiocarbon Age Calibration Curves 0–50,000 Years cal BP." *Radiocarbon* 55: 1869–1887.

Schiffer, Michael B. 1996. *Formation Processes of the Archaeological Record*. Salt Lake City: University of Utah Press.

Sergant, Joris, Philippe Crombé, and Yves Perdaen. 2006. "The 'Invisible' Hearths: A Contribution to the Discernment of Mesolithic Non-structured Surface Hearths." *Journal of Archaeological Science* 33: 999–1007.

Simek, J. F. 1987. "Spatial Order and Behavioral Change in the French Paleolithic." *Antiquity* 61: 25–40.

Simek, J., and R. R. Larick. 1983. "The Recognition of Multiple Spatial Patterns: A Case Study from the French Upper Paleolithic." *Journal of Archaeological Science* 10: 165–180.

South, Stanley. 1979. "Historic Site Content, Structure and Function." *American Antiquity* 44: 213–237.

Stevenson, M. G. 1991. "Beyond the Formation of Hearth Associated Artifact Assemblages." In *Interpretation of Archaeological Spatial Patterning*, edited by E. M. Kroll, and T. D. Price, 269–299. New York: Plenum Press.

Stout, Dietrich. 2002. "Skill and Cognition in Stone Tool Production: An Ethnographic Case Study of Irian Jaya." *Current Anthropology* 43: 693–722.

Surovell, Todd A., and Nicole M. Waguespack. 2007. "Folsom Hearth-Centered Use of Space at Barger Gulch, Locality B." In *Frontiers in Colorado Paleoindian Archaeology*, edited by Bonnie L. Pitblado and Robert H. Brunswig, 219–259. Boulder: University Press of Colorado.

Taylor, Barry, Ben Elliot, Chantal Conneller, Nicky Milner, Alex Bayliss, Becky Knight, and Mike Bamforth. 2017. *Proceedings of the Prehistoric Society* 83: 23–42.

Thorson, Robert M. 2006. "Artifact Mixing at the Dry Creek Site, Interior Alaska." *Anthropological Papers of the University of Alaska* 4: 1–10.

Vachula, Richard S., Yongsong Huang, William M. Longo, Sylvia G. Dee, William C. Daniels, and James M. Russell. 2019. "Evidence of Ice Age Humans in Eastern Beringia Suggests Early Migration to North America." *Quaternary Science Reviews* 205: 35–44.

West, Fredrick H. 1967. The Donnelly Ridge Site and the Definition of an Early Core and Blade Complex in Central Alaska. *American Antiquity* 32: 360–82.

Whallon, Robert J. 1973. "Spatial Analysis of Palaeolithic Occupation Areas." In *The Explanation of Culture Change*, edited by Collin R. Renfrew, 115–130. Pittsburgh: University of Pittsburgh Press.

Whallon, Robert J. 1974. "Spatial Analysis of Occupation Floors II: The Application of Nearest Neighbor Analysis." *American Antiquity* 39: 16–34.

Wygal, Brian T. 2009. "Prehistoric Colonization of Southcentral Alaska: Human Adaptations in a Post Glacial World." PhD dissertation, Department of Anthropology, University of Nevada, Reno.

Wygal, Brian T. 2011. "The Microblade/Non-Microblade Dichotomy: Climatic Implications, Toolkit Variability, and the Role of Tiny Tools in Eastern Beringia." In *From the Yenisei to the Yukon: Interpreting Lithic Assemblage Variability in Late Pleistocene/Early Holocene Beringia*, edited by Ted Goebel and Ian Buvit, 234–254. College Station: Texas A&M University Press.

Yesner, David R. 1996. "Human Adaptation at the Pleistocene-Holocene Boundary (Circa 13,000 to 8,000 BP) in Eastern Beringia." In *Humans at the End of the Ice Age: The Archaeology of the Pleistocene Holocene Transition*, edited by Lawrence G. Straus, Berit V. Eriksen, Jon M. Erlandson, and David R. Yesner, 255–276. New York: Plenum Press.

Yesner, David R. 2001. "Human Dispersal into Interior Alaska: Antecedent Conditions, Mode of Colonization, and Adaptations." *Quaternary Science Reviews* 20: 315–327.

Yesner, David R. 2007. "Faunal Extinctions, Hunter-Gatherer Foraging Strategies, and Subsistence Diversity among Eastern Beringia." In *Foragers of the Terminal Pleistocene in North America*, edited by Renee B. Walker and Boyce N. Driskell, 15–31. Lincoln: University of Nebraska Press.

Younie, Angela M., and Thomas E. Gillispie. 2016. "Lithic Technology at Linda's Point, Healy Lake, Alaska." *Arctic* 69: 79–98.

5

Spatial Analysis of a Clovis Hearth-Centered Activity Area at the La Prele Mammoth Site, Converse County, Wyoming

MADELINE E. MACKIE, TODD A. SUROVELL, SPENCER PELTON,
MATTHEW O'BRIEN, ROBERT L. KELLY, GEORGE C. FRISON, ROBERT YOHE,
STEVE TETEAK, BETH SHAPIRO, AND JOSHUA D. KAPP

INTRODUCTION

Large game hunting is often a cooperative endeavor among the members of one or more residential groups who together fulfill several labor-intensive roles related to pursuing, killing, processing, and preserving yields from animals. Following hunting success, cooperative hunting groups are faced with two mobility options: transport their kill back to a residential basecamp or move their camp to the kill. Among pedestrian foragers that hunt very large animals (e.g., proboscideans) or groups of large animals (e.g., bison herds), residential groups most often move to kill sites (e.g., Duffy 1984, 158–166; Fisher 1992, 1993; Turnbull 1961, 138), since the transport of yields from kill sites to base camps is an inefficient means of handling large quantities of animal products (Metcalf and Barlow 1992). Once relocated, hunt participants establish short-term camps near the kill site, which are used for domestic and processing activities (Fisher 1992, 68). Use of short-term camps near large animal kills is reflected in ethnographic (e.g., Fisher 1992) and archaeological (e.g., Frison 1967; Huckell et al., chapter 7) records of societies that practice terrestrial large-game hunting.

Most hunter-gatherer archaeologists distinguish between residential and kill sites, but the distinction may be blurred among foragers with high residential mobility adapted to generalized terrestrial hunting. These groups are instead expected to regularly establish camps adjacent to animal kills (Kelly and Todd

https://doi.org/10.5876/9781646422265.c005

1988; Spiess 1984). North American archaeologists have long alluded to the notion that early Paleoindian (i.e., Clovis) settlement may be characteristic of residentially mobile megafaunal specialists (Waguespack and Surovell 2003) who establish camps near their kills to house hunt participants and facilitate processing tasks (e.g., Fisher 1992, 76; Kelly and Todd 1988). Among foragers with frequent residential moves such as Clovis, kill and camp sites should often be one and the same.

Such a position would lead one to assume there are many Clovis campsites, but archaeologists have found relatively few in the North American West compared to animal kills, caches, and other types of Clovis sites (Cannon and Meltzer 2004). The small number of known Clovis campsites in the West are located where we might expect them, given high residential mobility settlement patterns and short-term occupations near animal kill sites. The Murray Springs site (Haynes and Huckell 2007) and El Fin del Mundo (Sanchez et al. 2014) meet the expectations of a high residential mobility settlement pattern because both sites contain Clovis camps within a couple hundred meters of proboscidean kill sites. The ephemeral camp at the Aubrey Clovis site may also be a good example of a high residential mobility settlement, though no animal kills were discovered at Aubrey (Ferring 2001). Other than these three, the North American West contains little evidence for Clovis campsites.

We suspect that archaeologists have found so few Clovis campsites because the camps of highly mobile foragers with curated toolkits are difficult to find. Given a high residential mobility foraging system, most Clovis campsites were likely not occupied long enough to accumulate much refuse (Kelly and Todd 1988, 236–238). Moreover, we should not expect Clovis foragers to have created features indicative of residential occupation, such as large hearths, house floors, or substantial structures, because they did not occupy camps for long before moving on to the next animal kill. If the residential sites of high mobility foragers contain very few artifacts and features, then how can archaeologists find them?

In this chapter, we identify an ephemeral Clovis household located adjacent to a mammoth kill at the La Prele Mammoth site using method and theory developed at the Barger Gulch Locality B (BGB) Folsom site. Specifically, we compare spatial patterns at La Prele to four hearth-centered activity areas previously identified at Barger Gulch. Based on the spatial patterning of artifacts, we suspect the invisible hearth in Block B occurred within an interior space. The presence of an interior space and associated domestic artifact suggests that the distinction between Clovis campsites and kill sites is not clear-cut.

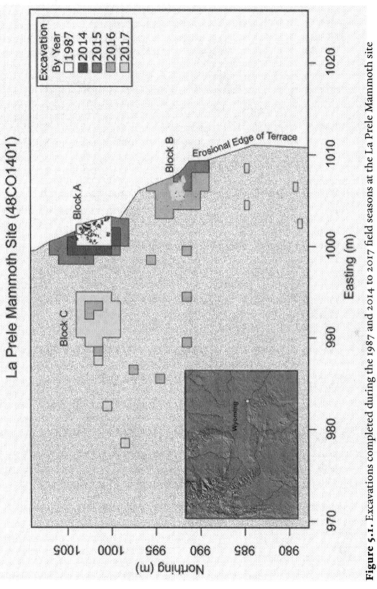

Figure 5.1. Excavations completed during the 1987 and 2014 to 2017 field seasons at the La Prele Mammoth site (48CO1401) in Converse County, Wyoming.

THE LA PRELE MAMMOTH SITE

The La Prele Mammoth (48CO1401) lies in an alluvial terrace of La Prele Creek approximately 12 km northwest of Douglas, Wyoming (figure 5.1). Initially called the Hinrichs Mammoth and later the Fetterman Mammoth, the site was discovered in 1986 and tested the following spring. George Frison and a crew from the University of Wyoming excavated the mammoth with a 3 × 4 m excavation block, recovering the partial remains of a juvenile mammoth (*Mammuthus* sp.) as well as a possible hammerstone, flake tool, and two in situ flakes (Walker et al. 1988). An additional seven flakes were found in the sediments surrounding the mammoth bones in plaster casts. During test excavations, in situ cultural materials were found at a slightly higher elevation than the mammoth bone bed, but the 1987 crew concluded that the mammoth and cultural remains were associated (Walker et al. 1988). Due to a dispute with the landowner, no further excavations occurred until 2014. In the intervening years, Byers (2002) revisited the site records and assemblage to analyze the security of the association between the mammoth remains and cultural materials. Byers (2002) concluded the association of cultural materials with the mammoth remains was suspect based on indications of multiple burial events, possible redeposition of cultural materials and mammoth remains, the small in situ artifact assemblage, and, most importantly, the elevation differences between cultural materials and faunal remains. We reopened the site in 2014 with the goal of resolving the question of Paleoindian exploitation of the megafaunal remains.

Between 2014 and 2017, we excavated just under 100 m² at the La Prele Mammoth site (figure 5.1). Newly excavated areas include multiple test units, expansion of the 1987 excavation block (Block A), and two excavation blocks in areas found to have relatively high artifact densities (Blocks B and C). We have recovered thousands of artifacts and significantly expanded the site area to account for these new discoveries. No cultural materials have been found above the mammoth, and a combination of stratigraphic profiles and hand augers show no appreciable slope to the surface on which the mammoth sits for at least 100 meters to the west, meaning no materials could have bioturbated downward to the level of the mammoth remains or been washed in from later occupations. All material classes (bone, lithics, ocher) show similar vertical distributions, with highest density of each artifact class occurring at the same elevation relative to the stratigraphy. This supports the hypothesis that all materials were on the same surface at deposition and have since been vertically distributed. Finally, no other archaeological occupations occur in the terrace. The chances of a mammoth dying in an unremarkable location, to be followed shortly by an unassociated human occupation, and then for the location to never be used again is exceedingly unlikely. Based on the new artifact assemblage, a better understanding of the site's post-depositional disturbances—particularly the presence of significant bioturbation—and absence of other archaeology in the site's vicinity, it is clear the cultural assemblage and mammoth remains are associated (Mackie et al. 2017).

Contamination of bone collagen has made dating difficult. This has been a problem since the discovery of the site, when the mammoth remains dated more than 2,000 years younger than our current dates (Byers 2002). We now have 14 dates that directly or indirectly date the site's occupation (Mackie et al. 2017). Considering it is more likely for bone collagen radiocarbon dates to be too young, we have the most confidence in our oldest mammoth bone collagen dates. The first was on ultrafiltrated collagen from the mammoth and dates to 11,066 ± 61 ^{14}C yrs BP (AA-108893). This estimate was corroborated by a second hydroxyproline date from a vertebra recovered in 1987 dating to 11,035 ± 50 ^{14}C yrs BP (OxA-X-2736-14; Devièse et al. 2018). These are consistent with a calcined bone date from Block B of 11,190 ± 130 ^{14}C yrs BP (AA-107104). These three radiocarbon dates average to 12,988 to 12,848 cal BP (11,053 ± 50 ^{14}C yrs BP), which places the La Prele site in the Clovis period as identified by Waters and Stafford (2007). The discovery of a nearly complete fluted projectile point in the same stratigraphic level as the mammoth approximately 17 m to the southeast of the bone bed confirms the cultural affiliation as Clovis.

The focus of this chapter is the excavation of Block B. This block lies approximately 10 m south of the mammoth remains and was first tested in 2015 after a large cobble tool was discovered protruding from the terrace south of the mammoth. The cobble tool tested positive for elephant antiserum during protein analysis (Mackie et al. 2017, Appendix B). The Block B excavation area includes 26.4 m^2 and its eastern boundary is formed by the modern terrace edge that truncates the archaeological deposits. The artifact assemblage from Block B includes 900+ flakes (64 point plots), 9 tools, 241 plotted bone fragments, and 1600+ mapped pieces of ocher. Stone tools include a large cobble tool, multiple flake tools, and a partial endscraper (figure 5.2b). Lithics are predominantly chert from the Hartville Uplift, located around 80 km southeast of the site. The majority of debitage is very small, averaging under a centimeter in length. There are 14 sizeable pieces of bone from Block B, but no identifiable mammoth remains. The lack of osteological landmarks on the highly fragmented faunal assemblage has prevented the identification of taxa, but samples from two fragments were identified as *Bison sp.* using ancient DNA at the University of California Santa Cruz Paleogenomics Laboratory.[1] While it may

---

[1] To confirm the taxonomic identity of the two unidentified remains, F54432 and F54627, we extracted, enriched, and sequenced DNA from powdered bone in the purpose-built ancient DNA facility at the University of California Santa Cruz Paleogenomics Laboratory. We

seem unusual for a bison to be present next to a mammoth bone bed, bison remains with strong evidence for use have been found at other mammoth kill sites (Haynes and Huckell 2007; Saunders 1977, 51).

Block B also contained artifacts generally not found in association with proboscideans in the New World, including abundant hematite ocher, bone needles, and a bone bead (figure 5.2). Near the center of the excavation block, ocher concentrations were so intense as to stain the sediments pink, forming a roughly oval stain. The stain encompasses a 3.2 m^2 area, including an approximately 2 × 1.5 m area reaching 15 to 20 m in depth. To map the ocher stain, we exposed it across all the affected units and created a scaled orthophoto with PhotoModeler software from photographs taken at various angles. Since the pink-stained sediment can be difficult to see in unaltered pictures, we used Dstretch to enhance the reds in site photographs (figure 5.2a). Within and just outside the ocher stain, we recovered the fragments of at least three bone needles and a bone bead. The needles measure 1.5 mm in diameter and the largest refitted fragment measures 17 mm in length (figure 5.2c). One fragment includes a portion of the eye. These needle fragments are likely the oldest needles recovered to date from the contiguous United States

---

extracted DNA following the method described by Dabney et al. (2013), and then turned extracted DNA into double-stranded libraries following Meyer and Kircher (2010). After shotgun sequencing a target of ~1 million reads per sample to assess library complexity and ancient DNA authenticity, we then enriched the prepared libraries for mammalian mitochondrial DNA using a bait set comprising 242 eutherian mammals (Slon et al. 2016) as described in Froese et al. (2017). We sequenced the enriched libraries on an Illumina MiSeq to a coverage of ~200,000 reads per sample.

To confirm the taxonomic ID of the samples, we first trimmed adapters and removed reads less than 30bp with SeqPrep (JstJohn 2009), removed low complexity sequences with PrinSeq (Schmieder and Edwards 2011), and then BLASTed the resulting data to the non-redundant nucleotide database on NCBI. This preliminary screening indicated that the majority of mammalian assignments were to *Bison* with fewer assigned to *Ovis*. We then used BWA (Li and Durbin 2009) to map to the *Bison* and *Ovis canadensis* nuclear genome. For sample F54627, 0.36% of the reads mapped to the Bison genome while 0.16% mapped to the *Ovis canadensis* genome. For sample F54432, 0.14% of reads mapped to *Bison* while 0.057% of reads mapped to *Ovis canadensis*. Reads mapping to *Bison* showed the characteristic patterns of ancient DNA decay, but reads mapping to Ovis did not. Focusing on mitochondria, we then mapped each library to an in-house reference dataset of eutherian mammal mitochondrial genomes that includes mammals present in Pleistocene and Holocene North America. Because the mitochondrial genome sequences are similar among the potential species, we restricted our results to retain only reads that map uniquely to one of the target mitochondrial genomes. For F54627, 149 reads mapped uniquely to the *Bison* mitochondrial genome, while 0 reads mapped to that for *Ovis canadensis*. For F54432, 27 reads uniquely mapped to *Bison* while 0 reads mapped to *Ovis canadensis*. We therefore conclude that both unidentified samples are most likely Bison in origin.

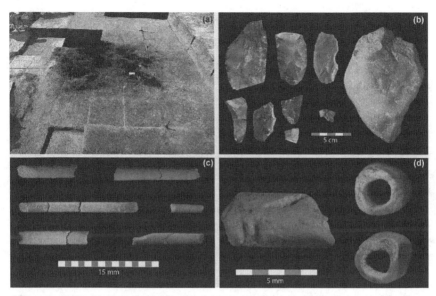

Figure 5.2. Notable finds from Block B: (a) Dstretch-enhanced photo of the ocher stain looking south, nails are spaced 1 m apart; (b) a selection of stone tools; (c) a selection of bone needle fragments including a portion of an eye on the lower left fragment; and (d) a bone bead.

(Lyman 2015; Osborn 2014). We also recovered a bone bead, which has rounded ends and two perpendicular grooves and measures 6.5 mm in length (figure 5.2d). Bone beads, needles, and ocher are artifact types that are generally associated with domestic activities, suggesting the use of Block B included activities other than mammoth butchery.

A COMPARATIVE CASE: BARGER GULCH LOCALITY B

Southeast of Kremmling, Colorado, in the western half of Middle Park, is Barger Gulch Locality B (BGB), a large Folsom campsite, which produced just over 75,000 chipped stone artifacts from 164 m² of excavations. Based on high artifact densities and a dominance of local lithic raw materials, the site is believed to have been a single, relatively long-term, and possibly cold season occupation (Surovell 2003, 2009; Surovell and Waguespack 2007; Waguespack and Surovell 2014). The lithic assemblage at BGB includes more than 200 diagnostic Folsom pieces in addition to a large diversity of tool and core forms, although debitage comprises more than 98 percent of the assemblage.

Four large contiguous areas were excavated at BGB, including three that pre-served hearth features. The Main Block contained two hearths, and the East and South Blocks each exhibited single hearths. Hearths at BGB are associated with high artifact densities (typically hundreds to thousands of artifacts per m²), although densities vary by excavation area. Because the site preserves hearth features associated with high densities of chipped stone artifacts, Waguespack and Surovell (2014) were able to identify robust and repetitive spatial patterning in near-hearth areas. Those patterns were largely identified on the basis of variation in artifact density (also see Puckett and Graf, chapter 4) and the relative frequency of burned artifacts and bone.

The first hearth identified at BGB became apparent after laboratory analysis of the chipped stone and bone assemblage (Surovell and Waguespack 2007). Its location was marked by high densities of burned artifacts and bone, particularly calcined bone. It was also characterized by high relative frequencies of burned artifacts. On the basis of ring and sector analysis (Stapert 1989), Surovell and Waguespack (2007) argued the hearth occurred within a structure. Two additional interior hearth features, one in the South Block and another in the East Block, were later identified in the field on the basis of very weak charcoal staining associated with high densities of burned lithics and bone. All three features had very weak geomorphic expression and could be characterized as "invisible hearths," as described by Sergant et al. (2006). The exterior hearth feature at BGB in the northeastern part of the Main Block was by comparison quite obvious; it was a shallow pit with abundant charcoal and burned cultural materials associated with oxidized sediments.

Later analysis showed that hearth locations could be identified by examining bivariate scatterplots comparing artifact densities to relative burning frequencies for 50 × 50 cm excavation quads (Waguespack and Surovell 2014). At BGB, these two variables regularly exhibited wedge-shaped distributions, and quads associated with hearth features occur as outliers exhibiting intermediate to high artifact densities with much higher densities of burning than would be expected based on the overall shape of the distribution.

Using a simple spatial simulation, Waguespack and Surovell (2014) showed that this wedge-shaped distribution can result from the cleaning of interior hearth features with secondary disposal of hearth contents in the "yards" outside of structural walls. Importantly, the emergence of this wedge-shaped distribution is only expected in the case of cleaning of hearth features. Outside refuse areas are characterized by relatively low artifact densities with a mixture of high and low percentages of burned artifacts. Interior work spaces are characterized by contiguous areas of high density and low relative frequency of burned artifacts of appropriate size and shape to be household features. These patterns are most identifiable in the case of hearth-centered activity areas with high artifact densities.

Patterns identified at BGB provide useful context for comparison to spatial distributions at the La Prele Mammoth site. Although artifact densities at La Prele are much lower than at BGB, similar artifact distribution patterns should be evident if similar processes governed the use of space in the hearth-centered activity area at La Prele. Furthermore, the presence of both interior and exterior hearth features at BGB provides the possibility of the direct comparison of spatial patterns associated with each kind of feature to the hearth area at La Prele.

THE LA PRELE HEARTH

Like the interior hearths at Barger Gulch, no sedimentological indications of a hearth (e.g., oxidation, charcoal staining) were present in Block B at the La Prele Mammoth site. This is expected, considering that the occupation was likely relatively short and that significant bioturbation is present. Rather, we identified the "invisible" Block B hearth using analytical techniques that explain frequencies and densities of burned materials across space (Sergant et al. 2006; Surovell and Waguespack 2007; Waguespack and Surovell 2014). To identify the location of the hearth feature at La Prele, we used three methods: (1) the geometric center of calcined bone, (2) the geometric center of burned lithics, and (3) the relationship between artifact density and percentage of burned artifacts. In Block B, we recovered 162 pieces of calcined bone weighing 2.36 g and 26 flakes that exhibit clear signs of burning, such as pot lids, crazing, and/or irregular fracture surfaces. Although these sample sizes are small, they show a nonrandom spatial distribution clustering near the center of the block, with the majority of burned materials coming from a roughly 2 m diameter area (figure 5.3a and b). We identified estimated hearth locations for each material type using weighted mean proveniences of point-plotted coordinates for artifacts recovered in situ and quad center coordinates for screen recovered artifacts. The distribution of calcined bone has a centroid at 1006.646 E 991.883 N. The burned lithic artifact centroid occurs less than 10 cm away at 1006.730 E 991.922 N. These locations also correspond spatially to the hearth location identified by the method developed at BGB. A plot of artifact density versus the percentage of burned artifacts for excavation quads at La Prele is shown in figure 5.3c. As at BGB, a wedge-shaped distribution of these variables is evident, with one quad occurring as a major outlier to the overall distribution at 1006.75 E 992.25 N (figures 5.3c and d).

All three methods of hearth identification return locations less than 40 cm apart. For additional analyses, we averaged these three locations (burned bone, burned lithics, and outlier quadrant for burned percentage/density) to 1006.709E 992.018N. This location is consistent with the densest concentrations of artifacts on site (figure 5.4). It also lies along the southern edge of the ocher stain and within a

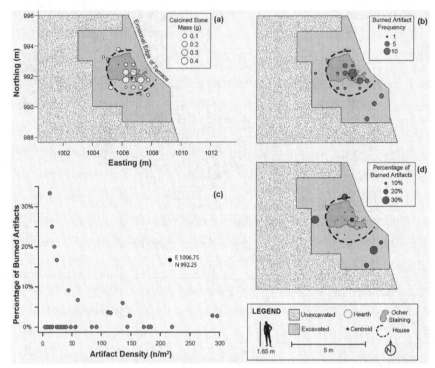

Figure 5.3. Map of Block B at La Prele site showing hearth positions determined using the (a) sum of calcined bone mass by quad, (b) frequency of burned artifacts by quad, (c) percentage of burned artifacts versus artifact density for each quad; black point shows likely hearth location, and (d) percentage of burned artifacts by quad; black circle corresponds to the black outlier from (c).

meter of the recovery locations of the bone needle fragments and bone bead (figure 5.3). It is worth noting that the archaeological deposits are truncated northeast of this location and the lack of artifacts and edge of the ocher stain in that area should be viewed as missing deposits, not the result of a lack of discard. All the following analyses use 1006.709 E 992.018 N as the hearth center point and all figures show the hearth as a 50 cm diameter circle centered on this point (figures 5.3 and 5.4).

USE OF HEARTH SPACE

We now turn to the question of whether the hearth occurred within an interior or exterior space. Although there is no direct architectural evidence of a structure at La Prele, interior versus exterior spaces should be identifiable based on artifact

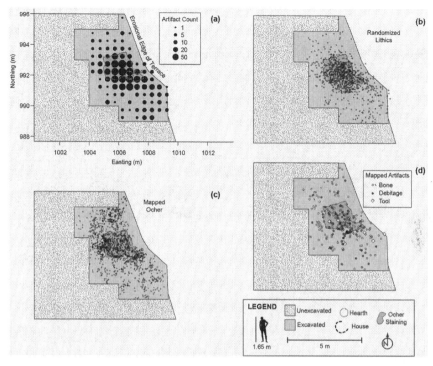

Figure 5.4. Map of Block B showing (a) lithic frequency by quad, (b) all lithics plotted with screen lithics randomized by quad, (c) point-plotted ocher nodules, and (d) in situ bone fragments, debitage, and tools.

distributions, since interior distributions are constrained by walls that act as obstacles to human and artifact movement (e.g., Stapert 1990; Surovell and Waguespack 2007; Waguespack and Surovell 2014). Stapert (1990) calls this phenomenon the *barrier effect*. In contrast, exterior hearths have no outlying constraints. In order to increase artifact numbers for this analysis, we assigned all screen-recovered lithics (n = 911) random point locations within the 50 × 50 cm quadrant from which they were recovered (figure 5.4). As in situ sample sizes for bone (n = 437) and ocher (n = 1658) were larger than point-plotted lithics, all analyses only use coordinates from artifacts recovered in place (figure 5.4).

We modified Stapert's (1989, 1990) ring analysis to include ring widths of 0.25 m expanding from the hearth centroid in Block B. Due to the small sample size at La Prele and the loss of materials from the northeast side of the hearth, we do not break the area around the hearth into radial sectors, but instead assume that the hearth

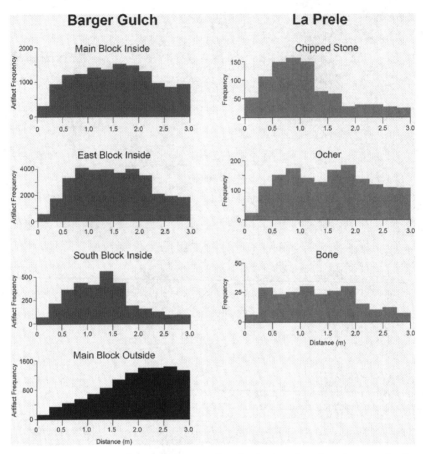

Figure 5.5. Frequency of chipped stone artifacts by distance from hearth center for four hearths from BGB and three material types at La Prele Block B.

is located in the approximate center of the activity area. We then compare the La Prele pattern to the three interior and one exterior hearths at BGB (Waguespack and Surovell 2014). To make the La Prele and BGB data more comparable, all lithic coordinates from BGB were randomized within the excavation quadrant from which they were recovered.

At BGB, there are clear differences in artifact distributions associated with interior and exterior hearth features. In terms of frequency, interior hearth features show unimodal or multimodal distributions, with the highest frequencies of artifacts occurring 1 to 2 m from hearth centers (figure 5.5). Note that this interpretation is different from Stapert (1989, 1991) who often associates unimodal distributions

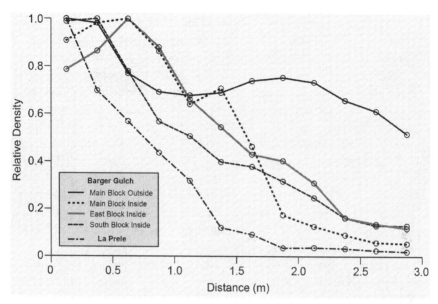

Figure 5.6. Distance from hearth versus relative density of all lithics for four hearths at the BGB and Block B at the La Prele Mammoth site.

with exterior hearths and bimodal distributions with interior hearths. The exterior hearth at BGB shows a very different pattern, with artifact frequencies gradually increasing with distance until plateauing at a distance of 2 to 3 m from the hearth center. When viewed with respect to artifact density, BGB's interior hearth features show a gradual trend of distance-decay out to 3 m, while densities associated with the exterior hearth decline to approximately 0.75 m from hearth center and then remain relatively unchanged at greater distance (figure 5.6).

The distributions of artifacts associated with the Block B hearth at La Prele strongly parallel the interior hearth features at BGB. At La Prele, frequencies of chipped stone, bone, and ocher show unimodal, bimodal, and multimodal distributions, respectively, peaking at distances of 0.75 to 2 m from the hearth center (figure 5.5). Secondary modes for bone and red ocher occur at approximately 1.75 to 2.0 m, suggesting a barrier effect. When examined with respect to lithic artifact density, chipped stone shows the typical distance decay pattern of interior hearth features at BGB, evidenced by a gradual decline in density out to 2 m (figure 5.6). Based on these distributions, we suggest that the hearth in Block B is more likely to have occurred within a structure than outside of one.

Identifying the size of this potential structure is complicated by erosion, which truncated the northeastern portion of this artifact cluster. Therefore, we cannot complete a formal sector analysis that would identify distance of the barrier effect by radial sector. However, the overall distribution of artifacts, in combination with the size and shape of the ocher stain, may provide some insight into wall positions. If walls acted to prevent or minimize artifact movement, it is possible that the spread of ocher would have been limited by the wall locations. Therefore, the distinct edge of the ocher-stained area might indicate the former position of a wall. There is precedent for ocher stains marking domestic spaces at multiple Upper Paleolithic sites (Roper 1992), most notably at Pincevent where ocher staining occurred around one side of three hearths thought to have been located within dwellings (Carr 1991, 241–243; Price 2013, 89–91; but see Stapert 1989). In the Paleoindian record, ocher staining was noted on the living floor at the Sheaman site (Frison and Stanford 1982, 144–145) and has also been found at multiple Folsom sites (Roper 1992). An oval was drawn around the ocher stain to include the areas of highest artifact density (figure 5.3 and 5.4). These areas are largely congruent in space, although high artifact densities extend to the south of the hearth, while the area of ocher staining does not. If this reconstruction is correct, it is important to note that quads with high percentages of burned artifacts but low artifact densities occur just outside of it (figure 5.3d), which is what would be expected if the hearth feature was cleaned and burned materials were moved outside (Waguespack and Surovell 2014). Supporting this interpretation is the presence of small quantities of calcined bone found in the same areas, more than 2 m away from the hearth feature to the north and south (figure 5.3a).

The northeastern open end of the proposed structure is not meant to represent a door but instead uncertainty from erosional truncation. The proposed structure has a diameter of roughly 3.3 m. The hearth sits off center in the southern portion of the structure. The distance between the hearth centroid and the highest frequencies of artifacts (northwest of the hearth) is approximately 1.98 m. This distance is consistent with the barrier effect observed in artifact frequencies and distributions at 1.75 to 2 m (figure 5.5). In summary, the frequency of artifacts with increasing distance from the hearth (figure 5.5), density decay trend (figure 5.6), and artifact patterning (figures 5.3 and 5.4) all suggest the hearth in Block B was located in an interior space.

DISCUSSION

Block B at the La Prele Mammoth site appears to represent an interior, hearth-centered activity area. Interestingly, none of the bone fragments found have been identified as mammoth, suggesting this area is not simply an extension of the mammoth butchery area (although many bones were too fragmentary for species identification). The presence of burned bone and select bison elements in close proximity to a hearth indicates these were used for subsistence purposes and brought onto the site from another location. The presence of an unusual amount of ocher is notable, and we are unsure of the ocher's function. However, its extent does offer a marker that might identify the location of an ocher-stained house floor, at least on the northern side of the hearth. Finally, the bone needles, a bone bead, an endscraper, and other flake tools suggest activities generally associated with domestic spaces. If found in isolation, this type of artifact assemblage would undoubtedly be identified as a Clovis campsite, making its presence next to a mammoth kill even more remarkable. Block B clearly represents a residential occupation which was created in association with the butchering of the La Prele mammoth. We believe there are other artifact concentrations on-site that may be additional activity areas or structures, although more excavation and analysis will be required to confirm this hypothesis.

The identification of a residential occupation at the La Prele Mammoth site is consistent with ethnographic accounts of groups moving to kills to butcher multi-ton animals (e.g., Duffy 1984, 156–158; Fisher 1992, 1993; Turnbull 1961,138). While the discovery of the campsite associated with a proboscidean kill should not be surprising (given the ethnographic record on elephant hunting) there have only been two other confirmed cases of campsites identified at Clovis proboscidean sites: Murray Springs (Haynes and Huckell 2007) and El Fin del Mundo (Sanchez et al. 2014). In the case of Murray Springs and El Fin del Mundo, the campsites were located significantly farther from the mammoth remains (> 75 m) than at La Prele, but this distance is not inconsistent with ethnographic reports (Fisher 1993). Given that there should be campsites near many, if not all proboscidean kill sites, why have more not been found? In the case of La Prele, the campsite was only identified because of a fortuitous find. The Block B cobble tool (figure 5.2b) was found protruding from terrace scarp while creating a path to carry buckets to the water screening area. It was immediately identified as a tool, and its in situ location was noted in the same stratigraphic position as the mammoth bone bed ~12 m to the north. We tested the area the following year and discovered stone tools, a bone needle, and the ocher stain. Without the discovery and identification of the cobble tool, it is unlikely we ever would have excavated Block B. While the assemblage would have eventually been exposed through erosion, it would have been difficult to identify due to its small average artifact size. The very low to non-existent artifact densities between the mammoth bone bed in Block A and Block B make it unlikely that the Block A excavation would have ever been expanded far enough to identify Block B without discovery of the cobble tool. We suspect that one reason why campsites have not been found at other proboscidean kill sites is that excavations tend to stop at the edge of bone beds when artifact counts decrease in density or disappear entirely. It is possible that more extensive testing beyond the edges of bone beds at other sites could result in the identification of additional residential occupations.

There are two possible, non-exclusive, explanations for the paucity of Clovis campsites in the American West. The first is that the classic settlement campsites exist (e.g., central residential places with extended occupations), but we have yet to locate one. This type of classic settlement may be present, but we should expect them to be less frequent in the record because Clovis likely produced far more sites with shorter occupations (e.g., campsites associated with kills), particularly if Clovis were a highly residentially mobile group who regularly pursued megafauna. The second possibility is that the view of campsites and kills as separate entities was blurred in the Clovis settlement system. In this case, the distinction between campsite and kill site may not be particularly informative if these site types largely overlap. In either case, Block B at the La Prele Mammoth site appears to represent interior hearth space with domestic artifacts, indicating the site is a mammoth kill with associated residential occupation.

Acknowledgments. We are very grateful to Jack and Zach Amen for allowing access to the site. We would also like to thank James and Shirley Baker for running the backhoe and fixing anything we managed to break. This work would not have been possible without our countless excavators, including many volunteers, undergraduate and graduate students, members of the Northern Arapahoe tribe, and four years of the University of Wyoming Field School (2014 to 2017). Thank you to Paul Sanders for volunteering countless hours in the lab. Thanks to K. C. Carlson and Lee Bement for the invitation to contribute to the SAA session in Vancouver and this chapter. Support for this project was provided by the Frison Institute of Archaeology and Anthropology, University of Wyoming Archaeological Field School, Shlemon Center for Quaternary Studies, National Geographic (grant no. 9896-19), Wyoming Cultural Trust Fund, and Quest Archaeological Research Program.

REFERENCES

Byers, David A. 2002. "Taphonomic Analysis, Associational Integrity, and Depositional History of the Fetterman Mammoth, Eastern Wyoming, USA." *Geoarchaeology* 17 (5): 417–440.

Cannon, Michael D, and David J Meltzer. 2004. "Early Paleoindian Foraging: Examining the Faunal Evidence for Large Mammal Specialization and Regional Variability in Prey Choice." *Quaternary Science Reviews* 23 (18): 1955–1987.

Carr, Christopher. 1991. "Left in the Dust: Contextual Information in Model-Focused Archaeology." In *The Interpretation of Archaeological Spatial Patterning*, edited by Ellen M Kroll and T Douglas Price, 221–256. New York: Springer.

Dabney, Jesse, Michael Knapp, Isabelle Glocke, Marie-Theres Gansauge, Antje Weihmann, Birgit Nickel, Cristina Valdiosera, Nuria García, Svante Pääbo, Juan-Luis Arsuaga, and Matthias Meyer. 2013. "Complete Mitochondrial Genome Sequence of a Middle Pleistocene Cave Bear Reconstructed from Ultrashort DNA Fragments." *Proceedings of the National Academy of Sciences of the United States of America* 110 (39): 15758–15763.

Duffy, Kevin. 1984. *Children of the Forest: Africa's Mbuti Pygmies.* New York: Dodd, Mead & Company.

Ferring, C Reid. 2001. "The Archaeology and Paleoecology of the Aubrey Clovis Site (41DN479) Denton County, Texas." Denton: University of North Texas Denton Center for Environmental Archaeology.

Fisher, JW. 1992. "Observations on the Late Pleistocene Bone Assemblage from the Lamb Spring Site, Colorado." In *Ice Age Hunters of the Rockies*, edited by Dennis J. Stanford and Jane S. Day, 51–81. Boulder: University Press of Colorado.

Fisher, Jack. 1993. "Foragers and Farmers: Material Expressions of Interaction at Elephant Processing Sites in the Ituri Forest, Zaire." In *From Bones to Behavior: Ethnoarchaeological and Experimental Contributions to the Interpretation of Faunal Remains*, edited by Jean Hudson, 247–262. Carbondale: Center for Archaeological Investigations, University of Southern Illinois Press.

Frison, George C. 1967. "The Piney Creek Sites, Wyoming." *University of Wyoming Publications* 33 (1).

Frison, George C., and Dennis J. Stanford. 1982. *The Agate Basin Site: A Record of the Paleoindian Occupation of the Northwestern High Plains.* New York: Academic Press.

Froese, Duane, Mathias Stiller, Peter D. Heintzman, Alberto V. Reyes, Grant D. Zazula, André E. R. Soares, Matthias Meyer, Elizabeth Hall, Britta J. L. Jensen, Lee J. Arnold, Ross D. E. MacPhee, and Beth Shapiro. 2017. "Fossil and Genomic Evidence Constrains the Timing of Bison Arrival in North America." *Proceedings of the National Academy of Sciences* 114 (13): 3457–3462.

Haynes, Caleb Vance, and Bruce B. Huckell. 2007. *Murray Springs: A Clovis Site with Multiple Activity Areas in the San Pedro Valley, Arizona.* Tucson: University of Arizona Press.

JstJohn. 2009. "SeqPrep." https://github.com/jstjohn/SeqPrep.

Kelly, Robert L., and Lawrence C. Todd. 1988. "Coming into the Country: Early Paleoindian Hunting and Mobility." *American Antiquity* 53 (2): 231–244.

Li, Heng, and Richard Durbin. 2009. "Fast and Accurate Short Read Alignment with Burrows-Wheeler Transform." *Bioinformatics* 25 (14): 1754–1760.

Lyman, R. Lee. 2015. "North American Paleoindian Eyed Bone Needles: Morphometrics, Sewing, and Site Structure." *American Antiquity* 80 (1): 146–160.

Mackie, Madeline E., Todd A. Surovell, Robert Kelly, Matthew O'Brien, and Spencer Pelton. 2017. "The 2016 Field Season at the La Prele Mammoth Site." On file with Quest Archaeological Research Program, Southern Methodist University, Dallas.

Metcalf, Duncan, and K. Renee Barlow. 1992. "A Model for Exploring the Optimal Trade-Off between Field Processing and Transport." *American Anthropologist* 94 (2): 340–356.

Meyer, Matthias, and Martin Kircher. 2010. "Illumina Sequencing Library Preparation for Highly Multiplexed Target Capture and Sequencing." *Cold Spring Harbor Protocols* 2010 (6): 5448.

Osborn, Alan J. 2014. "Eye of the Needle: Cold Stress, Clothing, and Sewing Technology during the Younger Dryas Cold Event in North America." *American Antiquity* 79 (1): 45–68.

Price, T. Douglas. 2013. *Europe before Rome: A Site-by-Site Tour of the Stone, Bronze, and Iron Ages.* Oxford: Oxford University Press.

Roper, Donna C. 1992. "A Comparison of Contexts of Red Ochre Use in Paleoindian and Upper Paleolithic Sites." *North American Archaeologist* 12 (4): 289–301.

Sanchez, Guadalupe, Vance T. Holliday, Edmund P. Gaines, Joaquín Arroyo-Cabrales, Natalia Martínez-Tagüeña, Andrew Kowler, Todd Lange, Gregory W. L. Hodgins, Susan M. Mentzer, and Ismael Sanchez-Morales. 2014. "Human (Clovis)–Gomphothere (*Cuvieronius* sp.) Association ~13,390 Calibrated yBP in Sonora, Mexico." *Proceedings of the National Academy of Sciences* 111 (30): 10972–10977.

Schmieder, Robert, and Robert Edwards. 2011. "Quality Control and Preprocessing of Metagenomic Datasets." *Bioinformatics* 27 (6): 863–864.

Sergant, Joris, Philippe Crombé, and Yves Perdaen. 2006. "The 'Invisible' Hearths: A Contribution to the Discernment of Mesolithic Non-Structured Surface Hearths." *Journal of Archaeological Science* 33 (7): 999–1007.

Slon, Viviane, Isabelle Glocke, Ran Barkai, Avi Gopher, Israel Hershkovitz, and Matthias Meyer. 2016. "Mammalian Mitochondrial Capture, a Tool for Rapid Screening of DNA Preservation in Faunal and Undiagnostic Remains, and Its Application to Middle Pleistocene Specimens from Qesem Cave (Israel)." *Quaternary International* 398: 210–218.

Spiess, Arthur E. 1984. "Arctic Garbase and New England Paleo-Indians: The Single Occupation Option." *Archaeology of Eastern North America* 12: 280–285.

Stapert, Dick. 1989. "The Ring and Sector Method: Intrasite Spatial Analysis of Stone Age Sites, with Special Reference to Pincevent." *Palaeohistoria* 31: 1–57.

Stapert, Dick. 1990. "Within the Tent or Outside? Spatial Patterns in Late Palaeolithic Sites." *Helinium* 30 (1): 14–35.

Surovell, Todd. 2003. "The Behavioral Ecology of Folsom Lithic Technology." PhD dissertation, Anthropology, University of Arizona, Tucson.

Surovell, Todd A. 2009. *Toward a Behavioral Ecology of Lithic Technology*. Tucson: University of Arizona Press.

Surovell, Todd A., and Nicole M. Waguespack. 2007. "Folsom Hearth-Centered Use of Space at Barger Gulch, Locality B." In *Emerging Frontiers in Colorado Paleoindian Archaeology*, edited by Robert H. Brunswig Jr. and Bonnie L. Pitblado, 219–259. Louisville: University Press of Colorado.

Turnbull, Colin M. 1961. *The Forest People*. London: Routledge.

Waguespack, Nicole M., and Todd A. Surovell. 2003. "Clovis Hunting Strategies, or How to Make Out on Plentiful Resources." *American Antiquity* 68 (2): 333–352.

Waguespack, Nicole M., and Todd A. Surovell. 2014. "A Simple Method for Identifying Households Using Lithic Assemblages: A Case Study from a Folsom Campsite in Middle Park, Colorado." In *Lithics in the West: Using Lithic Analysis to Solve Archaeological Problems in Western North America*, edited by Douglas H. MacDonald, William Andrefsky Jr., and Pei-Lin Yu, 35–49. Missoula: University of Montana Press.

Walker, Danny N., George C. Frison, David Darlington, Richard Reider, William R. Latady, and Mark E. Miller. 1988. "The Hinrichs Mammoth Site, Converse County, Wyoming." Amherst, MA: Tenth Biennial Meeting of the American Quaternary Association.

Waters, Michael R., and Thomas W. Stafford. 2007. "Redefining the Age of Clovis: Implications for the Peopling of the Americas." *Science* 315 (5815): 1122–1126.

Waters, Michael R., Charlotte D. Pevny, and David L. Carlson. 2011. *Clovis Lithic Technology: Investigation of a Stratified Workshop at the Gault Site, Texas*. College Station: Texas A&M University Press.

6

Analytical and Interpretive Challenges Posed by Late Paleoindian Activity Areas at the Water Canyon Site, West-Central New Mexico

ROBERT DELLO-RUSSO, ROBIN CORDERO, AND BANKS LEONARD

INTRODUCTION

Accuracy in the archaeological identification of early Holocene open activity areas requires that possible geological causes of spatial patterning as well as fine-grained chronological factors be considered before attempting to infer how any patterned archaeological remains might reflect human behavior. Such challenges in the interpretation of spatial patterning are exemplified at the Water Canyon Paleoindian site (figure 6.1). Here we describe the site and its geologic setting, and then briefly review the changing paleo-environments that helped drive the various geological formation processes at Water Canyon. From there we discuss the lithic artifact and bone assemblages recovered from the late Paleoindian component at Locus 1 North, and then go on to examine how post-depositional geomorphic processes may have affected the spatial patterning of the bone deposits and how issues with the dating of the deposits can affect subsequent interpretations of those patterns.

EARLY HOLOCENE ARCHAEOLOGICAL SITES IN NEW MEXICO

While there are a number of early Holocene (or late Paleoindian) archaeological sites known in New Mexico, very few have produced actual chronometric occupation dates. Among those that have been dated are the San Jon site with a Cody (originally termed Firstview[1]) occupation dating to 8,275 radiocarbon years before

---

[1] The Firstview projectile point type is currently believed to be a southern derivation of the Eden type of the Cody complex by Knell and Muñiz (2013, 11) while Fogle-Hatch (2015)

https://doi.org/10.5876/9781646422265.c006

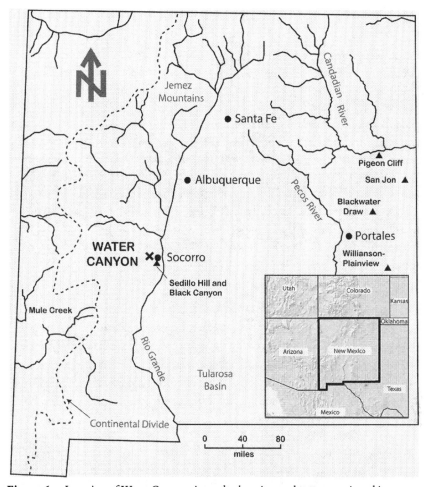

Figure 6.1. Location of Water Canyon site and other sites and areas mentioned in text.

present (^{14}C yr BP; Holliday et al. 1999), Blackwater Draw with a Cody occupation dating between ~8,690 and 8,970 ^{14}C yr BP (Holliday et al. 1999), Williamson-Plainview with a date on calcined bone of ~10,280 ^{14}C yr BP (Holliday et al. 2017), and Pigeon Cliff (Steen 1955, 1976) with a date of ~7,840 ^{14}C yr BP (figure 6.1). All of these sites are found in the eastern third of New Mexico and all, with the exception of Pigeon Cliff (a small rock shelter), are open sites.

---

argues that Firstview is metrically and morphologically similar enough to Scottsbluff and Eden types that it should no longer be considered a unique type. We accept Fogle-Hatch's conclusion in this paper.

The Water Canyon Site

Water Canyon (Dello-Russo et al. 2010) is a Paleoindian site located in west-central New Mexico, west of the city of Socorro (figure 6.1). This open-air site is eroding from within a large series of coalesced alluvial fans emanating from the Magdalena Mountains and its scientific significance derives from the following: (1) the site is extensive (covering over 9 hectares) and multicomponent, with solid evidence for Clovis, Folsom, Cody, other late Paleoindian and Archaic periods of human occupation; (2) portions of the site are stratified, intact, and dateable; (3) the site contains at least two *Bison* sp. bone beds; and (4) the cultural manifestations of the site are found both within and adjacent to a very extensive fossil wetland deposit, or black mat. The black mat (cf. Haynes 2008) was extant over the late Pleistocene-early Holocene (LP-EH) transition and contains an abundance of paleo-environmental proxy data (Dello-Russo et al. 2016a). Taken together, these attributes make this site unique in New Mexico west of the Pecos River. Interdisciplinary research has been on-going at Water Canyon since 2008 (Dello-Russo 2010, 2012, 2015).

The Water Canyon Geological Setting

Six different loci have been identified at the site, as seen in the plan map (figure 6.2), and most of the loci occupy either very stable settings on Pleistocene-age fan surfaces, such as Loci 2 and 6, or more dynamic colluvial slopes at the base of these landforms, such as Locus 1 South, Locus 3 and Locus 4. Locus 1 North and Locus 5 were revealed in buried, black mat sediments in the vicinity of No Name Arroyo, within the alluvial deposits of the Magdalena fan. Two additional drainages that cut through the site are the Big Wash and an unnamed arroyo at the south end of the site. These drainages are tributaries to the main Water Canyon drainage, which emanates from the Magdalena Mountains and drains, ultimately, into the Rio Grande to the east. The snow-melt and rain waters moving through the alluvial fan from the Magdalena Mountains emerge at the surface where the headward-eroding tributaries of the Water Canyon drainage incise into the Magdalena fan (figure 6.3).

The Water Canyon Paleo-Environment

The paleo-environmental reconstructions for the Water Canyon site, over the LP-EH transition (from ~14 kya to ~8 kya), are inferred from proxies including pollen, phytoliths, diatoms, land snails, microfossils, macro-botanicals, charcoal, and stable carbon isotopes that together provide a record of shifting environments for

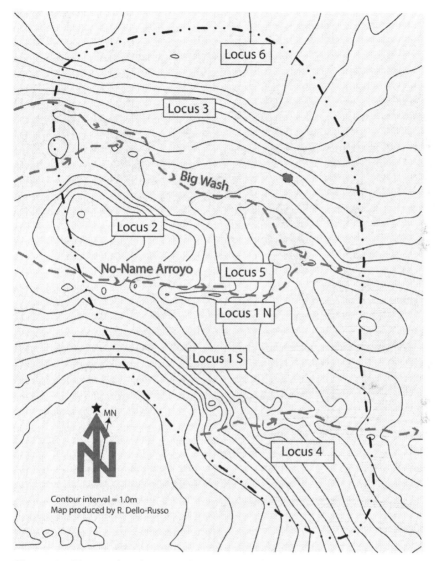

Figure 6.2. Topographic plan map of Water Canyon site.

the site over the 6,000-year interval (Dello-Russo et al. 2016b). During the Bolling-Allerod (~14,000 yr BP), the site setting was a relatively narrow riparian zone with abundant C_3 grasses and sedges surrounded by a juniper and C_4 grassland ecotone, which was in turn supported by greater-than-modern summer precipitation (Yost

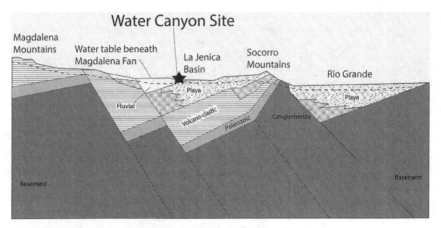

Figure 6.3. Schematic of Water Canyon site's geologic setting.

2016). By the termination of the Bolling-Allerod, during the latest Pleistocene into the earliest Holocene (~13,200–11,100 yr BP), there may have been a substantial drop in summer precipitation, a fluctuating water table and a concomitant reduction in C4 grasses. During this LP-EH transition, the proxy data suggest the presence of a wet meadow bordering a creek or interconnected pools interspersed with wetlands and marshy areas. The existence of fresh water, together with the variety of browse and forage shrubs, grasses and herbs, would have provided a strong attraction for bison and other game animals. By the early Holocene (~11,100–9,300 yr BP), the site was characterized by warm and wet environments with strong seasonal fluctuations that took the form of standing pools, cienega (or marsh) deposits or simply lush grasslands. The organic remains of these features are expressed today as the black mat. This was followed by a gradual warming and drying trend that culminated, by about 8,000 yrs BP, in the present-day Chihuahuan vegetational community at the site, which is represented by a dry juniper savannah.

LOCUS 1 NORTH BONE BED AND ARTIFACT SCATTER

This research focuses on the portion of the site designated as Locus 1 North, which contains at least one buried *Bison* sp. bone bed and has produced associated artifacts, charcoal, burned and calcined bones, and both chronometric and paleo-environmental samples. A total of 22 hand-excavated 1 m-by-1 m units and three backhoe trenches were opened between 2008 and 2016 in Locus 1 North, and the mapped locations of all the hand-excavated units and one backhoe trench (BT3) are illustrated in figure 6.4.

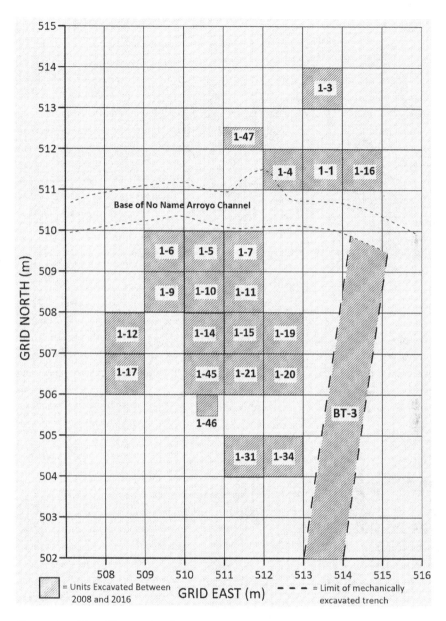

Figure 6.4. Map of Locus 1 North excavation units.

The faunal remains identified in Locus 1 North are attributed to *Bison* sp. on the basis of measurements of metacarpals, radii, and femora recovered during excavations between 2009 and 2015, and comparisons of those measurements to published metrics for the same elements for both *Bison antiquus* and *Bison bison* recovered at other archaeological sites in the region (Lewis 2003; McCartney 1983; Todd 1987). These biometric data are provided in table 6.1. The individuals represented in the Locus 1 North faunal assemblage tend to fall somewhere between *B. antiquus* and *B. bison* in size, and as such they could represent smaller individuals of a southern clade or a mountain-foothill population of *B. antiquus*. Due to their early Holocene age, they could also represent some of the first *B. bison* in the region. Given these issues, we have chosen to refer to these animals as *Bison* sp. The resolution of these issues is beyond the scope of this paper but might best be resolved by a DNA study where the Locus 1 North assemblage could serve as an excellent comparative data set between *B. bison* and *B. antiquus* genetic data sets collected from other archaeological sites in western North America (cf. Wilson et al. 2008).

Altogether, the cultural materials from Locus 1 North have been found between 48.43 m and 47.43 m grid elevation, although the vast majority were recovered above 47.82 m. This puts the bulk of the Locus 1 North deposits from 1.57 to 2.18 m below the grid surface elevation of 50.00 m. Table 6.2 lists the 60 identifiable faunal elements and fragments of the assemblage recovered to date, which represent at least 1–2 cows, 3 juveniles and at least 1 bull (table 6.2). A number of the recovered long bones exhibited percussion marks, bone flakes and green-bone fracture edges. Most of these fractures occurred at or near mid-shaft, suggesting that they had been processed for the recovery of marrow. It is possible that additional cultural materials will be encountered in some of the remaining unexcavated areas to the east of the Locus 1 North excavation grid, although no faunal or other cultural materials were encountered in BT3, which was excavated to a grid elevation of approximately 47.75 m.

Table 6.3 lists the lithic artifacts recovered from both surface and subsurface contexts in Locus 1 North, including 141 unutilized debitage flakes, three retouched or utilized flakes, four bifaces, and four multipurpose tools, five scrapers, and two projectile point fragments (table 6.3). These lithics include both those recovered as point-located artifacts and those recovered in screens during excavation. One of the projectile point fragments was recovered from the surface and is not believed to have been associated with the late Paleoindian component. The second is considered to be an artifact diagnostic of the component. The lithic raw materials that comprised this stone artifact assemblage are presented in table 6.4. These raw materials are dominated by obsidians and silicified rhyolites, which were procured from the nearby Sedillo Hill and Black Canyon quarries to the southeast (Dello-Russo 2004). While the majority of the obsidian artifacts had been procured from Rio

TABLE 6.1. Comparative post-cranial measurements for *Bison* sp. from Locus 1 North

| Element Name | FS No. | Measurement Location on Element | Measurement (mm) | Comparative collection or site (reference) | | | | | |
| | | | | HORNER II (TODD, 1987) | | LAMB SPRING (McCARTNEY, 1983) | | MODERN BISON (LEWIS 2003) | |
				MALE	FEMALE	MALE	FEMALE	MALE	FEMALE
Metacarpal	FS 1305	Maximum Length (MC1)	215	—	—	220±8.1	216.1±5.3	210.6±7.3	202.6±11.1
	FS 1528		214						
	FS 1305	Proximal Breadth (MC2)	82.26	—	—	80.4±4.4	67.3±4.0	74.8±3.9	63.7±4.4
	FS 1528		68.93						
	FS 1305	Proximal Depth	51.04	—	—	43.5±1.9	39.0±1.8		36.8±3.3
	FS 1528		43.21						
	FS 1305	Mid-Shaft Width	53.54	—	—	53.0±3.2	41.4±1.9	48.2±3.2	37.5±3.2
	FS 1528		37.73						
	FS 1305	Mid-shaft Breadth	32.23	—	—	34.3±1.9	29.2±0.8	32.6±2.3	26.8±2.3
	FS 1528		28.38						
	FS 1305	Distal Breadth (MT4)	82.93	—	—	—	—	75.3±2.7	63.7±3.5
	FS 1528		67.74						
Radius	FS 1508	Greatest Breadth of Proximal End (RD3)	95	—	88.5±2.8	—	—	—	—
	FS 1386		89						
	FS 1493		89						
	FS 1508	Greatest Breadth of Proximal Articular Surface (RD4)	91.7	—	85±2.4	—	—	—	—
	FS 1386		85.76						
	FS 1493		86.08						
Femur	FS 1585	Greatest depth of Proximal End (RD9)	50.83	57±2.8	48.7±2.3	—	—	—	—
	FS 1585	Greatest Length of Lateral Condyle (FM6)	65.14	73.2±2.2	65.8±2.1	—	—	—	—
	FS 1585	Greatest Breadth of Distal End (FM12)	103	118.3±3.3	107.5±2.1	—	—	—	—

TABLE 6.2. *Bison* sp. elements, Locus 1 North

Element	Total
Calcaneus	4
Cuneiform	2
Femur	7
Fused metacarpal	3
Fused metatarsal	8
Humerus	5
Long bone indeterm.	1
Middle phalange	3
Naviculo-cuboid	2
Pisiform	1
Proximal phalange	3
Radio-ulna	2
Radius	4
Rib indeterm.	3
Scaphoid	2
Tarsal indeterm.	1
Tibia	9
Ulna	4
Unciform	1
Total	60

Grande alluvial gravels to the east, one biface thinning flake came from the Mule Creek source area in southwest New Mexico, an air distance of ~225 km from the site (Shackley 2010a). One of the biface fragments recovered in Locus 1 North was made from a coarser rhyolite and the blood protein residue recovered from the artifact was identified as "bovine" (Yohe 2012), which conforms well with the associated *Bison* sp. bones.

Excavators also recovered a modified sandstone slab in association with the bones. This artifact's surfaces had both striations and planed high points, suggesting that it had been used for grinding activities. Numerous impact areas were also identified on the slab suggesting that it had also been utilized as an anvil stone. This latter functional interpretation was reinforced by the recovery of a spatially associated hammerstone. Preserved on the slab were both starch and lipid residues (Cummings 2016), suggesting that the slab had been used to process tubers and bone marrow, respectively.

The charcoal fragments documented in Units 1-11 and 1-15 of Locus 1 North (of which 10 were identified to multiple species and chronometrically dated) are thought to represent the ephemeral remains of a hearth and were designated as Feature 1. Their association with burnt and calcined bone fragments further supports this interpretation (Buenger 2003; Asmussen 2009) and may also suggest that the early Holocene occupants of Locus 1 North were using *Bison* sp. bones as fuel or were simply discarding processing debris into Feature 1. This latter interpretation is provisional, since the burnt and calcined bone fragments were too small to be identified to species. Alternatively, this feature could represent a dump following the clean-out of a hearth located elsewhere. While this is a plausible interpretation, it is difficult to understand why hunter-gatherers would dump such remains into a well-defined activity area, assuming there had been a clear temporal association between

TABLE 6.3. Lithic artifact types, Locus 1 North

| Raw Material | Locus 1 North | | |
	DEBITAGE FLAKES	TOOLS	Total
Andesite	-	1	1
Basalt	1	-	1
Chalcedony	9	5	14
Chert	7	2	9
Obsidian	31	2	33
Quartzite	5	1	6
Silicified Rhyolite	85	9	94
Sandstone	-	1	1
Sedimentary	2	-	2
Total			161

TABLE 6.4. Lithic raw material categories, Locus 1 North

Tool Type	Locus 1 North
Debitage Flakes	141
Projectile Points[a]	2
Bifaces	4
Multipurpose Tools	4
End Scrapers	3
Side Scrapers	1
Scrapers (Other, Indeterminate)	1
Retouched and/or Utilized Flakes	3
Anvil/ Ground Stone	1
Hammerstone	1
Total	161

[a] One point unassociated with the Late Paleoindian component.

the hearth, the butchering tools, and the butchered bones. In addition, the cleanout of a hearth, to us, suggests space maintenance inside a structure. At present, we have not yet discovered evidence at Locus 1 (or anywhere at the Water Canyon site) for a structure of any kind, so the rationale for the cleanout of a hearth is currently unsupported. Beyond this, a taphonomic argument for the presence of this concentration of charcoal and calcined bone is difficult to sustain, given the lack of aligned long bones in the deposit (signaling the directional effects of sheetwash dynamics in this particular region of the deposit) and the total lack of charcoal anywhere else in this same stratum in Locus 1. We had considered the possibility that the charcoal concentration had originated from a distant forest fire upstream, but the clear association of the charcoal with both burnt and calcined bone indicates to us that the most parsimonious interpretation of the feature is that of a hearth. Accordingly, we see that to be the most basic interpretation of the feature.

Thus, these assemblages and samples, taken together with Feature 1, are thought to represent the remains of a single open-air, early Holocene processing area. However, chronometric results also suggest the possible presence of more than one component. As such, these findings are reviewed and discussed further in the following sections of this chapter.

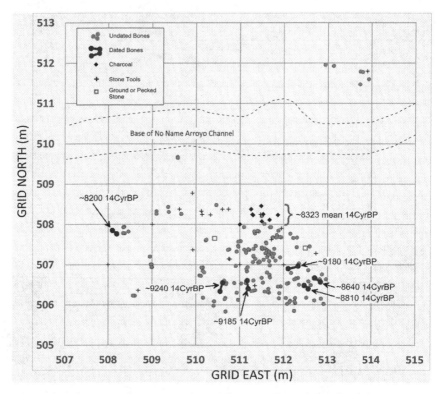

Figure 6.5. Plan View of Locus 1 North, with fauna, artifacts, charcoal and chronometrics.

SPATIAL DISTRIBUTION OF CULTURAL MATERIALS IN LOCUS 1 NORTH

The positions of all the point-located artifacts, faunal remains, and selected charcoal and chronometrically dated samples are illustrated in plain view in figure 6.5. By constructing "back plots" (where the locations of all artifacts from the excavated units of Locus 1 North are projected onto vertical planes), we are able to illustrate the spatial relationships among the same point-located items along two major sets of cardinal orientations: South-to-North arrayed against grid elevation (figure 6.6) and West-to-East arrayed against grid elevation (figure 6.7). The circles in the plots represent undated small bone fragments and end-points of undated, larger bone elements while the circles connected by lines represent larger elements that have been radiocarbon dated. The bones in Locus 1 North occur primarily along the south side of the present-day No Name Arroyo, although a few of the *Bison* sp. bones were found near the base of the north side of No Name Arroyo. Those were the northern- and easternmost remnants of the Locus 1 North faunal assemblage (figures 6.5 and 6.6).

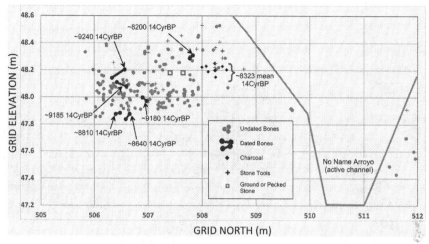

Figure 6.6. South-to-North back plot of Locus 1 North, with fauna, artifacts, charcoal and chronometrics.

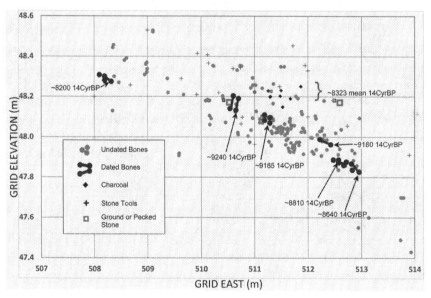

Figure 6.7. West-to-East back plot of Locus 1 North, with fauna, artifacts, charcoal and chronometrics.

The initial chronometric dates for the Locus 1 North deposit came from collagen in a femur diaphysis fragment recovered in Unit 1-12 at a grid elevation of 48.31 m (which is in the upper portion of the assemblage), and from the previously mentioned suite of charcoal fragments found in Unit 1-11 between 48.15 and 48.25 m grid elevation (Feature 1). The bone collagen, which was not subjected to any form of pre-treatment prior to dating, returned a radiocarbon date of ~8200 ^{14}C yr BP (FS 1037; table 6.5). When the wood species of the 10 charcoal fragments were identified, they were found to include juniper, pine, ponderosa pine, oak and unknown hardwood (Dello-Russo 2012:40, table 6.4). These fragments (FS 1036, 1049, 1051–1055, 1058, 1059a, 1059b) returned dates that were all statistically similar and produced a pooled mean radiocarbon date of ~8,323 ^{14}C yrs BP (table 6.5). These radiocarbon dates suggest that the age of the nearby bone is too young to be contemporary with the hearth, which is not unexpected given the collagen's lack of pretreatment.

After the 2015 University of New Mexico archaeological field school at the Water Canyon site, an additional radiocarbon date was returned from the Locus 1 North *Bison* sp. bone bed. This date, of ~8,640 ^{14}C yrs BP (FS 1625c; table 6.5), was returned on collagen from a tibia recovered at 47.84 m grid elevation. This collagen was also not pre-treated before being dated. This dated tibia from the lower portion of the bone bed was thus approximately 440 years older than the dated femur from the upper portion of bone bed and suggests one of several possibilities: (1) the bone bed actually represents the remains of two early Holocene bone processing events and the bone dates are relatively correct; (2) the bone bed represents only one early Holocene bone processing event and at least one of the collagen dates is incorrect, perhaps due to the lack of laboratory pre-treatment prior to the dating of the bone collagen; or (3) the bone bed represents one Holocene bone processing event where the charcoal dates are correct and each bone collagen date is incorrect—one too young and one too old.

We sought to address these possibilities by selecting new dateable samples from the bone bed to examine whether the previous bone collagen dates were incorrect. The results of these efforts are presented in the following section.

RENEWED CHRONOMETRIC DATING OF THE LOCUS 1 NORTH BONE BED

New dates have recently been returned on four additional *Bison* sp. bone collagen samples from Locus 1 North. These collagen samples (FS 1510, 1528, 1605, 1613) were taken from bones (tibia, metacarpal, femur, and tibia, respectively) that were selected from a range of vertical positions within the lower bone bed (from 48.17 to 47.88 m grid elevation). The locations of these dated samples are plotted together with the Locus 1 North bones and previously dated bones in figures 6.5, 6.6, and 6.7.

Collagen samples were purified using ultrafiltration and XAD resin protocols (Waters et al. 2015; Hoggarth et al. 2016), and the measurements of the carbon stable isotope ratios (^{13}C/^{12}C) were undertaken to calculate sample purity and the effects of fractionation. The samples were then reduced to carbon dioxide and then to dateable

TABLE 6.5. Radiocarbon dates, Locus 1 North and Locus 5

Field Sample (FS) Number	Unit, Level	Grid North (m)	Grid East (m)	Grid Elevation (m)	Material Dated	Radiocarbon Age[a]	13C/12C (‰)	Calibrated Age BP (2 sigma)[b]	Laboratory Number
1037	1-12, L6	507.833	508.101	48.310	Collagen	8200 ± 40	-12.3	9027–9278	Beta-292053
1036	1-11, L6	508.236	511.869	48.251	Charcoal	8354 ± 48	-20.6	9254–9486	AA-94458
1049	1-11, L6	508.079	511.498	48.231	Charcoal	8349 ± 49	-10.2	9250–9484	AA-94459
1051	1-11, L6	508.405	511.192	48.223	Charcoal	8314 ± 56	-23.4	9189–9464	AA-94460
1052	1-11, L6	508.381	511.255	48.229	Charcoal	8447 ± 64	-21.7	9395–9540	AA-94461
1053	1-11, L6	508.235	511.299	48.201	Charcoal	8324 ± 52	-19.5	9321–9469	AA-94462
1054	1-11, L6	508.458	511.482	48.203	Charcoal	8385 ± 48	-21.5	9285–9499	AA-94463
1055	1-11, L6	508.246	511.287	48.199	Charcoal	8346 ± 51	-21.1	9243–9485	AA-94464
1058	1-11, L7	508.112	511.668	48.123	Charcoal	8338 ± 48	-21.4	9242–9477	AA-94465
1059a	1-11, L7	508.112	511.668	48.123	Charcoal	8280 ± 50	-23.4	9122–9279	Beta-288067
1059b	1-11, L7	508.254	511.528	48.149	Charcoal	8186 ± 47	-23.9	9017–9147	AA-94466
1625c	1-20, L5	506.585	512.840	47.839	Collagen	8640 ± 40	-24.9	9635–9682	ICA16B/0713
1613	1-20 / L4	506.163	512.111	47.998	Collagen	9180 ± 60	-9.7	10,234–10,500	PSU-3564
1510	1-45, L2	506.334	510.545	48.141	Collagen	9240 ± 50	-10.2	10,258–10,524	PSU-3565
1528	1-21, L4	506.599	511.166	48.089	Collagen	9185 ± 50	-10.5	10,240–10,442	PSU-3566
1605	1-20, L5	506.333	512.477	47.884	Collagen	8810 ± 70	-9.3	9621–10,161	PSU-3567
5096	5-01, L3	521.774	527.581	45.673	SOM	8955 ± 57	-23.9	9912–10,228	AA-104050

[a] All radiocarbon assays completed by accelerator mass spectrometry (AMS).

[b] Calibration of radiocarbon dates utilized Calib 7.1 / IntCal 13 calibration curve (Reimer et al. 2013).

graphite. All the aforementioned work was completed at the University of New Mexico Environmental Archaeology Laboratory and Center for Stable Isotopes. The radiocarbon dating of the purified samples was then completed using the Accelerator Mass Spectrometry (AMS) method at the Penn State University AMS laboratory.

The reported dates are provided in table 6.5 and include, from the sample with uppermost grid elevation in the bone assemblage to that with the lowest grid elevation, ~9,240, ~9,185, ~9,180 and ~8,810 ^{14}C yrs BP. The date for the sample at the lowest grid elevation (FS 1605) is older than the previous date on collagen from the lower part of the bone bed, ~8,640 ^{14}C yrs BP (FS 1625c; table 6.5), recovered nearby at 47.839 m grid elevation. This does support the idea that un-pretreated collagen samples produce slightly younger radiocarbon dates than those that are pretreated. The locations of the other three newly acquired radiocarbon dates on bone collagen fall within the middle, vertically speaking, of the Locus 1 North bone deposit (at 48.141, 48.089 and 47.998 m grid elevation, respectively), yet are definitely older than the other bone collagen dates or the pooled mean charcoal date for the hearth, with the age differences ranging between 540 and 1,040 years.

These results, at first glance, still suggest the possibility that more than one bone bed might exist at Locus 1 North, but the locations of the dates are stratigraphically inconsistent,–with the younger dates (~8,640 and ~8,810 ^{14}C yrs BP) occurring stratigraphically below the older dates. In order to better understand this situation, we examined the possibility that geomorphic processes had somehow impacted the bone deposits in Locus 1 North. The results of these investigations are briefly described below.

GEOLOGICAL SITE FORMATION PROCESSES AND THE NATURE OF THE BONE BED AT LOCUS 1 NORTH

Because the site is located within and on the Magdalena alluvial fan, the sediments forming the site have been subjected to repeated sheet-wash and cut-and-fill dynamics since the middle Pleistocene. The results of these dynamics are reflected in the schematic cross-section of the south-to-north stratigraphy between Locus 1 North and Locus 5 (figure 6.8), which is based on mechanical core data and backhoe trench profiles. The complex nature of this stratigraphy is a consequence of the incision, development, and subsequent burial of paleo-channels within the Magdalena alluvial fan over time. Not only did paleo-channels develop within the fan, but sheet-washing events episodically scoured, eroded and remodeled the surface of the fan throughout the Late Pleistocene and Holocene. In the process, such sheet-washing events could have removed sediment and the cultural materials embedded within that sediment.

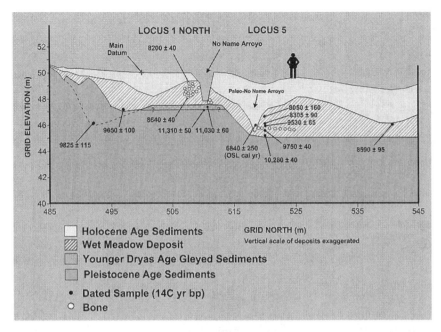

Figure 6.8. South-to-North stratigraphic cross-section schematic from Locus 1 through Locus 5.

In the case of Locus 1 North, it is important to recognize that the cultural event (or events) responsible for the Locus 1 North bone bed (or beds) took place while the paleo-No Name Arroyo was in place, prior to the existence of No Name Arroyo itself (see figure 6.8). The paleo-No Name Arroyo came into being after ~8,955 ^{14}C yrs BP (see discussion below about the resharpened Eden point in Locus 5) and began to refill ~6,840 years ago (middle Holocene). During the earliest Holocene, we believe that the cut and fill dynamics of the Magdalena fan could have removed and shifted sediment and bones from some portion of the bone bed in Locus 1 North, possibly creating a gap, or unconformity, between a lower and an upper cultural deposit (see figures 6.6 and 6.7).

As part of a standard methodological protocol during excavations, all bone elements and artifacts longer than 5 cm were mapped in place with at least two provenience points, using a total station. Each provenience point generated coordinates in three-dimensional space and thus enabled us to later reconstruct the three-dimensional position of each long bone element or artifact. As a consequence of this field methodology, we can say that those portions of the bone beds that were mapped and recovered by our excavators were only modestly affected by the actions of sheetwash events.

While the excavators noted small gravels piled against some bones in the bone beds, indicating the fluvial transport of such gravels, the energy flows during those events were not strong enough to orient long bones in the direction of those flows. Bones remaining in the bone beds were oriented in random patterns, indicating that they were not significantly affected by geomorphic processes like sheetwash. Much higher energy events must have removed or damaged other parts of the bone beds, leaving deep channels and disconformities. Beyond these observations, it remains outside the scope of this paper to spatially disentangle the processing events that created the bone deposits in Locus 1 North if, as it appears, more than one occurred.

CHRONOLOGICAL SUMMARY

At this point, three of the four new bone collagen dates (those at ~9,200 ^{14}C yrs BP), together with the ten charcoal dates for the Feature 1 hearth, provide the most secure radiocarbon ages for Locus 1 North. While it is tempting to see at least the uppermost of the three, younger bone collagen dates as providing support for the idea that the *Bison* sp. bone bed in Locus 1 North represents two early Holocene (late Paleoindian) bone processing events, we feel that the most conservative interpretation at this point is that there is only one well-dated *Bison* sp. bone bed (at ~9,200 ^{14}C yrs BP) in Locus 1 North and only one well-dated hearth (at ~8,323 ^{14}C yrs BP) that may or may not have been associated with a second bone bed. There is certainly provocative support for the idea of a second bone bed, since the hearth is associated with burnt and calcined bone, a grinding stone/anvil with bone marrow lipid residue, and a biface with bovine blood residue. Nevertheless, we currently view the three younger bone collagen dates (for FS1037, 1625c and 1605 at ~8,200, ~8,640 and ~8,810 ^{14}C yrs BP, respectively) as slightly problematic. Neither of the samples for FS1037 and FS1625c were subjected to any form of pretreatment, and the sample for FS1605 was extremely small, at 0.15 mg, where the laboratory indicates an optimal sample size of 0.7 mg. Therefore, at this point we see the ages derived from these three samples as equivocal and unacceptable.

This situation clearly provides a warrant for future research. It is possible that future dating efforts will find that bones at the top of the deposit will generate dates contemporary with the pooled mean date for the Feature 1 hearth (at ~8,323 ^{14}C yrs BP), and thus provide solid evidence for the presence of a second bone bed. Similarly, future dating efforts, where we use larger sample sizes and uniform pretreatment protocols, may bring the ages of the bones at the base of the deposit in line with the currently accepted age of the bone bed (at ~9,200 ^{14}C yrs BP).

The most notable of the artifacts to be associated with the hearth (the most recent event) is the slab ground stone/anvil. As this slab is most closely associated with the pooled mean charcoal date of ~8,323 ^{14}C yrs BP, it becomes for now the oldest known ground stone artifact in New Mexico. Clearly, a number of bones and other lithic artifacts (including the rhyolite biface with bovine blood residue[2]) are associated with Feature 1, particularly when the hearth is viewed in figures 6.6 and 6.7. There does appear to be a slight gap, or unconformity, between this assemblage of bones, artifacts, and hearth and the older dated bone bed below, but specifying precisely whether the gap is real or perceived and which artifacts and bones belong to which deposit must await additional chronometric clarification.

The age of the upper portion of the Locus 1 North deposit, based on the age of the hearth, could be seen as contemporary with an Allen-Frederick occupation with a date range of 7,900–9,350 ^{14}C yrs BP (Pitblado 2007, 313). To shed additional light on this matter, it is worth noting that a late Paleoindian projectile point fragment (figure 6.9) was recovered from the surface in Locus 1 North at a location 25 m south of the bone bed. While made from siltstone and quite damaged, this fragment still retains some parallel diagonal flake scars that are hallmarks of the Allen-Frederick point style (Pitblado 2007, 320). Allen-Frederick occupations are well-documented in the Great Plains and southern Rocky Mountains (Pitblado 2007; Bamforth 2007; Hofman 2010) but there are no dated Allen-Frederick sites currently known in New Mexico. There are, however, a small number of projectile points with parallel diagonal flaking patterns that have been identified in New Mexico, including one in the Jemez Mountains to the north of Water Canyon (personal communication, Ana Steffen, Valles Caldera National Monument, 2009), one in the Tularosa Basin of southeastern New Mexico (Shackley 2010b) and several at the nearby Black Canyon rhyolite quarry (observed by the lead author during field trips to the site), among others. Given these, together with the parallel-diagonally flaked point fragment illustrated in figure 6.9 and dates in the upper Locus 1 North bone bed within the Allen-Frederick date range, it is perhaps not unlikely that Allen-Frederick people, or perhaps other late Paleoindian people contemporary with the Allen-Frederick culture and using similarly flaked points, may have processed *Bison* sp. at the Water Canyon site. If so, we could argue at this point that the ~8,323 ^{14}C yrs BP pooled mean charcoal age from the Feature 1 hearth in the upper-most part of Locus 1 North at Water Canyon may represent the first Allen-Frederick date in New Mexico. Of further interest, we also suggest that much or all of the bone deposit in Locus 1 North (at ~9,200 ^{14}C yrs BP) represents an open-air processing event contemporary with Cody (Eden) occupations in the region (which have a date range of 7600–9,649 ^{14}C yrs BP; Knell and Muñiz 2013, 11–12). This constitutes the first

---

[2] This artifact was discovered in Unit 1-11 between 48.284 and 48.413 m grid elevation, immediately above Feature 1. It was recovered after excavation in the screen and was not point-located.

Figure 6.9. Blade fragment of siltstone projectile point from Locus 1 with parallel diagonal flaking pattern.

well-dated Cody (Eden) occupation west of the Pecos River in New Mexico.

In addition, these dates may conform closely to the estimated age of an apparent Cody-era bone bed in Locus 5 at Water Canyon. That Locus 5 bone bed, found embedded in the fossil wetland stratum within a probable paleo-channel of the Big Wash, has not yet been directly dated. The bone preservation is extremely poor and no dateable collagen has been recovered to date. However, a resharpened Eden projectile point (figure 6.10) was recovered in situ, in direct association with the bone bed (in Unit 5-1, Level 3, 45.698 m grid elevation) and a dateable sample of soil organic matter (SOM; FS5096) was recovered in association with tooth enamel and lithics near the projectile point (4.21 m to the northeast and 2.5 cm below). Because the black mat deposit in which both the Eden point and the Locus 5 bone bed were embedded slopes downward from the southwest to the northeast (Dello-Russo 2015, 31), we believe that the point and the SOM sample were close to the same stratigraphic level. The SOM sample dated to ~8,955 ^{14}C yrs BP (table 6.5), which is well within the Cody date range. The near contemporaneity of this date in Locus 5 and of the bone bed date in Locus 1 North is thus intriguing and points to a possible functional relationship between the two bone beds where remains of a *Bison* sp. kill were deposited in Locus 5 and then high utility meat-bearing elements were transported to Locus 1 North, where they were further processed. Clearly, this suggests another possible avenue for future research.

CONCLUSION

It is clear that site formational processes at the Water Canyon site have complicated the stratigraphy of Locus 1 North and thus both our functional interpretations and our chronological assignments of the archaeological remains. We can securely infer the presence at Locus 1 North of one well-dated, early-Holocene (~9,200 ^{14}C yrs BP) *Bison* sp. bone bed and one well-dated early-Holocene (~8,323 ^{14}C yrs BP) hearth with an associated grinding slab/ anvil (possibly associated with another *Bison* sp. bone bed). We argue that the hearth-centered activity area was likely created by a late Paleoindian group that was contemporary with the regional Allen-Frederick culture, whereas the well-dated bone bed and its associated processing area can be seen as contemporary with Cody (Eden) late Paleoindian groups and perhaps further associated with another Cody (Eden) bone bed in Locus 5.

These findings underscore another important aspect of the Water Canyon site. The availability of fresh water, wildlife, plant

Figure 6.10. Resharpened Eden projectile point from Locus 5.

foods, fuel and other subsistence resources made the Water Canyon site a "persistent place" on the landscape that attracted foragers repeatedly over time. This is evident archaeologically by the range of diagnostic artifacts left behind by ancient foragers, representing a period of over 5,000 years and including those from Clovis, Folsom, Cody-Eden, possibly Allen-Frederick and other late Paleoindian eras. The presence of stemmed Gypsum-style points in Locus 2 at the site indicates yet another hunter-gather visit to the site during the middle-to-late Archaic period.

In terms of future research, the existence of a possible unconformity in Locus 1 North underscores the need for further chronometric, geomorphic, and archaeological studies to clarify the nature of the Locus 1 North bone bed(s). Moving ahead, we point out that such interdisciplinary approaches to the analysis of open activity areas can be instrumental in helping to design future investigations, not just at Locus 1 North but also at other activity areas across the Water Canyon site and other sites in similar alluvial fan settings.

Acknowledgments. The authors would like to thank a number of people and organizations who have helped improve the understanding of Locus 1 North at the Water Canyon site. First and foremost, this research could not have been completed without the continuing, generous financial support of Art and Susan Hurley, Roland and Martha Mace, Mike Abernathy and Carolyn Galceran, Mr. and Mrs. Dennis

Zeunert, George and Carol Price, Larry and Sherye Boylan, Gerald McElvy, Lois Lockwood, Gary Grief and Dorothy Wells, Dr. Sally Davis, Dr. Richard Kozoll, John Guth, Marilyn Guida, Jayne Chromy, Mary Ann Sanborn, and Mr. and Mrs. Stephen Matthews. The laboratory pretreatment of bone collagen samples for radiocarbon dating was completed by Keith Prufer and Clayton Meredith of the UNM Department of Anthropology. Graphical assistance was provided by Scott Gunn from OCA. Jeff Thomas assisted with the selection of dateable faunal samples. The continued efforts in the field came about through ongoing collaborations with the New Mexico Historic Preservation Division, the New Mexico Tech Energetic Materials Research and Testing Center, and the University of Arizona Argonaut Archaeological Research Fund (Vance Holliday, Director). Professional colleagues who have helped collect key data from or clarify many of the complicated aspects of Locus 1 North include Nancy Akins, Jesse Ballenger, Mike Collins, Linda Scott Cummings, Patrice Dello-Russo, Jim Dixon, Paul Goldberg, Rusty Greaves, Steve Hall, C. Vance Haynes, Vance Holliday, Evan Kay, Les McFadden, Dave Meltzer, Susan Mentzer, Gary Morgan, Susie Smith, Christian Solfisburg, Evan Sternberg, Chad Yost, and Barbara Winsborough. Insights and contributions from all were greatly appreciated. Comments and suggestions from Victor Thompson and one anonymous reviewer helped us clarify some aspects of the paper. Finally, thanks go to Lee Bement and K. C. Carlson for their gracious invitation to the SAA symposium. The authors are responsible for any errors or omissions.

REFERENCES

Asmussen, Brit. 2009. "Intentional or Incidental Thermal Modification? Analysing Site Occupation via Burned Bone." *Journal of Archaeological Science* 36: 528–436.

Bamforth, Douglas B., ed. 2007. *The Allen Site: A Paleoindian Camp in Southwestern Nebraska*. Albuquerque: University of New Mexico Press.

Buenger, Brent A. 2003. "The Impact of Wildland and Prescribed Fire on Archaeological Resources." PhD dissertation, Department of Anthropology, University of Kansas, Lawrence.

Cummings, Linda Scott. 2016. "Pollen, Phytolith, Starch, and Organic Residue (FTIR) Analysis of a Sandstone Slab from the Water Canyon Paleo Indian Site (LA 134764), Socorro County, New Mexico." *Technical Report 2016–061*. Golden, CO: PaleoResearch Institute.

Dello-Russo, Robert D. 2004. "Geochemical Comparisons of Silicified Rhyolites from Two Prehistoric Quarries and 11 Prehistoric Projectile Points, Socorro County, New Mexico, U.S.A." *Geoarchaeology: An International Journal* 19 (3): 237–264.

Dello-Russo, Robert. 2010. "Archaeological Testing at the Water Canyon Site (LA 134764), Socorro County, New Mexico: Interim Report for the 2008 and 2009 Field Seasons." *Escondida Research Group Report Number 2009-09*. Santa Fe, NM.

Dello-Russo, Robert. 2012. "Continued Interdisciplinary Research at the Water Canyon Paleoindian Site (LA 134764), Socorro County, New Mexico: Interim Report for the 2010 Field Season and Data Recovery Plan for the 2012 Season." *Office of Archaeological Studies Preliminary Report 42*. Santa Fe: Museum of New Mexico.

Dello-Russo, Robert. 2015. "Archaeological Excavations at the Water Canyon Paleoindian Site (LA134764), Socorro County, New Mexico. Interim Report for the 2012 and 2013 Field Seasons." *Office of Contract Archeology Report No. 185-1174*. Albuquerque: Maxwell Museum of Anthropology, University of New Mexico.

Dello-Russo, Robert D., Susan J. Smith, and Patrice A. Walker. 2016a. "The Black Mat at the Water Canyon Paleoindian Site near Socorro, New Mexico: A Paleoenvironmental Proxy Data Archive for the Pleistocene-Holocene Transition." In *New Mexico Geological Society, Guidebook, 67th Field Conference: The Geology of the Belen Area*, edited by Bonnie A. Frey, Karl E. Karlstrom, Spencer G. Lucas, Shannon Williams, Kate Zeigler, Virginia McLemore, and Dana S. Ulmer-Scholle, 491–500. Socorro: New Mexico Bureau of Geology and Mineral Resources.

Dello-Russo, Robert D., Susan J. Smith, Chad Yost, Barbara Winsborough, Stephen Hall, Pamela McBride, and Owen Davis. 2016b. "The Black Mat at the Water Canyon Paleoindian Site and a New Paleoenvironmental Record for the Pleistocene-Holocene Transition in West-Central New Mexico." Poster presentation at the American Quaternary Association 24th Biennial Meeting: Retooling the Quaternary to Manage the Anthropocene / Section III. Paleoecology: Tools, Models and Novel Approaches. Santa Fe, NM, June 28–July 2, 2016.

Dello-Russo, Robert D., Patricia A. Walker and Vance T. Holliday. 2010. "Recent Research Results from the Water Canyon Site, a Clovis and Late Paleoindian Locale in West-Central New Mexico." *Current Research in the Pleistocene* 27: 72–75. Center for the Study of the First Americans, College Station: Texas A&M University.

Fogle-Hatch, Cheryl. 2015. "Explanations for Morphological Variability in Projectile Points: A Case Study from the Late Paleoindian Cody Complex." PhD dissertation, University of New Mexico, Albuquerque.

Haynes, C. Vance, Jr. 2008. "Younger Dryas 'Black Mats' and the Rancholabrean Termination in North America." *Proceedings of the National Academy of Sciences* 105 (18): 6520–6525.

Hill, Matthew E., Jr., Matthew G. Hill, and Christopher C. Widga. 2008. "Late Quaternary Bison Diminution on the Great Plains of North America: Evaluating the Role of Human Hunting versus Climate Change." *Quaternary Science Reviews* 27 (17–18): 1752–1771.

Hofman, Jack L. 2010. "Allen Complex Behavior and Chronology in the Central Plains." In *Exploring Variability in Early Holocene Hunter-Gatherer Lifeways, University of Kansas Publications in Anthropology* 25, edited by Stance Hurst and Jack L. Hofman, 135–152. Lawrence: University of Kansas.

Hoggarth, J. A., B. J. Culleton, J. J. Awe, and D. J. Kennett. 2014. "Questioning Postclassic Continuity at Baking Pot, Belize, Using AMS ^{14}C Direct Dating of Human Burials." *Radiocarbon* 56 (3): 1057–1075.

Holliday, Vance T., Eileen Johnson, James Warnica, and C. Vance Haynes Jr. 2017. "The Williamson-Plainview and Type Milnesand Sites on the Southern High Plains, New Mexico." *PaleoAmerica* 3 (2): 122–149.

Holliday, Vance T., Eileen Johnson, and Thomas W. Stafford Jr. 1999. "AMS Radiocarbon Dating of the Type Plainview and Firstview (Paleoindian) Assemblages." *American Antiquity* 64: 444–454.

Knell, Edward J., and Mark P. Muñiz. 2013. "Introducing the Cody Complex." In *Paleoindian Lifeways of the Cody Complex*, edited by Edward J. Knell and Mark P. Muñiz, 3–28. Salt Lake City: University of Utah Press.

Lewis, Patrick John. 2003. "Metapodial Morphology and the Evolutionary Transition of Late Pleistocene to Modern Bison." PhD dissertation, Department of Biological Anthropology and Anatomy, Duke University, Durham, NC.

McCartney, Peter Howard. 1983. "An Archaeological Analysis of Bison Remains from the Cody Paleo-Indian Site of Lamb Spring, Colorado." MA thesis, Department of Anthropology, University of Arizona, Tucson.

McDonald, Jerry N. 1981. *North American Bison: Their Classification and Evolution.* Berkeley: University of California.

McPherron, Shannon J. P. 2005. "Artifact Orientations and Site Formation Processes from Total Station Proveniences." *Journal of Archaeological Sciences* 32: 1003–1014.

Pitblado, Bonnie L. 2007. "Angostura, Jimmy Allen, Foothills-Mountain: Clarifying Terminology for Late Paleoindian Southern Rocky Mountain Spearpoints." In *Frontiers in Colorado Paleoindian Archaeology: From the Dent Site to the Rocky Mountains*, edited by Robert H. Brunswig and Bonnie L. Pitblado, 311–337. Boulder: University Press of Colorado.

Reimer, P. J., M. G. L. Baillie, E. Bard, A. Bayliss, J. W. Beck, P. G. Blackwell, C. B. Ramsey, C. E. Buck, G. S. Burr, R. L. Edwards, M. Friedrich, P. M. Grootes, T. P. Guilderson, I. Hajdas, T. J. Heaton, A. G. Hogg, K. A. Hughen, K. F. Kaiser, B. Kromer, F. G. McCormac, S. W. Manning, R. W. Reimer, D. A. Richards, J. R. Southon, S. Talamo, C. S. M. Turney, J. Van der Plicht, and C. E. Weyhenmeyer. 2009. "Intcal09 and Marine09 Radiocarbon Age Calibration Curves, 0–50,000 Years Cal BP." *Radiocarbon* 51: 1111–1150.

Shackley, M. Steven. 2010a. "Source Provenance of Obsidian Small Debitage from the Water Canyon Paleoindian Site (LA 134764), Socorro County, New Mexico." Report prepared for Dr. Robert Dello-Russo, Office of Archaeological Studies, Museum of New Mexico, Santa Fe, by Geoarchaeological XRF Laboratory, University of California, Berkeley.

Shackley, M. Steven. 2010b. "Source Provenance of Artifacts from Boca Negra Wash and White Sands National Monument." Report prepared for Dr. Bruce Huckell, University of New Mexico, Albuquerque by Geoarchaeological XRF Laboratory, University of California, Berkeley.

Steen, Charlie R. 1955. "The Pigeon Cliffs Site: A Preliminary Report." *El Palacio* 62 (5–6): 174–180.

Steen, Charlie R. 1976. "Excavations at Pigeon Cliff." In *Collected Papers in Honor of Marjorie Ferguson Lambert, Papers of the Archaeological Society of New Mexico*: 3, edited by Albert H. Schroeder, 19–36. Albuquerque: Albuquerque Archaeological Society Press.

Todd, Lawrence C. 1987. "Bison Bone Measurements." In *The Horner Site*, edited by George C. Frison and Lawrence C. Todd, 371–403. New York: Academic Press.

Waters, M. R., T. W. Stafford, B. Kooyman, and L. V. Hills. 2015. "Late Pleistocene Horse and Camel Hunting at the Southern Margin of the Ice-Free Corridor: Reassessing the Age of Wally's Beach, Canada." *Proceedings of the National Academy of Sciences* 112 (14): 4263–4267.

Wilson, Michael C., Leonard V. Hills, and Beth Shapiro. 2008. "Late Pleistocene Northward-Dispersing *Bison antiquus* from the Bighill Creek Formation, Gallelli Gravel Pit, Alberta, Canada, and the Fate of *Bison occidentalis*." *Canadian Journal of Earth Sciences* 45: 827–859.

Winsborough, Barbara. 2016. "Diatom Paleoenvironmental Analysis of Sediments from the Water Canyon Paleoindian Site (LA134764)." Report prepared for Dr. Robert Dello-Russo, Office of Archaeological Studies, Museum of New Mexico, Santa Fe, by Winsborough Consulting, Leander, TX.

Yohe, Robert M., II. 2012. "An Analysis of Protein Residue of One Artifact from the Water Canyon Paleoindian Site." Report prepared for Dr. Robert Dello-Russo, Office of Archaeological Studies, Museum of New Mexico, Santa Fe by the Laboratory of Archaeological Sciences, California State University, Bakersfield.

Yost, Chad L. 2017. "Phytolith Analysis of Late Pleistocene and Early Holocene Sediments from the Water Canyon Paleoindian Site, LA134764, New Mexico." Technical Report 16003 prepared for Dr. Robert Dello-Russo, UNM Office of Contract Archeology by Paleoscapes Archaeobotanical Services Team, LLC, Bailey, CO.

7

Boca Negra Wash

Investigating Activity Organization at a Shallowly Buried
Folsom Camp in the Middle Rio Grande Valley of New Mexico

BRUCE B. HUCKELL, CHRISTOPHER W. MERRIMAN,
AND MATTHEW J. O'BRIEN

Anthropologists have long been interested in how hunter-gatherers organized the use of space within the limits of their residential sites. Beginning with the Harvard Kalahari Project in the 1960s and1970s (Yellen 1977), and becoming a focal point of cross-cultural investigations in the 1970s through the1990s (Binford 1978, 1983, 1991; Gamble and Boismier 1991; Kroll and Price 1991; O'Connell et al. 1991), intrasite spatial studies have flourished. Ethnographic studies of spatial organization—relying on features such as hearths, domestic structures and shelters, and refuse areas—provide strong examples of ways in which hunter-gatherers may choose to organize their residential sites. Stepping back in time to assess archaeological spatial organization in the absence of direct observation of people living in a site, the identification of spatial patterning becomes far more difficult.

The challenges of working with open-air campsites created by mobile hunter-gatherers are well known to archaeologists—we are often confronted by small samples of artifacts, partial excavation and exposure of potentially large occupational areas, poor organic preservation, and the impacts of post-occupational natural and sometimes cultural site formation processes. For archaeologists interested in the organization and use intrasite of space by hunter-gatherers, combinations of these factors may confound efforts to reconstruct patterning. Our purpose here is to share our efforts to examine whether a small, shallowly buried Folsom site in the Middle Rio Grande Valley retains any traces of spatial patterning in activity organization.

https://doi.org/10.5876/9781646422265.c007

Since the 1960s, it has been clear that the Middle Rio Grande Valley near Albuquerque contains a significant number of Paleoindian sites, especially those of the Folsom technocomplex. The pioneering work of Jim Judge and Jerry Dawson (Dawson and Judge 1969; Judge and Dawson 1972; Judge 1973), as well as amateur archaeologists such as Ele Baker and his son Tony (LeTourneau and Baker 2002), brought professional attention to these sites. These sites are virtually all in upland environments dominated by eolian processes and long-term soil formation rather than in stratified alluvium. As such, the sites offer the advantage of being discoverable through surface survey, but at the same time their principal drawbacks are their shallow depth of burial, potentially complex history of burial, exposure, reburial, and bioturbation. Judge and subsequent investigators including Dan Amick (1994, 1996, 1999) and Phil LeTourneau (2000) worked almost exclusively with surface-collected artifact assemblages; no excavations were undertaken due to the uncertainties surrounding the history of their occupation and the integrity of their depositional contexts. However, in the late 1960s, Jerry Dawson's excavations at the Rio Rancho Folsom site (Dawson and Judge 1969: 156–159; Huckell and Kilby 2002; Huckell et al. 2001) demonstrated that although shallow (10–20 cm below surface), two of the three major loci were single component Folsom occupations. However, his investigations were focused primarily on artifact assemblage composition and he did not attempt to explore issues of internal site organization of activities. Given the challenges to site integrity noted above, can these shallowly buried sites contribute to our understanding of how these ancient hunter-gatherers organized the spaces within which they pursued particular tasks?

THE BOCA NEGRA WASH SITE

An opportunity to evaluate this question came to us by chance in June of 1997, when Huckell had the good fortune to stumble across a previously unknown Folsom site. It was named the Boca Negra Wash site, given its proximity to an ephemeral wash with that name located along the eastern side of the Albuquerque Volcanoes (figure 7.1). The site was positioned in sandy, pedogenically modified eolian sand resting atop a 0.14 Ma (150,000-year-old) basalt flow emanating eastward from the Albuquerque Volcanoes (Crumpler 1999). It consisted of two loci at the eastern and southern margins of a playa (dry lake) (Holliday et al. 2006). At an elevation of 1,661 m, local vegetation today is desert grassland punctuated with scattered juniper (*Juniperus osteosperma*) trees. Dominant shrubs include sand sage (*Artemesia filifolia*), saltbush (*Atriplex canescens*), and winterfat (*Krashennikovia lanata*); grasses include three awn (*Aristida* spp.), galleta (*Hilaria jamesii*), ricegrass (*Achnatherun hymenoides*), dropseed (*Sporobolus* sp.), burrograss (*Scleropogon brevifolis*, limited

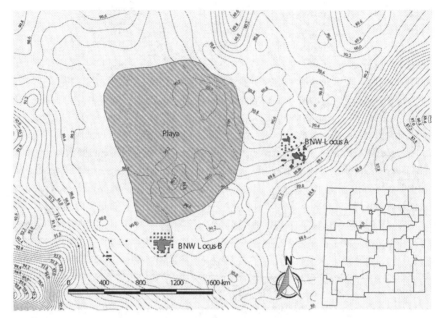

Figure 7.1. General location and map of the Boca Negra Wash site

to the playa surface), needle and thread grass (*Stipa* spp.), and grama (*Bouteloua* spp.). Narrowleaf yucca (*Yucca angustissima*) and succulents including prickly pear (*Opuntia*), multiple species of cholla (*Cylindropuntia*), and pincushion (*Coryphantha*) are also present. Initial surface exploration revealed first one, and then the second, spatially discrete concentrations of flaked stone artifacts (figure 7.1). The more easterly, Locus A, had been truncated by the construction of natural gas pipelines and a dirt road; some 100 m to the southwest was Locus B, which had escaped twentieth-century disturbance. Based on artifact morphology and lithic material representation, both loci appeared to represent Folsom occupations (Huckell and Kilby 2000; Huckell et al. 2002; Huckell et al. 2003).

The discovery of the Boca Negra Wash site thus afforded a chance to investigate some important questions. Specifically, the research was focused on three issues: (1) reconstruction of lithic technological organization; (2) definition of intrasite spatial patterning of task areas; and (3) reconstruction of paleoenvironmental conditions.

The Boca Negra Wash site was excavated using a system of 1 m grid squares, with individual unit coordinates established as being the number of meters north and east of an arbitrary local site datum. An arbitrary vertical datum served to control vertical provenience, with subdatums tied to it used for local control of excavations within units. Excavation began with systematic sampling of both loci with 1 m units spaced 2 m apart. Judgmental units were excavated to expand around test units that produced more artifacts, and ultimately additional contiguous, judgmental units were excavated to create an extensive exposure. Each unit was excavated entirely with trowels in 50 cm-by-50 cm quarters and in arbitrary 5 cm levels. Changes in sediment color and texture were recorded on unit level forms. The goal was to locate all artifacts in place to the extent possible; to ensure complete recovery of artifacts, all excavated sediments were dry-screened through 1/4-inch and 1/16-inch mesh hardware cloth. When found in situ, artifact provenience was determined using the x-y-z grid coordinate format; those recovered from screening were located to the quarter and level of the unit.

After surface mapping and artifact collection, test pits were excavated in Locus A; they revealed subsurface debitage extending to depths of 10–20 cm below the modern surface. In 2000 and 2001, the UNM archaeological field school excavated both Loci A and B. At Locus A, 95 1 m-by-1 m units were excavated within a 20 m east-west-by-32 m north-south area. Eight sherds and a few pieces of fire-cracked rock indicated a minor later component. Excavations continued in 2003 with a smaller paid and volunteer crew, but the main focus shifted to Locus B. In 2004 only Locus B was excavated. We will not consider Locus A further in this study due to the impact of twentieth-century construction of the road and gas line.

Locus B produced approximately 1,600 artifacts and faunal remains from 104 1 m-by-1 m grid units. Excavation began with a systematic sampling pattern of 1 m units spaced at 2 m intervals; judgmentally placed units expanded in areas where higher artifact densities were encountered in the sample units. The excavations covered an area 30 m east-west by 23 m north-south, near the west center of which was a large, irregular block of contiguous units covering an area approximately 10 m east-west by 11 m north-south (figure 7.1).

One of the research objectives posed at the outset concerned intrasite organization and use of space. We focus on that aspect of the research, specifically at Locus B.

DEPOSITIONAL CONTEXT

The deposits containing the Folsom occupation at Locus B were shallow; artifacts occurred from the modern surface to depths of less than 20 cm. Within this vertical space there were two eolian deposits affected to varying degrees by pedogenesis (Holliday et al. 2006). The older of the two is a well-sorted eolian sheet sand, OSL-dated to ca. 24,000 ka, with its upper portion pedogenically modified and showing a prominently columnar-structured, reddened, clay-rich Btb horizon, underlain by a Btkb and Bkb carbonate horizons. We have interpreted this as a late Pleistocene

Figure 7.2. Soil stratigraphy at the Boca Negra Wash site

soil, truncated by erosion sometime during the Holocene. Resting unconformably atop it is a second sheet sand deposit, the base of which exhibits a poorly consolidated red sand identified as a Bw horizon. Finally, a thin A/C horizon of weak, reddish brown color tops the red sand. Figure 7.2 illustrates the relationships among these horizons. Folsom artifacts occur from within the upper few centimeters of the Btb through the Bw and A/C horizons. The Folsom occupation likely took place atop the surface of an A horizon developed on the Pleistocene soil; it was removed by Holocene erosion and the artifacts reburied within the loose red sand. Subsequent bioturbation, particularly by burrowing rodents, amplified the effects of the eolian processes (also see Holliday et al. 2006).

This paper presents our efforts to determine whether Locus B artifacts and faunal materials show any spatial patterning and thus possible evidence of intrasite organization of particular tasks attributable to the Folsom occupants. To be clear, we make two important assumptions at the outset of this study: (1) we assume that Locus B represents a single occupation and is not a palimpsest composed of more than one use of the area (Folsom or otherwise), and (2) we assume that activities conducted in Locus B originally were segregated spatially to some degree (e.g., there is patterning to seek). We first present a description of the roughly 1,600 specimens recovered from Locus B. This will be followed by presentation of the distribution of these specimens within the locus, and the results of our quantitative analysis aimed at detecting spatial patterning in these distributions. We offer inferences about the significance of the distribution and what Locus B may tell us about organization of activities within intrasite space, and conclude with comparisons to other similar studies at other Folsom sites.

THE LOCUS B ARTIFACT ASSEMBLAGE

As shown in table 7.1, Locus B produced more than 1,600 specimens. Fifty-one Folsom weaponry-related artifacts—finished point fragments, preform fragments, channel flakes, and one small pseudo-fluted point—were recovered (figure 7.3). As seen here, basal fragments of finished points are most common, and include basal corner fragments (figure 7.3b-d) and edge fragments (figure 7.3a and g) from five different points, as well as a full-width basal fragment (figure 7.3e) and a tip fragment (figure 7.3f). All display breaks are impact-related, and it is probable that the basal corner and edge fragments broke within the spear haft. A final specimen, figure 7.3h, is the basal portion of a so-called "pseudo-fluted" point, first reported from Lindenmeier (Wilmsen and Roberts 1978: figure 110). Preform fragments are nearly as common as finished point fragments; the three examples shown here are all second flute failures and include two longitudinally split fragments (figure

TABLE 7.1. Artifacts recovered from Locus B, Boca Negra Wash site

Artifact Type	Freqency	Percent of Complete Assemblage	Percent of Lithics
finished point	8	0.5	0.6
preform	6	0.4	0.5
pseudo-fluted point	1	0.1	0.1
channel flake	27	1.7	2.1
biface	2	0.1	0.2
end scraper	1	0.1	0.1
graver	1	0.1	0.1
retouched flake	7	0.4	0.5
scraper	1	0.1	0.1
utilized flake	2	0.1	0.2
cobble tool	2	0.1	0.2
debitage	1229	75.6	95.5
tooth enamel	296	18.2	—
bone	42	2.6	—
Total	1625		

7.3j and k) and one with a hinge-through break (figure 7.3i). More than three times as many channel flake fragments as preforms are present (table 7.1). In addition to the weaponry-related artifacts, other tools of several kinds were present in relatively small numbers. The most common tool type in this latter group is unifacially retouched flakes, five examples of which are shown in figure 7.4. Four of those illustrated are flakes with unifacial retouch along a lateral margin (figure 7.4a, c, d, and e), while the other (figure 7.4 b) is a graver. Two large, igneous, presumably local cobble tools were also recovered from the site (figure 7.5); similar tools have been reported from Folsom components or sites such as Agate Basin (Frison and Stanford 1982: 55–67) and Stewart's Cattle Guard (Jodry 1999: Figs. 105, 108). Neither exhibits any modification, and we suspect that they served some role in the butchering process, perhaps bone breakage. Unsurprisingly, debitage accounts for almost 75 percent of the assemblage.

Several different lithic material types and sources are represented. The two most abundant are obsidian (Shackley 2005) and Pedernal chert (Bryan 1939; Church and Hack 1939; Smith and Huckell 2005), both derived from the Jemez Mountains some 75 km to the north; together they comprise 71 percent of the assemblage. Of the 16 XRF-sourced obsidian artifacts, 15 are from the Valle Grande Member/Cerro del Medio geochemical group sources (Huckell at al 2011). Accounting for 12 percent of the assemblage are cherts from sources between 100 and 300 km distant, including Chuska chert, available in the Chuska Mountains on the northwestern Arizona-New Mexico border; Zuni China chert and Zuni Spotted chert, both from the Zuni Mountain range and its environs west of Grants, New Mexico (LeTourneau 2000). All of these sources occur to the north, west, and northwest of the site. Approximately 19 percent of the assemblage is composed of various cherts, chalcedonies, quartzite,

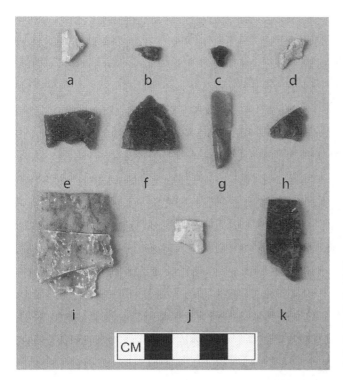

Figure 7.3.
Folsom point fragments (a-h) and preform fragments (i-k) from Locus B of the Boca Negra Wash site

Figure 7.4.
Miscellaneous, unifacially retouched flake tools from Locus B of the Boca Negra Wash site. Flakes with lateral retouch (a, b-e) and a graver (b)

Figure 7.5. Igneous cobble tools from Locus B of the Boca Negra Wash site

and petrified wood. Some of these are almost certainly local, available as cobbles in exposures of alluvium less than 1 km north and west of the site.

THE LOCUS B FAUNAL ASSEMBLAGE

Faunal remains were also recovered, amounting to approximately 300 pieces of tooth enamel morphologically and metrically consistent with bison cheek teeth (Mullen 2007). As one student excavator wryly observed, most Folsom sites contain bone beds; at Locus B we seemed to have an enamel bed. Also recovered were three dozen matchstick-like fragments of weathered bone lacking clear original exterior or interior surfaces. All that could be determined was that they were derived from bones with shaft thicknesses greater than 1–2 mm, and, given their association with the tooth enamel, that would most likely mean bison.

Taken together, the lithic artifact assemblage and the scant faunal assemblage suggest that the Folsom occupation of Locus B most likely consists of a bison kill and a short-term camp. We base this inference on the presence of impact-damaged points—including tip fragments and broken and shattered basal fragments (figure 7.3)—as well as processing tools (figure 7.4 and 7.5) and the remnants of bison, which we see as consistent with a kill. What we interpret to be camp-related activities are reflected by the Folsom point preforms and channel flakes, as well as abundant debitage from tool manufacture. This general pattern of bison tooth enamel and small bone splinters associated with broken Folsom point fragments as well as Folsom point performs, channel flakes, and flake tools has also been found at one other partially excavated Middle Rio Grande Valley Folsom site, known as Deann's (Huckell and Ruth 2004). Similar assemblages, but with better preservation of bison remains, are known from the San Luis Valley, Colorado; these include sites such as Linger (Dawson and Stanford 1975; Hurst 1943), Reddin, and Cattle Guard (Jodry 1999a and b). On the Great Plains, the Folsom component of Area 2 of the Agate Basin site in Wyoming also exhibits similar co-occurrence of bison remains, an assemblage containing tools for butchering, and extensive evidence of point manufacture (Frison and Stanford 1982).

Thus, the assemblage composition from Locus B tells us about the kinds of activities that took place. But what about their intrasite distribution?

INVESTIGATION OF SPATIAL PATTERNING

The first observation is that post-occupational disturbance has had limited effects on the spatial distribution of artifacts—or at least on some of the larger, heavier pieces—in Locus B. In two instances, refitting pieces of the same artifact were present within the same 1 m-by-1 m unit. This includes two fragments of a Folsom point preform that broke on the second flute attempt (figure 7.3i) that were within 1–2 cm of one another. Three pieces of the same unifacially retouched flake tool were also present (figure 7.4c). It is possible that these artifacts were broken by trampling sometime after the Folsom occupation—presumably bison continued to visit the playa when it held water, and they might have been heavy enough to break the artifacts against the exposed argillic horizon. It is unlikely that truly large artifacts like the cobble tools (figure 7.5) have moved very far from their place of deposition.

It is also worth considering whether there is any evidence of size-sorting within the assemblage. One concern is that over the millennia, eolian processes may have disrupted the initial cultural patterning. If this were the case, then the debitage should be size-graded relative to the prevailing winds. The prevailing wind direction today—and in the past, as shown by Pleistocene longitudinal dunes within the Middle Rio Grande Valley—is from the southwest. The largest flakes thus should be the farthest upwind, grading to smallest at the downwind end of the block. Given this wind pattern, one might expect that if eolian size-sorting of the assemblage occurred, it would be shown by a general decrease in lithic artifact size in the downwind (northeast) direction. To assess this possibility, we measured maximum flake length and then plotted the distribution of flakes by their length, as shown in figure 7.6. The largest black dots represent the flakes with the greatest lengths, while the smallest white dots stand for the flakes with the smallest lengths. The distribution of debitage size within the main block is mixed, not patterned, indicating limited or

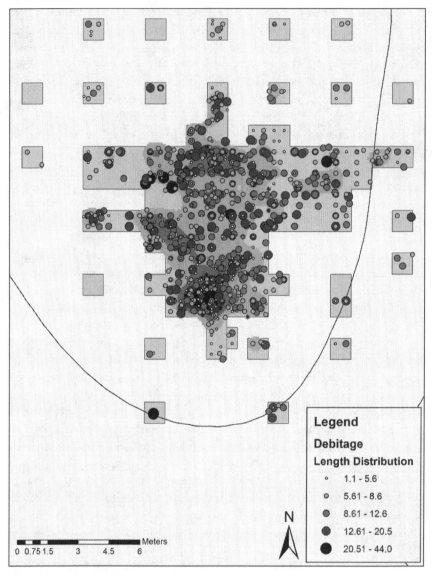

Figure 7.6. Lithic artifact size within Locus B of the Boca Negra Wash site

no size-grading. We interpret this to mean that eolian processes did not fundamentally alter the original spatial distribution of artifacts. To tackle the identification of spatial patterning for the locus as a whole, we are of course limited by the realities of excavated space. Essentially, we do not truly know the actual distribution of all

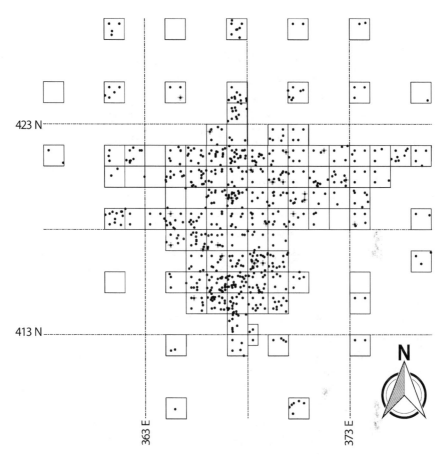

Figure 7.7. Spatial distribution of all artifact classes at Locus B of the Boca Negra Wash site

cultural materials, and the general excavation approach of "chasing" units with more artifacts often leads to a spatial bias. This precludes use of a number of spatial analytical tools common to GIS, such as Nearest Neighbor Analysis, which assumes that all artifact locations are known. Yet, even if those tools were available to us, what might they really tell us? We are less interested in whether distributions are clustered or not, but more interested in why there is clustering. So, instead, we use the spatial relationships tested for correlation between artifact types as a mechanism to extract meaning from the heterogeneous distribution seen in scatterplots and backplots.

As opposed to point-based analysis, our approach to the Locus B spatial analysis relies on grid-based analysis using the 1 m-by-1 m excavation units as the fundamental unit of measurement. Given the relatively low density and dispersed nature of the artifacts, we rely on the same 1 m-by-1 m grid used for excavation to tally counts of various lithic artifact categories of the site. With sufficient sample sizes, we then examine correlations using Spearman's Rank Correlation as a means to test whether relationships exist between different lithic raw materials, artifact types, and non-lithic materials recovered from the excavations. In other words, we want to know if artifacts are spatially grouped by type or raw material. The goal is to elucidate trends and suggest possible explanations for any patterning observed. The distribution of artifacts can often reveal patterns of spatial behavior that complement or contradict interpretations of site function. To study spatial patterns, we rely on the assemblage recovered from the excavation units between N408 to N428 and E358 to E378. This assemblage includes 1,132 pieces of debitage, 15 flake tools, 12 points and preforms, and 32 channel flakes for a total 1,191 artifacts distributed over 104 excavation units, referred to as the *main block* (figure 7.7). The artifact density across the main block is 11.4 artifacts per unit. The distribution seen in figure 7.7 appears to be patterned. Using Orton's (1980) approach to isopleth mapping, we can take twice the variance of artifact counts divided by the mean density values to determine whether this pattern could be the result of randomness. Values closer to one approximate a random distribution and larger values suggest clustering. Using our two densities values from above, BNW has variance-to-mean ratio of 12.9, respectively, which means that the distribution is not random. This seems fairly intuitive given the scatterplot of artifacts; however, clustering alone does not differentiate between causal mechanisms, such as anthropogenic and/or natural processes. The following subsections will provide a highlight of some of the spatial patterns found at Locus B, and plausible explanations for these patterns.

LITHIC ARTIFACT DISTRIBUTION

Any discussion of spatial patterning is limited by the scale of excavation—we can only speak of what we see. These limitations hamper analytical analysis when we cannot observe the entire space of the occupation. As such, we rely primarily on identifying trends of patterning within the excavated area, using statistical verification when possible.

The most obvious pattern in the densities of artifacts is the high concentration of artifacts located at N414 to N416 and E366 to E368 in the southern part of the main block, where density averages 36 artifacts per m² (figure 7.8). The only other area sharing similar density levels is 6 m north in unit N421, E367. What does this distribution tell us? Although Mackie et al. in chapter 5 use the presence of charcoal and burned flakes to identify the location of a hearth and a structure, we lack clearly

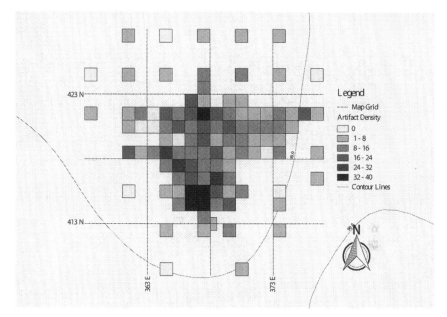

Figure 7.8. Artifact density at Locus B of the Boca Negra Wash site

burned artifacts and only 14 small charcoal fragments were recovered. These had no clear association with the Folsom occupation or even definitive cultural origins.

The first analysis of the lithic assemblage examines the relationship between the primary raw materials. Their distribution suggests at least two discrete reduction areas that cannot be seen when looking at the composite assemblage. Obsidian and Pedernal chert from the Jemez Mountains to the north dominate an otherwise diverse suite of raw materials. The other non-local raw material that is fairly common is Chuska chert from the Chuska Mountains to the northwest, along the border of Arizona and New Mexico. Figure 7.9 shows the distribution and relative abundance of obsidian, Pedernal chert, and Chuska chert.

To examine the distribution of these raw materials, we first needed to address a concern about sample size and area. A simple method would be to average the density for one material at increasing increments of another material. However, this confounds the importance of areal density over what we are really interested in, which is the relative frequencies of one material over another. We instead chose to devalue the area and examine the relationships by looking at the percentage of one material in the assemblage based on incremental intervals of another. For example, how many artifacts of Pedernal chert are found when there are no obsidian artifacts, versus when there is one obsidian artifact, two obsidian artifacts, and so forth?

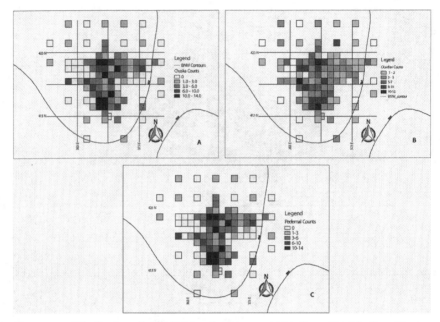

Figure 7.9. Distribution of major lithic material types within Locus B of the Boca Negra Wash site

Because Pedernal chert is the most common material, we set it to proportional value of zero-to-one by dividing each grid cell tally of Pedernal by the total number of Pedernal artifacts in the main block assemblage. Then, this was summed over the different frequencies of both obsidian and Chuska chert (figure 7.10). Essentially, we wanted to see whether relationships exist between raw materials without biasing this comparison if distributions are similar across the site or vary spatially. Stronger correlations among all of the materials would support the inference that those materials were reduced by people in the same space—that is, there were no discrete reduction areas where particular material types were flaked. Alternatively, uncorrelated material spacing would suggest separate and discrete reduction areas. In the case of obsidian, there is a general positive relationship indicating that where we find increases in obsidian, there is a corresponding, albeit not significant, increase in Pedernal chert ($rs = 0.467$, $p = 0.178$). Chuska chert, on the other hand, exhibits a slightly inverse relationship with the percentage of Pedernal chert ($rs = -1.000$, $p = 0.083$), but this too is not significantly correlated. The implications of these trends are that the deposition of obsidian and Pedernal occurred in similar spaces, whereas Chuska was discarded discretely. This distinction supports the notion that the site still possesses spatial integrity despite some artifacts' post-occupational movement.

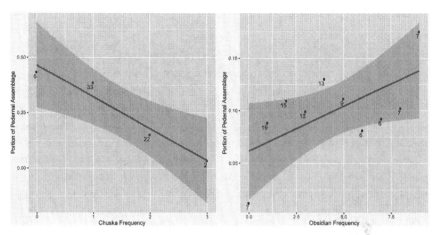

Figure 7.10. Plot of lithic material density of Pedernal chert against obsidian and against Chuska chert

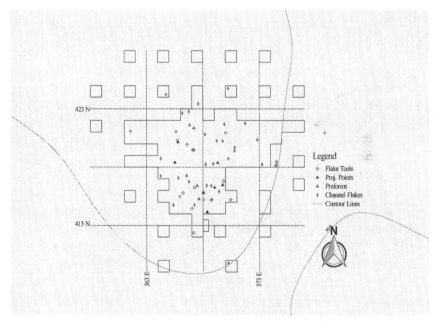

Figure 7.11. Distribution of flake tools and weaponry-related artifacts within Locus B of the Boca Negra Wash site

When we separate the tool assemblage into flake tools and weaponry, including channel flakes, we see distributions similar to those among the debitage (figure 7.11). The average flake count in units without tools is 7.9 artifacts per m² and 16.2

artifacts per m² in units with tools present, which is a significant difference (t = −4.88, df = 58, p = 0.0001). At a very basic level, this makes sense. Debitage is the discarded byproduct of tool manufacture and maintenance. Yet, this overlooks the possibility that the places where tools are manufactured are not necessarily where they are discarded. This inference would hold unless something else is tethering the occupants to particular locations.

The lithic assemblage shows demonstrable spatial structure. The distribution of the artifact assemblage is primarily found concentrated at the southern end of the main block, but moderate densities can also be found elsewhere throughout the block. The analysis of common raw materials shows overlapping but distinct reduction areas, and the tool assemblage shows that there is more debitage in areas with tools than without. In the absence of additional information, we are still left with a basic question of why these patterns occur where they do. To address this question, we turn our attention to the faunal material.

BONE FRAGMENTS, TOOTH ENAMEL, AND DEBITAGE SPATIAL DISTRIBUTIONS

As noted above, hearths and domestic structures are great aids in assessing the use of space within an archaeological site. Two prominent Folsom sites where activity structure was reconstructed include Barger Gulch Locality B in Middle Park, Colorado (Surovell and Waguespack 2007), and the Mountaineer site in the vicinity of Gunnison, Colorado (Morgan and Andrews 2016; Stiger 2006). At Barger Gulch Locality B, hearths were identified in part by concentrations of burned lithic artifacts; at Mountaineer, shallow remnants of structures were observed. Other chapters in this volume (Jochim, chapter 2; Puckett and Graf, chapter 4; Mackie et al., chapter 5; Bement et al., chapter 8) reinforce the importance of hearths and habitation structures in structuring space use at forager camps. However, Boca Negra Wash Locus B lacks obvious hearths, and the lithic assemblage is not helpful in defining hearth areas; only two burned flakes were identified. This suggests that perhaps hearths were not present, or they were not correlated with production or tool repair tasks, or they may have been located outside the excavated areas. The obvious question is how activities at Locus B were structured if not centered around hearths. What was the focal point of activity at the site, and what evidence can be brought to bear to understand how Folsom people spatially organized their activities?

The assemblage of small bone fragments and tooth enamel derived from bison is a valid starting point. If the site is a kill site and the carcass(es) served as the focal point of activity, then we would expect the lithic assemblage to track with the spatial distribution of the faunal remains. One could envision Folsom hunters working

to butcher and perhaps disarticulate the carcass(es) for consumption or transport, and, as needed, repair, replace, or resharpen their tools to accomplish these
tasks. Without the impact of post-depositional disturbances, and in the absence of
intentional cleanup around the kill site, there should be a close spatial correlation
between the fauna and lithics.

The faunal assemblage consists of 339 total pieces of bone and tooth enamel fragments, of which 297 have specific provenience. When bone is present, it averages
5.9 fragments per excavation unit and ranges from 1 to 28 pieces per square meter
(figure 7.12). After excluding sterile units, debitage was also tallied. The average frequency was 9.6 pieces of debitage per unit, ranging between 1 and 41 pieces per
square meter.

When looking at the density plots for faunal remains, there are 58 units with
either bone or tooth enamel. Most units with faunal remains have 1 to 5 specimens
of bone and/or tooth enamel, but there is a primary concentration located in the
southern portion of the main block with an increase in frequency near N421, E364.

Comparisons between the faunal and lithic materials also reveal an interesting
pattern. Seventy-two percent of the artifacts are found in excavation units that had
faunal remains. This would suggest that the processing of the bison carcass(es) coin-
cided with locations of tool, use, repair, and manufacture. Yet, the density of faunal
material per unit does not directly influence the density of artifacts—units with
more bone and tooth enamel do not contain more artifacts ($rs = -0.3$, $p = 0.437$)
(figure 7.13). One could imagine that standing on top of a bison carcass while repair-
ing your tool kit would be less ideal than doing so beside the carcass. This suggests
some post-occupational disturbance of the materials that led to their intermingling,
but we remain confident that this movement did not drastically alter the spatial
patterning derived from behavior. To summarize, we interpret the distribution
of flaked stone artifacts and faunal remains at Locus B to reflect a set of carcass-
centered, as opposed to hearth-centered, activities.

DISCUSSION

Moving beyond the intrasite spatial analysis, it is important to explore how Boca
Negra Wash Locus B contributes to our understanding of Folsom lifeways. Recent
excavations and publications have shown that Folsom sites are much more diverse
in terms of site function, duration of occupation, size, and contents than was appreciated twenty years ago. There are of course "classic" bison kill sites, such as the
Folsom-type site (Cook 1927; Meltzer 2006) and Cooper (Bement 1999), where
projectile points and butchering tools comprise the lithic assemblage. One can also
recognize what appear to be large-area, recurrently occupied residential sites with

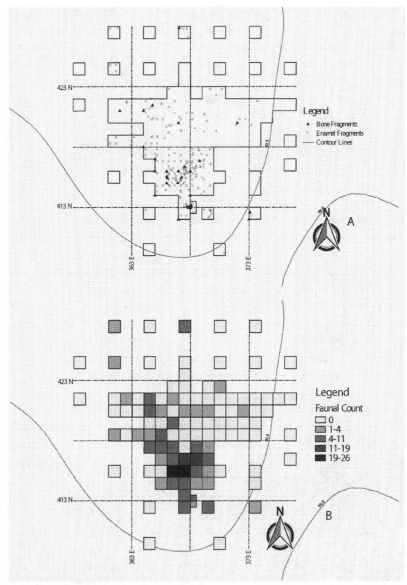

Figure 7.12. Distribution of bone and tooth enamel fragments within Locus B of the Boca Negra Wash site

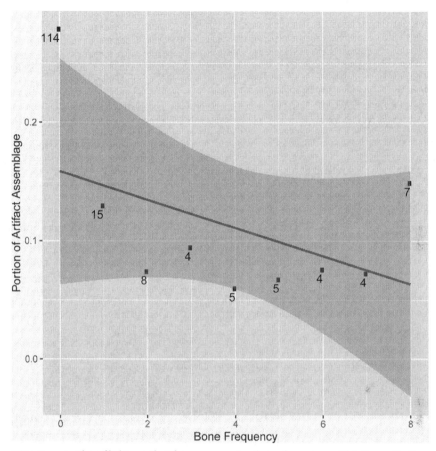

Figure 7.13. Plot of lithic artifact frequency against bone frequency within Locus B of the Boca Negra Wash site

large, diverse lithic assemblages, such as Lindenmeier (Roberts 1935, 1937; Wilmsen and Roberts 1978) and possibly Rio Rancho (Huckell and Kilby 2002). However, there are also smaller sites that appear to be relatively long-term residential localities with structures and large, diverse lithic assemblages, such as Agate Basin (Frison and Stanford 1982), Barger Gulch Locality B (Surovell and Waguespack 2007), and Mountaineer (Morgan and Andrews 2016; Stiger 2006). Stewart's Cattle Guard shows a series of localized clusters of suites of tools adjacent to bison carcasses that Jodry (1999) interpreted as family residential localities. Finally, there are sites that appear to be short-term residential occupations associated with bison kills and fairly diverse but numerically small lithic assemblages. We emphasize that the site type categories also show overlap—with a decision to make a short-term stay at a kill site, a kill/camp results. Further, large residential sites like Lindenmeier are likely to be palimpsests of many small kill/camp types of occupations.

One of the issues worth considering is how human activities are structured at sites occupied by mobile foragers. We can consider some simple scenarios in hypothetical terms. At kill sites, the carcasses of the animals killed clearly become the immediate focus of activity. However, once butchering is completed, the hunters are faced with a decision about whether to continue other activities relating to the carcasses, such as cooking and consuming meat, processing hides, obtaining marrow, etc. This would also include decisions about where to conduct such activities—at the place where the animals lay or somewhere else, possibly nearby. A subsequent decision would be where to pursue other activities that might be carried out at or near the place where the kill was made. Such activities might include weaponry refurbishment and tool manufacture or maintenance. Again, a decision would have to be made regarding the location of such activities, whether in proximity to the kill or away from it. There may also be a secondary set of decisions pertaining to the spatial relationships between non-carcass-related activities (such as discrete knapping locations). The results of such hypothetical decisions could result in a range of site "types," all related to the locations of the carcasses as an original landscape element to provide structure for subsequent human activities.

How does the carcass-centered pattern of activities detected at Locus B compare with what is seen at other Folsom sites? Although we have not attempted to conduct any spatial statistical analyses for other sites, we can offer some observations about the association of flaked stone tools, weaponry repair/replacement, and bison bone at a few other sites. Examination of the published site maps for Lindenmeier Area I Units A and B (Wilmsen and Roberts 1978: figure 160–161) suggests the presence of a pattern, in parts of these areas, like the one seen at Boca Negra Wash Locus B. For example, the six 5 ft-by-5 ft grid units in Unit B in the range of 1D to 01D (east-west) and 0D to 0F (north-south) show an area some 15 ft by 10 ft revealing bones, a few channel flakes, and a handful of points and preforms (Wilmsen and Roberts 1978: figure 161). Similar associations can be seen on other Lindenmeier maps, such as Area II, Unit G (Wilmsen and Roberts 1978: figure 164). We recognize that the cultural deposit at Lindenmeier is thicker than that at Locus B, and reducing the bones and artifacts to a single occupation plane may combine things that were vertically distinct. This is particularly the case for Unit G, where three stratigraphically distinct occupational components may be present (Wilmsen and Roberts 1978: figure 52). However, in the absence of evidence to the contrary, we suggest that Lindenmeier Area I Unit A likely represents, at least in part, a situation similar to that seen at Locus B.

Further assessment of the degree to which the clusters identified using the spatial analysis reflect behaviorally discrete activity areas in Locus B will require refitting analysis. One category of artifacts that would be particularly useful in this regard is channel flakes. This might help shed additional light on the existence of what seem to be two spatially distinct areas of fluted point production. The relative abundance and small size of Pedernal chert and obsidian debitage makes any refitting of flakes of these materials very challenging.

There is some indication that raw material types appear concentrated, possibly reflecting preserved individual reduction episodes. The spatial distribution of three minor materials—Chuska, China, and Zuni Spotted chert—offer additional insight into the distribution patterns seen for Pedernal chert and obsidian. Specifically, while China and Zuni Spotted chert do not show any clear differences in distribution from Pedernal and obsidian, Chuska chert does. As the most distant raw material from the site, one would expect the supply of Chuska chert to be relatively depleted in comparison to materials from sources closer to the site. Although we note that Chuska is slightly more abundant than either China or Zuni spotted, this may be a product of sampling error or the generally poor understanding of the range of variation in the properties of Zuni Mountains chert sources. In any case, there is clearly a greater abundance of Chuska artifacts in the northeastern part of the locus.

Low density near-surface sites make it difficult to build spatial arguments about internal organization, and certainly Locus B at Boca Negra Wash underscores these challenges. The task is made more difficult by the amount of area that has been excavated relative to what may remain unexcavated. Nevertheless, our analysis suggests that there are indications that despite these challenges, some of the initial patterning in the distribution of artifacts and faunal remains is recognizable. We cannot determine what may have structured Folsom choices about where particular activities took place, although it is potentially the case that decisions were made based on where bison were killed and fell. At Locus B and other Folsom sites, there does seem to be a tendency for weaponry manufacture and repair to take place relatively close to animal carcasses or parts of carcasses. This is seen in the Folsom occupation of Area 2 at Agate Basin as well as sites such as Cattle Guard.

CONCLUSIONS

Despite the potentially confounding effects of erosion, bioturbation, and shallow depth of burial, Locus B does seem to retain indications of spatial patterning in the distribution of activities. Further, statistically significant differences in the distribution of artifacts and faunal remains can be detected, so these patterns can be detected by objective means. The composition of the artifact assemblage and its spatial patterning reveal empirical support for our initial interpretation that Boca Negra Wash Locus B was a short-term kill/camp site. Moreover, it does show differential use of space by the Folsom group that created it. The frequency of artifacts that correlate with the location of bone and tooth enamel suggests that activities centered on killing bison, carcass butchering, and retooling. The low artifact counts relative to some other Folsom sites, as well as the high proportion of non-local raw materials, also support our interpretation that the occupation was short-term. The highly fragmented archaeofauna indicates at least one bison was killed and that the carcass remained exposed to prolonged subaerial weathering. Undoubtedly, some of the faunal material likely experienced some post-occupational translocation, but concentrations are present, such as the one found in the area around N415, E366. The density of lithics in this area indicates that tool manufacture and maintenance was done as needed during or after the butchery. At the same time, some individuals began efforts to repair and re-equip their weaponry, as evidenced by the presence of broken preforms and channel flakes. This rearmament spatially overlaps with the proposed butchery location but is also centered on a second area some 6 m north around N421, E367. Unlike the more southerly concentration of activity, we currently have no empirical evidence to explain why occupants chose this northern locale. Was it chosen because it offered protection from the wind or benefitted from tree shade? We may never know, but it remains intriguing to speculate.

As a final point, the investigation of the Boca Negra Wash site demonstrates that shallowly buried Folsom sites in eolian contexts can repay careful excavation and analysis of the distribution of artifacts and minimal faunal remains with information concerning how these ancient hunter-gatherers organized their activities.

Acknowledgments. We are indebted to numerous people for their efforts to explore the Boca Negra Wash site. Thanks first to the students who participated in the 2001 and 2002 University of New Mexico archaeological field schools. Their careful work under hot and windy conditions for six weeks was greatly appreciated. Supervising the field school students as graduate student teaching assistants were Briggs Buchanan, Marcus Hamilton, David Kilby, and Susan Ruth; they ensured that the excavations proceeded smoothly. In 2003 and 2004, excavations were conducted by a small professional crew composed of student archaeologists from UNM and the University of Arizona. We are grateful to Vance Holliday for the generous financial support of the 2003 and 2004 fieldwork through the Argonaut Archaeological Research Fund (AARF) at the University of Arizona. Karen Price of UNM's Maxwell Museum photographed the artifacts that appear in figures 7.3–7.5, and we thank her for her excellent work. Thanks as well go to the New Mexico

Historic Preservation Division for their support of the investigations. We are greatly indebted to K. C. Carlson and Lee Bement for their invitation to participate in this project on open-air camps of mobile hunter-gatherers.

We dedicate this paper to the memory of Patrick Orion Mullen, who excavated at the site as a UNM field school student in 2002 and was part of the professional crew in 2004.

REFERENCES

Amick, Daniel S. 1994. "Technological Organization and the Structure of Inference in Lithic Analysis: An Examination of Folsom Hunting." PhD dissertation, University of New Mexico, Albuquerque.

Amick, Daniel S. 1996. "Regional Patterns of Folsom Mobility and Land Use in the American Southwest." *World Archaeology* 27: 411–426.

Amick, Daniel S., ed. 1999. *Folsom Lithic Technology: Exploration in Structure and Variation*. Archaeological Series, 12. Ann Arbor, MI: International Monographs in Prehistory.

Binford, Lewis R. 1978. "Dimensional Analysis of Behavior and Site Structure: Learning from an Eskimo Hunting Stand." *American Antiquity* 43: 330–361.

Binford, Lewis R. 1983. *In Pursuit of the Past: Decoding the Archaeological Record*. New York: Thames and Hudson.

Binford, Lewis R. 1991. "When the Going Gets Tough: Nunamiut Local Groups, Camping Patterns, and Economic Organisation." In *Ethnoarchaeological Approaches to Mobile Campsites*, edited by Clive S. Gamble and W. A. Boismier, 25–138. Ann Arbor, MI: International Monographs in Prehistory.

Bryan, Kirk. 1939. "Stone Cultures near Cerro Pedernal and Their Geological Antiquity." *Bulletin of the Texas Archeological and Paleontological Society* 11: 9–42.

Church, Fermor S., and John T. Hack. 1939. "An Exhumed Erosion Surface in the Jemez Mountains, New Mexico." *The Journal of Geology* 47: 613–629.

Crumpler, L. S. 1999. "Ascent and Eruption at the Albuquerque Volcanoes: A Physical Volcanology Perspective." In *Albuquerque Geology*, edited by Frank J. Pazzaglia and Spencer G. Lucas, 221–233. Socorro, NM: Fiftieth Annual Field Conference, New Mexico Geological Society.

Dawson, Jerry, and W. J. Judge. 1969. "Paleo-Indian Sites and Topography in the Middle Rio Grande Valley of New Mexico." *Plains Anthropologist* 14: 149–163.

Dawson, Jerry, and Dennis J. Stanford. 1975. "The Linger Site: A Reinvestigation." *Southwestern Lore* 41 (4): 22–28.

Frison, George C., and Dennis J. Stanford, eds. 1982. *The Agate Basin Site: A Record of the Paleoindian Occupation of the Northwestern High Plains*. New York: Academic Press.

Gamble, Clive, and W. A. Boismier, eds. 1991. *Ethnoarchaeological Approaches to Mobile Campsites*. Ann Arbor, MI: International Monographs in Prehistory.

Holliday, Vance T., Bruce B. Huckell, James H. Mayer, and Steven L. Forman. 2006. "Geoarchaeology of the Boca Negra Wash Area, Albuquerque Basin, New Mexico." *Geoarchaeology* 21: 765–802.

Huckell, Bruce B., and J. David Kilby. 2000. "Boca Negra Wash, a New Folsom Site in the Middle Rio Grande Valley." *Current Research in the Pleistocene* 17: 45–47.

Huckell, Bruce B., and J. David Kilby. 2002. "Folsom Point Production at the Rio Ranch Site, New Mexico." In *Folsom Technology and Lifeways*, edited by John E. Clark and Michael B. Collins, 11–29. Lithic Technology Special Publication No. 4. Tulsa, OK: Department of Anthropology, University of Tulsa.

Huckell, Bruce B., J. David Kilby, Briggs Buchanan, Marcus J. Hamilton, and Susan Ruth. 2002. 2001 "Excavations at the Boca Negra Wash Site, North-Central New Mexico." *Current Research in the Pleistocene* 19: 39–40.

Huckell, Bruce B., J. David Kilby, and Marcus J. Hamilton. 2003. "2002 Investigations at the Boca Negra Wash Site, North-Central New Mexico." *Current Research in the Pleistocene* 20: 33–35.

Huckell, Bruce B., and Susan Ruth. 2004. "Test Investigations at Deann's Folsom Site, North-Central New Mexico." *Current Research in the Pleistocene* 21: 48–50.

Huckell, Bruce B., M. Steven Shackley, Matthew J. O'Brien, and Christopher W. Merriman. 2011. "Folsom Obsidian Procurement and Use at the Boca Negra Wash Site, New Mexico." *Current Research in the Pleistocene* 28: 49–52.

Hurst, C. T. 1943. "A Folsom Site in a Mountain Valley of Colorado." *American Antiquity* 8: 250–253.

Jodry, Margaret A. 1999a. "Paleoindian Stage." In *Colorado Prehistory: A Context for the Rio Grande Basin*, by Marilyn A. Martorano, Ted Hoefer, III, Margaret A. Jodry, Vince Spero, and Melissa L. Taylor, 45–114. Denver: Colorado Council of Professional Archaeologists.

Jodry, Margaret A. 1999b. "Folsom Technological and Economic Strategies: Views from Stewart's Cattle Guard Site and the Upper Rio Grande Basin." PhD dissertation, American University, Washington, DC.

Judge. W. James. 1973. *Paleoindian Occupation of the Central Rio Grande Valley in New Mexico*. Albuquerque: University of New Mexico Press.

Judge, W. James, and Jerry Dawson. 1972. "Paleo-Indian Settlement Technology in New Mexico." *Science* 176: 1210–1216.

Kroll, Ellen M., and T. Douglas Price, eds. 1991. *The Interpretation of Archaeological Spatial Patterning*. New York: Plenum Press.

LeTourneau, Philippe D. 2000. "Folsom Toolstone Procurement in the Southwest and Southern Plains." PhD dissertation, University of New Mexico, Albuquerque.

LeTourneau, Philippe D., and Tony Baker. 2002. "The Role of Obsidian in Folsom Lithic Technology." In *Folsom Technology and Lifeways*, edited by John E. Clark and Michael B. Collins, 31–45. Lithic Technology Special Publication No. 4. Tulsa: Department of Anthropology, University of Tulsa.

Morgan, Brooke, and Brian Andrews. 2016. "Folsom Stone Tool Distribution at the Mountaineer Block C Dwelling: Indoor and Outdoor Spaces as Activity Areas." *Paleoamerica* 2: 179–187.

Mullen, Patrick O. 2007. "You Are What You Eat: Younger Dryas Grass Flora." *The Artifact* 45: 29–50.

O'Connell, John F., Kristen Hawkes, and Nicholas Blurton Jones. 1991. "Distribution of Refuse-Producing Activities at Hadza Base Camps: Implications for Analysis of Archaeological Site Structure." In *The Interpretation of Archaeological Spatial Patterning*, edited by Ellen M. Kroll and T. Douglas Price, 199–220. New York: Plenum Press.

Orton, C. 1980. *Mathematics in Archaeology*. Cambridge: Cambridge University Press.

Shackley, M. Steven. 2005. *Obsidian, Geology and Archaeology in the North American Southwest*. Tucson: University of Arizona Press.

Smith, Gary A., and Bruce B. Huckell. 2005. "The Geological and Archaeological Significance of Cerro Pedernal, Rio Arriba County, New Mexico." In *Geology of the Chama Basin*, edited by S. G. Lucas, K. E. Zeigler, V. W. Lueth, and E. E. Owen, 425–431. 56th Field Conference Guidebook. Socorro: New Mexico Geological Society.

Stiger, Mark A. 2006. "A Folsom Structure in the Colorado Mountains." *American Antiquity* 71: 321–352.

Surovell, Todd A., and Nicole M. Waguespack. 2007. "Folsom Hearth-Centered Use of Spacer at Barger Gulch, Locality B." In *Frontiers in Colorado Paleoindian Archaeology: From the Dent Site to the Rocky Mountains*, edited by Robert H. Brunswig and Bonnie L. Pitblado, 219–259. Boulder: University Press of Colorado.

Wilmsen, Edwin N., and Frank H. H. Roberts Jr. 1978. *Lindenmeier, 1934–1974*. Smithsonian Contributions to Anthropology Number 24. Washington, DC: Smithsonian Institution Press.

Yellen, John E. 1977. *Archaeological Approaches to the Present: Models for Reconstructing the Past*. New York: Academic Press.

8

The Late Paleoindian Occupation at the Bull Creek Site

Comparing and Contrasting Seasonal Site Structure and Resource Procurement Strategies

LELAND C. BEMENT, KRISTEN A. CARLSON, AND BRIAN J. CARTER

INTRODUCTION

This chapter investigates seasonal variation in site structure at the Bull Creek camp by comparing and contrasting artifact assemblages and features identified in disparate areas across the stratified occupations. Central to the comparisons are inter- and intra-component artifact and animal bone distributions and their possible associations with cooking features. In addition, the Bull Creek camp components are compared to the bison kill components at the nearby, large-scale Ravenscroft bison arroyo trap to further explore late Paleoindian use of seasonally structured bison resources.

The late Paleoindian Period is a culture historical construct that includes the Plainview, Frederick/Allen, Scottsbluff, and Eden cultures, all of which produced lanceolate-shaped projectile points (Carlson and Bement 2017; Hurst and Hofman 2010; Knell and Muniz 2013; Pitblado 2003). These cultures adapted to the North American Great Plains and Rocky Mountains. Where faunal remains are preserved, bison appears to be the focal animal of these societies, although seasonal use of other resources, including small-bodied game and plants, is also indicated (LaBelle 2010). Site types during this broad time period include large camps such as the Allen site (Bamforth 2007), Jim Pitts (Sellet, Donohue, and Hill 2009), Hell Gap (Larson, Kornfeld and Frison 2009), Osprey Beach (Johnson and Reeves 2013), Jurgens (Wheat 1979), and Lime Creek (Davis 1962), and large-scale bison kills, including Perry Ranch (Hofman and Todd 1997), Allen (Mulloy 1959), Horner

https://doi.org/10.5876/9781646422265.c008

(Jepsen 1953), Plainview (Sellards, Evans, and Meade 1947), Bonfire Shelter (Dibble and Lorrain 1968), Olsen-Chubbuck (Wheat 1972), and Lubbock Lake (Johnson 1987). Additional site types include lithic procurement sites, small camps, and isolated artifact finds (Bamforth 2002; LaBelle 2010). Models of late Paleoindian land use and subsistence structure depict late Paleoindian groups as mobile hunter/gatherers targeting bison and smaller prey in season as well as collecting plant resources (Bamforth 2007; LaBelle 2010; Hill 2010; Hollenbach 2010). Seasonal moves between resource areas define the mobility pattern for these groups. Only large base camps are typically reoccupied (LaBelle 2010). Large-scale bison hunting is generally a winter activity, spanning late fall through early spring (Hill 2010; Hill and Knell 2013). The timing of large-scale bison hunting is thought to coincide with bison mobility patterns and the annual cycle of bison herds. The structure of early Holocene bison mobility is only beginning to be understood (Boehm 2016; Widga, Walker, and Stockli 2010). Observed variability in stable carbon isotope ratios between individuals in a kill site equate high variability in isotope values with migrant herds and low variability with resident herds. The winter targeting of resident herds suggests late Paleoindians were relying on local bison resources to provision winter camps (Boehm 2016; Hill 2010).

STUDY AREA

Bull Creek is a third-order drainage to the Beaver River in western Beaver County, Oklahoma panhandle (figure 8.1). A series of high terraces (T3) with deposits dating to the late Pleistocene and early Holocene flank the now intermittent, meandering stream channel. Previous work within the Bull Creek valley has reconstructed the environment from 33,000 years ago to the present (Arauza et al. 2016; Bement et al. 2007; Sudbury 2010), identified landform/terrace and soil development along the Bull Creek drainage (Alexander 2013; Conley 2010; Woldearegay et al. 2012), investigated the possible presence of markers for an extraterrestrial impact in initial Younger Dryas and other age deposits (Bement et al. 2014; Kennett et al. 2009), and documented cultural sites of various time periods, ranging from Clovis to Late Prehistoric times (Bement, Schuster and Carter 2007; Bement 2014). These studies provide the local environmental, geologic, and cultural context for the project area.

The Bull Creek site (34BV176) is buried 2.5 m below the modern surface in a T3 terrace remnant approximately 16 km upstream from the Beaver River confluence. Meandering of the Bull Creek channel cut into this terrace, exposing a 5 m high cutbank. The deposits contain three litho-stratigraphic layers overlying Permian-age redbed bedrock. Stratum I is coarse sands and gravels of late Pleistocene age based on the presence of mammoth tooth and long bone fragments. Stratum II is

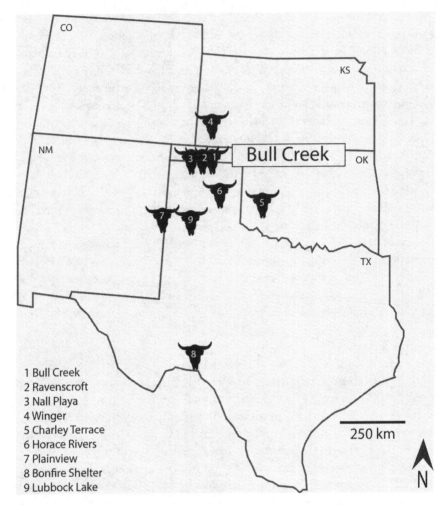

Figure 8.1. Location of the Bull Creek site and other sites mentioned in text.

fine-grained alluvium, including several well-developed buried soils. Stratum III is aeolian or reworked aeolian silt, also containing several buried soils. These three stratigraphic units are easily traced across the cutbank exposure of the Bull Creek site terrace and other T3 terraces along Bull Creek (Arauza et al. 2016; Conley 2010). Pollen and phytolith samples recovered from these various strata provide a baseline environmental reconstruction spanning the late Pleistocene through late Holocene times (Bement et al. 2007; Sudbury 2010), chronicling shifts between cool, mesic-adapted grasslands and warm, xeric grasslands. A dark buried soil dating ~12,900 cal BP contains a spike in nanodiamonds consistent with the proposed Clovis comet extinction event at the end of the Pleistocene and coinciding with the termination of the Clovis cultural period (Kennett et al. 2009; Bement et al. 2014; Firestone 2009). A second spike in nanodiamonds occurred in the near-surface deposits of the Late Archaic age and may be related to the regional impact of the Brenham meteorite in southwest Kansas (Bement et al. 2014).

Cultural deposits associated with this terrace remnant include a ~2,000 cal BP Late Archaic camp site within the upper 20 cm of the Stratum III surface deposits and the ~10,000 cal BP late Paleoindian camp in Stratum II deposits at an average depth of 2.5 to 3.0 m below the modern surface (Carlson and Bement 2017). Bone preservation is good in these deposits, although little organic content suitable for radiocarbon dating is preserved in the lowest deposits. Additional cultural deposits have been identified within the Bull Creek drainage and include Late Archaic as well as Paleoindian-age sites (Bement, Schuster, and Carter 2007). Among the oldest is the JS Cache (34BV180), where 110 Clovis blade and biface tools were buried in the lower deposits of a T3 terrace remnant (Bement 2014). Another Paleoindian-age discovery consists of an extremely well-made lanceolate dart point bearing elephant protein residue (Puseman 2004). This projectile point eroded from the Stratum II deposits of a T3 terrace located approximately 1 km upstream from the Bull Creek camp.

A late Paleoindian-age site that is contemporaneous to the Bull Creek camp is the Ravenscroft arroyo trap bison kill site, located approximately 1 km south of the Bull Creek camp on the high interfluve of a first-order tributary to Bull Creek (Bement, Buehler and Carter 2012). Ravenscroft provided the early Holocene bison isotope samples for a southern plains environmental reconstruction, tracking climate change across the Younger Dryas (YD) (Carlson et al. 2017). The reconstruction documents a shift from warm, wet conditions to hot, dry conditions at the end of the Allerød (Clovis drought, Haynes 1991), followed by an onslaught of increasingly cooler and wetter conditions, reaching the maximum at the height of the YD. Later, there is a return to hot, dry conditions during the initial early Holocene (terminal Folsom drought, Holliday 2000), and those conditions are more firmly established in the early Holocene. The multiple Ravenscroft bison kill components figure prominently in the reconstruction of the use of the Bull Creek camp in the following analysis.

The cultural deposits at the Bull Creek camp and Ravenscroft bison kill are investigated to address the research questions proposed below concerning the layout of open-air camps and the structure of late Paleoindian subsistence adaptations in this area. The presence of late Paleoindian lanceolate projectile points consistent with those found at the Bull Creek camp and Ravenscroft bison kill in area surface collections, as well as the identification of additional sites of late Paleoindian age (Hofman 2010), indicate a persistent late Paleoindian presence in the Oklahoma panhandle and neighboring portions of Texas and Kansas and the expectation that the results of our analyses are applicable to a broader region.

Archaeological investigation at the stratified Late Paleoindian Bull Creek camp-site, Oklahoma panhandle, is guided by two research questions: (1) How did Late Paleoindian (9,000–10,000 years ago) groups arrange activity areas at large camps, and (2) how did this organization differ during various seasons of the year? These research questions require the recovery of detailed information including the age, season, composition (including species richness tabulations), and distribution of activity areas within the Late Paleoindian components of the Bull Creek site, as well as the contemporaneity of intra-site activity areas and the contemporaneity of Bull Creek components with the large-scale bison-hunting sites in the project area. With these data, we are able to compare and contrast the seasonally specific aspects of activity areas.

One of the difficulties in defining the layout of large open-air sites lies in establishing contemporaneity in the use of disparate activity areas. We employ a multi-scale approach to ascertain various levels of co-occurrence, including stratigraphic consistency, radiocarbon alignment, seasonality convergence, mirrored faunal resource exploitation, and artifact refit patterns. Once patterns of contemporaneity are established, activity area divergences become important in reconstructing inter- and intra-group interactions, household composition, and possible social hierarchies.

METHODS

Analyses to address these questions and identify discrete activity areas begin with considerations of site formational and taphonomic processes (Cannon and Meltzer 2004, 2008; Grayson 1984, 1989; Hill et al. 2011; Lyman 1994). Taphonomic data gathered during excavation includes the 3D piece-point plotting of all in situ artifacts and bones; documentation of strike (compass orientation) and dip (slope aspect) attributes of all bones and artifacts. These datasets are combined with photographic documentation to assess the possibility that post-depositional factors may affect bone preservation and distribution. All bones have been assessed in the lab according to degree of weathering, root etching, carnivore and gopher modification, sediment abrasion, and trampling, as well as cultural modifications, including cutmarks, helical fractures, and bashing. All faunal remains have been identified to the lowest taxonomic level possible through comparisons with the comparative faunal collection housed at the University of Oklahoma (OU), as well as published identification guides (e.g., Casteel 1976; Gilbert 1973; Gilbert et al. 1981; Leonard 1959); and also to element, side, level of development (fusion, etc. Bement and Basmajian 1996), age, and sex; and standard measurements (Von den Dreisch 1976). Once these tasks are completed, the faunal remains associated with each excavation area and level are tallied for use in Species Richness analysis (Grayson 1984). These results are then compared across activity areas and stratigraphic components to determine the seasonal variation in hunting/gathering activities at the Bull Creek site.

A scaled approach is used to identify activities conducted and the possible association of these activities within specific areas of the site. Site formation processes must be identified and considered before meaningful associations between artifact assemblages, faunal remains, and defined cultural features can be made. Further consideration is necessary to determine if artifact, bone, and feature associations are the result of discard patterns or the presence of intact, discrete activity areas. The identification of discrete activities relies on the context within which particular activities are performed. For instance, the cutmarks or other indicators of butchery found on articulated animal skeletal segments reflect systematic, discrete activity as opposed to an accounting of all butchery marks across entire excavation-area assemblages, which could represent a palimpsest of activities. Similarly, artifact refits indicate the temporal or sequential relatedness of an activity. Refit artifacts found in close proximity indicate a discrete activity, whereas proximity of two objects could be the result of post-depositional factors of downslope movement of objects or discard patterns.

Several tasks were performed in assessing site structure. These included radiocarbon assay of multiple samples from each depositional component to identify broad contemporaneity of deposited materials. Stable isotope analysis of bison bone was likewise performed on multiple samples to establish contemporaneity of bison remains. The radiocarbon and stable isotope assays were performed on the same materials at the same laboratory. Only bison bone results with atomic stable isotope ratios consistent with modern bones were accepted for comparisons.

Attempts were made to refit flaking debris to identify sequential reduction actions of the same source material. As mentioned above, refits in close proximity may not verify the location where flint knapping took place; however, widely scattered refits are an indication that materials have been moved around the site either intentionally or by post depositional processes.

Differences in the subsistence organization of the components was determined by an accounting of the number of animal species identified for each occupation. Seasonality was determined through a combination of incremental growth metrics (bison tooth eruption and wear, fetal growth stage) and known seasonal presence/absence patterns of particular species. Stable carbon and nitrogen isotopic analysis of bison remains was employed to distinguish between highly mobile (migratory) bison, represented by high coefficient of variation (CV) levels, and resident herds, represented by low coefficient of variation values (Carlson and Bement 2013).

Materials used for these analyses were obtained from the 2009, 2015, 2016, and 2017 excavations at the Bull Creek camp (34BV176) and the 2008, 2009, 2013, 2015, 2016, and 2017 excavation at the Ravenscroft bison kill site. Excavations at these sites followed established excavation methods, including sub-meter horizontal and vertical provenance of all excavated materials in relationship to a permanent site datum and within 1 m-by-1 m horizontal grid coordinates. All excavated sediment was passed through 3 mm (1/8 inch) mesh hardware cloth; the resultant high graded residue was picked for bones and artifacts. Sediment samples were collected for additional analysis, including water screening and flotation. Individually mapped specimens were assigned individual field numbers. All excavated materials are housed at the Oklahoma Archeological Survey, University of Oklahoma, Norman, awaiting final curation at the university's Sam Noble Oklahoma Museum of Natural History.

RESULTS

Four field seasons between 2009 and 2017 at the Bull Creek camp excavated an estimated 54 m² area of the late Paleoindian-age deposits. These excavations documented 5 cooking or heating features, 8 post holes, and ~2,000 individually piece-plotted bone or stone cultural materials distributed between four stratigraphic levels, numbered from oldest (I) to youngest (IV). The sequence of archaeological investigation is detailed first, followed by a description of the content and structure of each level. Each component is then described and compared and contrasted within the site and between the Bull Creek camp and the nearby Ravenscroft bison kill site.

THE BULL CREEK SITE

Identifying a Paleoindian camp site that has evidence of occupation during multiple seasons of the year is rare. Rarer still is to find the various seasons of occupation in stratified contexts where one component aligns with the season of large-scale bison hunting activities and a second component aligns with the season of small-scale bison kills and broad-spectrum hunting-gathering subsistence pattern targeting multiple animal species. The Late Paleoindian-age (ca 9,000 to 10,000 radiocarbon years ago) deposits in the Bull Creek site (34BV176) appear to be just this type of camp site (figure 8.2). Limited excavations in 2009, 2015, 2016, and again in 2017 indicate that the Bull Creek site is a large camp extending for at least 100 m by 60 m (6,000 m²), buried 2.4–2.9 m below the surface within a high terrace bordering the now-intermittent Bull Creek channel. A Late Archaic (~2,000 year old) cultural deposit

Figure 8.2. Aerial view of the Bull Creek camp, 34BV176, looking east.

is found within the upper 20 cm of the terrace, and stratified Paleoindian deposits are found between 2.5 and 3.6 m below the terrace surface (Carlson and Bement 2017).

Investigation of the Bull Creek site began in 2003 with the documentation of Profile 1 (figure 8.2), a ~6 m tall profile inset 1 m into the cutbank exposure (Bement et al. 2007a) that documented three litho-stratigraphic units over bedrock. The bedrock consists of the Permian-age sandstone of the Cloud Chief Formation (Gustavson et al. 1991). Immediately above the bedrock is Unit I, consisting of coarse sand and gravel alluvium. Unit II consists of finer grain clasts, indicating a shift from rapid to slower stream flow with overbank deposition and colluvium. The Paleoindian cultural deposits are contained in Unit II. The upper portion of Unit II contains a thick (> 1 m) cumulic soil known locally as the Bull Creek soil. Above Unit II is Unit III. Unit III consists of wind-blown silts that continue to the surface of the profile. A Late Archaic cultural level is contained in the upper 15 cm of the Unit III aeolian deposits. The transitions or breaks between each of these depositional units are visible along the entire ~100 m cutbank exposure (figure 8.3) and have been documented in three additional profiles associated with each of the three block excavations at the Bull Creek site. This depositional sequence, including the Bull Creek soil, has been documented in four additional high-wall terrace exposures along the lower 9 km reach of Bull Creek to its confluence with the Beaver River (Alexander 2013; Arauza et al. 2016; Conley 2010; Woldearegay et al. 2012). Unit I dates to the late Pleistocene; Unit II dates from the latest Pleistocene to early Holocene; Unit III dates from middle to late Holocene (Arauza et al. 2016).

Figure 8.3. Bull Creek site cutbank exposure and location of described profiles. Looking southeast.

Within the Bull Creek site terrace remnant, this sequence occurs continuously over an area of at least 2 ha, including the 0.6 ha of known cultural material (Carlson and Bement 2017). Ground-penetrating radar imaging of the site area documented the presence of continuous deposits without any sign of disruptions by erosional discontinuities. Coring by bull-probe and Giddings Rig across the terrace surface documented deeply buried (~ 2.5 m) cultural material at least 60 m from the cutbank edge.

Profile descriptions of Unit II deposits describe stacked cumulic soils with multiple buried A-horizons. Contained within these soils are well-preserved pollen and phytolith assemblages, depicting the development of grass-dominated plant communities during Unit II deposition (Bement et al. 2007). Phytoliths in these same deposits show the grassland was dominated by warm-season C_4 short grasses, although intervals of increased C_3 cool-season grasses are seen immediately preceding the Late Paleoindian-bearing deposits.

Excavations into the Bull Creek site deposits include the 2003 excavation of a 1 m-by-1 m test unit to salvage bison bones eroding from the cutbank exposure of the site; the 2009 excavation of an 18 m^2 block that was expanded in 2015 by another 12 m^2; the 2016 excavation of a 12 m^2 block in an area south of the previous block excavations, and the 2017 excavation that deepened and expanded the 2016 excavation block, removed a line of units separating the 2009 and 2015 blocks, and opened areas adjacent to the west trench on the cutbank face between the 2015 and 2016 blocks (figure 8.4). The 2009 and 2015 blocks identified two stratified

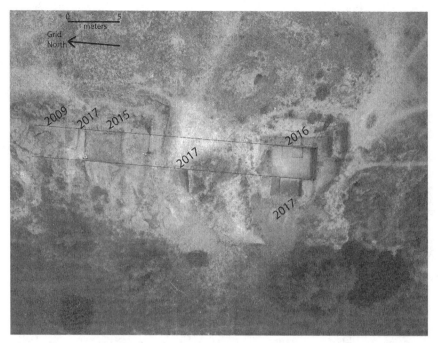

Figure 8.4. Location of excavation blocks by year of excavation. The 2003 test pit is not shown.

Late Paleoindian components. These two components converge at the northern edge of the site but are separated by increasingly thicker (up to 15 cm) fine-grain alluvial deposits toward the south. The change in amount of separation is attributed to the closer proximity to the valley wall of the northern area of the site, compared with the more distant downslope area of the south-central portion of the site. Continued investigations in 2017 identified a lower, still-undated component and an ill-defined upper late Paleoindian component.

DESCRIPTION OF BULL CREEK CAMP COMPONENTS

The following sections describe the composition, distribution of artifacts and features, radiocarbon ages, and stable carbon and nitrogen content of bison bone for the various components at the Bull Creek camp. As mentioned above, the components are numbered sequentially from oldest (I) to youngest (IV) and are described in that order.

BULL CREEK COMPONENT I

The lowest component at the Bull Creek camp consists of bones and a single flake located in fine sandy sediments approximately 1 m above bedrock. This component was discovered when an exposure of bison bone was noticed on the face of the cutbank in the area between the 2016 and 2017 excavation blocks. This area, identified as the West Trench, was investigated initially by opening a ~1 m-by-1 m excavation unit above several bison ribs eroding from the cutbank face. This excavation was subsequently expanded into an elongated excavation block 2 m north-south by 5 m east-west. The west trench is an expansion of an earlier high-wall profile described in 2015. A profile description of the eastern terminus of the trench documented the stratigraphy of the site from the bedrock to the modern surface, including all lithostratigraphic divisions previously documented at the site.

Initial investigation of this area uncovered 23 bison bones, including multiple ribs, phalanges, and thoracic vertebrae. Continued excavation in this area during the summer of 2017 uncovered additional bison axial elements and a single piece of turtle carapace. The faunal material consists of a total of 47 bison elements, predominantly ribs and thoracic vertebrae, s well as a single turtle carapace fragment. The bison elements represent a minimum number of individuals (MNI) of three based on the development stage and size differences in first phalanges. The proximal epiphysis on the bison first phalanges fuse by two years of age (Bement and Basmajian 1996). The three individuals include one large adult, one small adult, and one juvenile younger than two years old.

The dorsal spine on one thoracic vertebra measured 55 cm from dorsal tip to vertebral process. This size suggests the animal is in the *Bison antiquus* species size range. All of the bones in this level are coated with a thin layer of calcium carbonate. No cutmarks or green bone breaks have been documented from this level. Any possible cutmarks are likely obscured by the calcium carbonate coating on all specimens.

The only definite cultural material found with these bones is a single chert tertiary flake tool. The lithic material type is tentatively identified as Edwards Plateau chert from central Texas, although a definitive attribution of material source is hampered by a continuous coating of calcium carbonate. This flake tool has been submitted for protein residue analysis.

Four attempts to radiocarbon date bison bone from this level have failed. No collagen is preserved. A single attempt to radiocarbon date the soil organic matter from the sediment yielded an age of 11,588 ± 34 radiocarbon years before present (^{14}C BP) or a 2 σ calendar year range before present (cal BP) of 13,314–13,488 cal BP (UGAMS A26150) (table 8.1). This date is considered a maximum possible age for this deposit.

TABLE 8.1. Radiocarbon assays for Bull Creek camp

Site name	Site no.	Bone no.	Element	$\delta^{13}C$	$\delta^{15}N$	%C	%N	C:N atomic	Lab #	^{14}C	±	Occ. group
Bull Creek	34BV176	2015	pelvis	−8.6	9.1	14.4	5.2	3.26	P2475	9020	35	5
Bull Creek	34BV176	1190	petrous	−10.7	8.6	42.8	14.7	3.39	P2489	9195	35	4
Bull Creek	34BV176	232	humerus	−12.1	7.5	−	−	3.24	136075	9230	30	4
Bull Creek	34BV176	185	–	−	−	−	−	−	90952	9280	25	3
Bull Creek	34BV176	727	petrous	−9.0	9.3	29.9	10.5	3.31	173186	9290	30	3
Bull Creek	34BV176	512	humerus	−9.8	8.9	42.3	15.2	3.25	166047	9300	35	3
Bull Creek	34BV176	–	soil	−	−	−	−	−	A26150	11,588	34	1

ᵃ No prefix letter: UCAIMS; P: Penn State; A: UGAMS

BULL CREEK COMPONENT II

Bull Creek Component II is buried in fine sandy loam and is best represented in the lower levels in the 2015 and 2017 excavation blocks (figure 8.5). Component II is difficult to separate from the overlying Component III materials in the 2009 excavation block at the north end of the site, but increasingly gains vertical separation in the southern excavation blocks. A total of ~1,100 bones consisting of bison and canids have been individually mapped from this component. The bison remains represent an MNI of seven bison. An additional four bison fetuses are also represented in the assemblage but not included in the overall MNI. The bison fetuses are at the five- to six-month gestation level. If these bison followed the same annual reproductive cycle as modern bison (~July rut, ~May calving), then this stage of fetal development indicates a winter-time occupation of the site.

The bison bones display evidence of marrow processing in the form of extensive green bone fracturing to expose the marrow cavity (Carlson and Bement 2017). Cutmarks are distributed over the surfaces of leg bones to remove meat and periosteum. The helical fractures truncate many cutmarks, supporting the logical progression of butchering where hide and meat were removed before the bones were broken for marrow extraction. Cutmarks found on fetal elements indicate the fetuses were intentionally processed at the camp. A bison skull was bashed in the frontal to expose the brain case, allowing removal of the brain.

The sole occurrence of bison in this level suggests this occupation may be associated with a pattern of large-scale bison hunting exemplified at nearby kill sites, including Ravenscroft and the Winger site in southwestern Kansas (Hofman 2010). At the Ravenscroft site, located only 1.5 km from Bull Creek, fetal material of the same developmental stage was found in two adjacent arroyo trap bison kills (Bement, Buehler and Carter 2012). If excavations reveal that bison continue to be the sole resource transported to the camp and that the seasonality continues to correlate with the seasonality of contemporaneous large-scale bison kill sites, then this occupation level could represent site layout patterns associated with a base camp during periods of specialized bison hunting and reflect decision-making strategies related to moving animal parts from kill to camp and associated processing at the secondary location (Hill 2005, 2008).

Features within Component II consist of a single hearth and two post holes. The hearth consists of a central stained area devoid of bones and other debris surrounded by charred and uncharred bison bones, including bison fetal material (figure 8.5). The hearth area is 45 cm in diameter and forms a shallow bowl approximately 10 cm deep at the center. No in situ charcoal was found, only charred bone and stained sediment.

The post holes indicate that two posts were placed, somewhat randomly, 70 cm apart. The filled holes are 8 cm in diameter and extend 10 cm into the substrate, where each abruptly ends. The purpose of these post holes is purely conjecture and is hypothesized to be some sort of drying rack, roasting support, or wind break near the hearth.

Artifacts resulting from the bifacial reduction of an Alibates biface (discussed below) were deposited near this hearth and may indicate a discrete activity associated with the hearth or a single dump pile of flintknapping debris from somewhere else on site. The sequential refit of flakes within a spatially restricted area (less than 50 cm²) on the north side of the hearth suggests that site disturbance by occupation and post-depositional processes has not broadly distributed this material since the time of its deposition.

Lithic artifacts from Component II include one heavily reworked and broken lanceolate projectile point and a concentration of Alibates chert biface reduction flakes. The broken projectile point fragment is made of Alibates chert and displays flaking patterns depicting several episodes of use, breakage, re-shaping, use, and breakage. Only a small portion of the basal element of this projectile point displays its original flaking pattern (figure 8.6).

A total of 118 bifacial reduction flakes were found in a 50 cm diameter area on the north edge of a hearth. The flakes average 9.1 mm by 7.7 mm by 1.3 mm in length,

Figure 8.5. Hearth in Late Paleoindian component II at Bull Creek camp. Pedestalled artifacts depicted here all sit at the same elevation. The pedestalling can be visually misleading.

width, and thickness, respectively, and represent a mid- to late-level of biface reduction where thinning the biface was important and loss of width was also minimalized. A total of three refit series (two, three, and six flakes, each) of sequential flakes have been identified in this concentration and the length and width of these refit flakes are shown in figure 8.7 to show the consistency of flake size in this reduction sequence. The refit of six sequential flakes illustrates the reduction sequence along a 3.3-cm length of the biface edge (figure 8.7, Refit 2). This reduction sequence is also displayed on an Alibates chert projectile point preform recovered after it eroded from the site cutbank during the spring of 2017 (figure 8.6d). Although the preform cannot definitely be assigned to the Component II occupation, it is described here

Figure 8.6. Artifacts from Bull Creek site, including heavily reworked lanceolate point from 2009 excavation area (A), two points (B and C) that eroded from the cutbank face, and (D) projectile point preform from the north end of the site.

because of the similarity in biface reduction sequence between the preform and the Alibates chert bifacial reduction flake concentration.

The biface is a projectile point preform; its tip and one proximal corner were broken during the bifacial reduction sequence. The resulting object's dimensions are 10.51 cm long, with a maximum width of 3.08 cm and maximum thickness of 1.27 cm. The reduction process evident on this preform includes steep unifacial beveling of lateral edges through percussion, followed by straightening of the edges and further thinning by removal of long, narrow, tightly spaced pressure flakes that terminate at or slightly over the midline. The resulting flaking pattern is described as parallel oblique transverse flaking. In the area where re-alignment of the beveled edge to the center line of the biface through pressure flaking occurred, the biface width was reduced by ~2 mm. Had this reduction process continued along

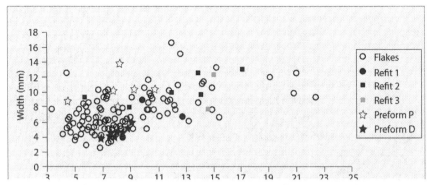

Figure 8.7. Flake metrics and preform flake scar metrics. Three refit sequence biface reduction flakes and preform proximal (P) and distal (D) flake scars are designated.

the entire length of the preform, the resulting biface would have been ~28 mm wide at its proximal end, with an overall estimated length in excess of 100 mm and a thickness of ~7.5 mm.

The dimensions of the bifacial thinning flakes from the flake concentrations are consistent with the shape and size ranges of flake scars on the preform, indicating that the flake concentration could be the result of thinning and shaping a projectile point preform. Several of the flakes in the flake concentration match the dimensions of the parallel oblique transverse pressure flaking displayed on the preform. The measurement of platform angle on the flakes from the concentration also compare well with the flake scar angles displayed on the preform, ranging from 84 degrees for large percussion flakes to 62 degrees for pressure flakes. The platform angle/flake scar angle similarity suggests that the same beveling technique was employed by the knapper responsible for the flake concentration.

Unifacial beveling in bifacial reduction serves two purposes. First, it conserves width loss incurred with each sequence of edge reduction. Bifacial reduction removes twice as much width compared to unifacial reduction. Second, moving the edge to opposing unifacial beveling positions creates a flatter, wider preform across the diagonal. A flatter preform is less susceptible to overshot flaking during pressure flaking, which greatly reduces the width of the final biface by removing the opposite edge. The result is a wider projectile point with lenticular cross section and oblique parallel transverse flake scars. Of course, when the process removes the tip and one basal corner, the result is a discarded preform like the one from the Bull Creek camp.

A 0.5 g sample of sediment from the flake concentration contained 30 pieces of micro-debitage less than 2 mm in greatest dimension. All micro-debitage was Alibates chert. The recovery of micro-debitage suggests the in situ reduction of a biface preform as these tiny fragments are less likely to be swept and transported in cleaning activities. Micro-debitage can be transported if flintknapping occurred on an impervious material such as an animal hide that was then picked up and dumped in another location (Gallagher 1977).

Radiocarbon dating of the Component II level consists of three assays on bison bone (two petrosals and one humerus) (table 8.1). The mean of the three samples is 9288 ± 17 ^{14}C BP (10,475–10,561 cal BP). These three assays are statistically the same at 95 percent confidence interval (T = 0.224222, Xi^2 (0.05) = 5.99, df = 2) (Reimer et al. 2013). Stable carbon and nitrogen isotopes on two of the samples (table 8.1) yielded an average of $\delta^{13}C$ = −9.4 ‰, and $\delta^{15}N$ = 9.1 ‰, with a CV($\delta^{13}C$) = 3.1. The low CV suggests the bison were from a resident herd (Carlson and Bement 2013).

Bull Creek Component III

Bull Creek Component III co-mingles with Component II at the north end of the site, yet separates into a distinct stratum as excavations moved south. At its greatest separation from the underlying Component II, Component III lies 25 cm above Component II and is separated by a darker soil. In the south 2016/17 excavation block, the Component III sediment is a tan, fine, sandy loam.

A total of ~1,350 bones distributed among 19 taxa have been individually mapped from this component. Bison is the largest animal in this component and probably accounts for the greatest amount of animal resources. A MNI of three bison have been identified in Component III. A significant number of other animal taxa have been identified, including medium and small mammals, reptiles, amphibians, birds, and mollusks (table 8.2). The presence of neonate bison, deer fawns, and warm-season reptiles and amphibians suggests this occupation of the site occurred during late spring through summer (Carlson and Bement 2017).

Artifacts from this component include large lithic flake tools of Alibates chert and quartzite, and bone tools including eyed needles and expedient bison-bone butchering tools. The eyed needles are small, with maximum diameters of 2 mm (Lyman 2015).

Features for this component include four hearths, six post holes, and one bison butchering area. The four hearths range in form from the 30-cm diameter, 8-cm deep feature 1 located in the 2009 excavation block (Carlson and Bement 2017) to the scattered hearth areas of features 2 through 4 that were identified in the 2015 excavation block. All four hearth areas appear to have been blown out and scoured by downslope washing and then filled with fine-grained sediments, possibly of aeolian origin. At the core of each scattered hearth are patches of oxidized sediment with embedded charcoal flecks and small fragments of burned bone, suggesting each is the locus of a shallow hearth and not the refuse from hearth cleanout activity.

Table 8.2. Component III taxa

Taxa	Common name	Screen NISP	Mapped NISP	Total NISP
Bison antiquus occidentalis	Bison	110	177	287
	Burned Bison	–	16	16
	Fetal Bison	13	14	27
	Bison/Deer	–	826	826
	Bison/Deer Burned	54	2	56
Odocoileus sp.	Deer	13	3	16
	Deer Burned	–	9	9
	Deer/Pronghorn	–	9	9
Antilocapra americana	Pronghorn	–	5	5
Sylvilagus floridanus	Cottontail rabbit	–	4	4
Lepus californicus	Jackrabbit	–	1	1
Microtus sp.	Microtus sp.	–	2	2
Dipodomys sp.	Kangaroo Rat	–	1	1
Taxidea taxus	Badger	–	1	1
Canid sp.	Wolf-size	–	4	4
	Coyote-size	–	1	1
Large Bird	Sandhill Crane	–	1	1
Small Bird		–	1	1
	Small Bird Burned	–	1	1
Croatalus sp.	Rattlesnake	–	2	2
	Non-Pit Viper Snake	–	2	2
Trachemys scripta	Slider Turtle	10	4	14
Terrapene carolina	Box Turtle	43	3	46
	Box Turtle Burned	–	5	5
Lampsilis teres	Freshwater Mussel	–	2	2
Snail	Snail	–	12	12
Total		243	1,108	1,351

The six post holes were identified in the 2016/17 southern excavation block in the vicinity of the bison butchering feature. The post holes range in size from 8 to 10 cm in diameter and 6 to 10 cm deep. The distribution of post holes appears

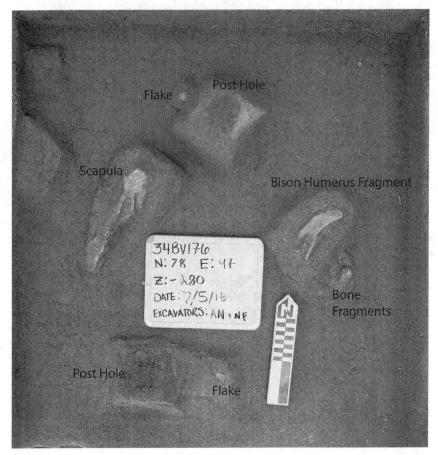

Figure 8.8. Two of three post holes and two possible bison bone tools from the 2016 Bull Creek excavation area. Artifacts and features are pedestalled and sit on the same elevation in relation to each other.

random (figure 8.8) and may result from the construction of possible drying racks, hide working racks, or a wind break.

The bison feature consists of a bison anterior axial segment including fourth and fifth lumbar vertebrae, all thoracic vertebrae, all cervical vertebrae, cranium, both mandibles, and ribs from the right and left sides (figure 8.9). All lumbar and thoracic vertebrae bear blow marks indicative of butchery accomplished with the aid of a pick or mattock-style implement that produced long progressive insertions and sudden circular compressive stops (figure 8.10). The uniformity in the diameter of the stroke terminations or compression suggests that a single tool was used on

Figure 8.9. The bone feature in the 2016 excavation area at Bull Creek, looking south.

this animal. The distribution of these marks indicate that the tool was employed to remove the muscle masses of the hump and back strap along both sides of the carcass. Similar compressive marks were documented on some of the ribs, indicating similar chopping motion to loosen muscle masses of the shoulders, muscle attachments along rib heads, and the blanket of flesh on the ribs. No butchery marks were observed on the cervical vertebrae. A single slash mark on the occipital condyle at the back of the skull suggests a sharp implement, probably a stone tool, was used to sever the head from the atlas vertebra. With the exception of the slash mark on the back of the skull, no stone tool cutmarks have been identified, although several medium-sized quartzite flakes suitable for use in butchering were recovered in this area. Maxillary tooth eruption and wear indicate the skeletal remains are from a mature animal. The smooth, slender horn core base suggests the animal was female. A second bison cranium, also smashed to gain access to the brain case, was uncovered approximately 2 meters east of the butchering feature and indicates the presence of a second bison. The age and sex of this animal could not be determined.

Associated with the post holes are 20 quartzite flakes, a hammerstone, and two bone tools. The quartzite flakes are tertiary flakes that are less than 5 cm in maximum

Figure 8.10. Composite bison bone feature expanded in 2017 excavation.

dimension. The larger flakes may have served as butchering/cutting tools, and several have been submitted for protein residue analysis to aid in determining their possible use as tools and to identify the range of possible materials processed using these flakes.

The lithic debris in this area was dominated by quartzite flakes, possibly used in the butchering of the bison remains. The dominance of quartzite flakes (11% Alibates chert to 89% Dakota quartzite) (figure 8.11) in this area stands in stark contrast to the lithic assemblages contained in the 2009 and 2015 excavation blocks where Alibates chert dominated the flake material (91% Alibates chert to 9% Dakota quartzite). Comparable shifts in preferred lithic material have been interpreted at other camps as an indication of the presence of more than one group, each represented by the dominant stone material type (Wilmsen and Roberts 1978). An alternative interpretation may be that the shift in tool stone type represents a shift in task, where the use of quartzite is superior to the use of chert or where quartzite is used for everyday tasks and exotic Alibates is relegated to curated tool (e.g., projectile point) manufacture.

Radiocarbon dating of the Component III level consists of two assays on bison bone (one petrosal and one humerus) (table 8.1). The mean of the two samples is 9215 ± 23 ^{14}C BP (10,269–10,437 cal BP). These two assays are statistically the same at 95 percent confidence interval ($T = 0.5764706$, Xi^2 (0.05) = 3.84, df = 1) (Reimer et al. 2013) and statistically different from the radiocarbon ages of the lower component II and overlying component IV occupations. Stable carbon and nitrogen isotopes on the two samples (table 8.1) yielded an average of $\delta^{13}C = -11.4$ ‰, and $\delta^{15}N$ = 8.1 ‰, with a $CV(\delta^{13}C) = 8.7$. The relatively high CV suggests the bison were from a comparatively more mobile herd compared to the tight CV of the underlying,

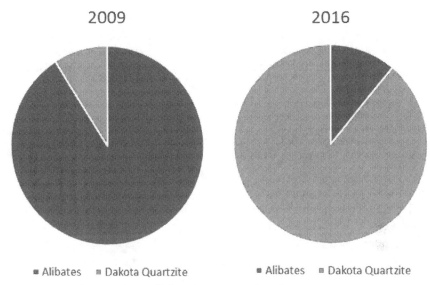

Figure 8.11. The percentage of lithic source materials in the 2009 and 2016 excavation blocks.

winter-occupation bison of Component II. This higher CV is consistent with values obtained from animals in a migrant herd (Carlson and Bement 2013).

BULL CREEK COMPONENT IV

Bull Creek Component IV was documented in the West Trench excavation area during the 2017 investigations (figure 8.4) and consists of a bison pelvis and proximal sesamoid. These materials are located in fine sandy loam overlying the Bull Creek III component level in the 2016/17 south excavation block. The limited exposure provided by the West Trench excavations precludes any further association of these faunal remains with other site components, with the exception of Component I, which lies ~1.5 m below Component IV. Component IV was not seen in the excavation blocks to the north or south of the West Trench area. Additional excavation is planned to investigate this component.

The pelvis was lying flat but on its dorsal surface. The sacrum and caudal vertebrae are missing. No cutmarks or other evidence of butchery were found. No artifacts were recovered in proximity to these bones and no seasonality can be gleaned from these elements. The size of the pelvis suggests it belonged to a mature cow.

A single radiocarbon assay on the pelvis yielded an age of 9020 ± 35 ^{14}C BP (10,169–10,241 cal BP) (table 8.1). This assay is statistically different at a 95 percent confidence level from the radiocarbon dates obtained for the Bull Creek Component III occupation (T = 22.42149, Xi^2 (0.05) = 5.99, df = 2). Stable carbon and nitrogen values for the pelvis are $\delta^{13}C$ = –8.6 ‰ and $\delta^{15}N$ = 9.1 ‰, respectively (table 8.1), plotting at the margin of the Component II winter-occupation bison values.

INTRA-SITE COMPARISON OF COMPONENTS

The various attributes of each Bull Creek camp component are tabulated to facilitate intra-site comparisons. The number of bison within Components I, II, III, and IV are 3, 7, 3, and 1, respectively. The number of other faunal taxa for each component is 1, 2, 19, and 1. The number of identified hearths for each component is 0, 1, 4, and 0. The number of post holes for each component is 0, 2, 6, and 0. The season of site use could only be determined for Components II and III, with seasonal determinations of winter and summer, respectively. Duration of site occupation by component could not be determined. Similarly, the number of individual occupations or repeat visits for each component remains unknown.

To illustrate intra-site diversity of artifact and faunal remains, bone and flake density maps were generated for Component II and Component III levels in the two major excavation areas of the site. The north block consists of an area of 12 m^2 excavated in 2015. The south block is a 12 m^2 area excavated in 2016 and 2017 (figure 8.12). These two areas of the site are separated by a linear distance of 20 meters that is yet to be excavated. The contour interval is 1 bone or flake for each density map. A total of 180 bones were plotted in the North Block at an average density of 15 bones /m^2. Maximum and minimum densities were 27/m^2 and 5/m^2, respectively. Only 40 bones were plotted in South Block at an average density of 3.3 bones/m^2 and maximum and minimum densities of 9/m^2 and 0/m^2, respectively. Plotted bones in the North Block of Component III totaled 194 bones at an average density of 16 bones /m^2 and maximum and minimums of 35/m^2 and 0/m^2, respectively. In the South Block, a total of 81 bones were plotted at an average density of 6.75 bones/m^2 and maximum and minimum densities of 38/m^2 and 0/m^2, respectively. Bone densities are highest in the North Block units for both components. An increase in bone density in the northeast corner of the South Block is related to the butchering of a single bison axial skeletal unit.

Flake density in Component II is dominated by a single concentration of biface thinning flakes along the north central area of North Block. A total of 21 flakes were recovered from a single unit. An additional 97 flakes, including 3 refit sequences of 2 flakes, 3 flakes, and 6 flakes, were recovered in the 2017 expansion of this excavation to include the next unit north (not included in the North Block analysis presented here). An average density for Component II North Block is 1.75 flakes/m^2 with

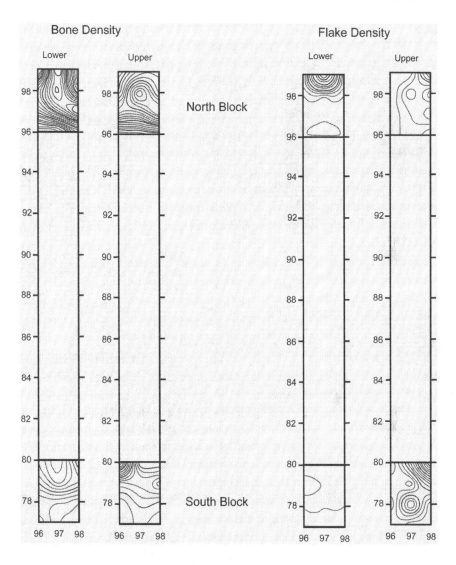

Figure 8.12. Bone and flake density maps for components II and III at the Bull Creek camp. For comparative purposes, only the 12 m² 2015 north block and 12 m² 2016/17 south block are graphed.

maximum and minimum densities of 21/m² and 0/m², respectively. Only 3 flakes were recovered from the South Block Component II, providing an average density of only 0.25 flakes /m², with maximum and minimum densities of 2/m² and 0/m², respectively. The reverse is seen in Component III, where the North Block flake recovery totaled 10 flakes at an average density of 0.83 flakes /m² with maximum and minimum densities of 4/m² and 0/m², respectively, and the South Block contained 20 flakes at an average density of 1.7 flakes /m² with maximums and minimums of 8/m² and 0/m², respectively. The disparity in lithic material types between the North Block and South Blocks described above is maintained even in this comparison of a smaller number of excavation units (see figure 8.12).

The winter season occupation exemplified by Component II is centered on the hunting of bison. Bison remains not only dominate but monopolize the winter component faunal assemblage. Marrow extraction appears to be the dominant site activity represented by the fractured nature of long bones brought to camp (Carlson and Bement 2017). Bifacial reduction of a late stage Alibates biface is represented by a dense accumulation of flaking debris near a hearth.

Component III contained four hearths surrounded by bone tools (needle and awl) and processed animal remains from a diverse fauna, including bison, deer, pronghorn, rabbit, turtle, and freshwater mussel. A light scatter of lithic reduction debris, also dominated by Alibates chert, indicates that tool manufacture and maintenance activities occurred somewhere on site but outside the excavation area. The presence of turtle and young deer suggest a summer season of occupation for this site component. The diversity of animals brought to the site during the Component III occupation is significantly different than that seen in the Component II level and is consistent with a more generalized subsistence mode similar to that seen at the Horace Rivers site in the Texas panhandle (Mallouf and Mandel 1997) and the Medicine Creek sites in Nebraska (Bamforth 2007; Davis 1953, 1962; Roper 2002) The mixed fauna at the O. V. Clary site, also in Nebraska, was interpreted as a multi-seasonal base camp associated with small-scale bison kills and other non-subsistence activities (Hill et al. 2011; May et al. 2008). Component III of the Bull Creek site could represent the site layout pattern associated with periods of broad-spectrum foraging over an extended occupation of more than one season.

An interesting parallel shared by the various excavation areas includes the recovery of the bison carcass segment mentioned above for Component III (figure 8.10) consisting of an articulated segment of cervical vertebrae, disarticulated thoracic vertebrae, and disarticulated ribs from both right and left sides. This re-occurring package suggests that part of the decision to transport bison portions from the kill location to the camp includes the anterior axial portion of animals. This commonality of body portion may be part of the "shared" apportionment to ensure all camp inhabitants (perhaps representing nuclear family units) receive a sizeable quantity of quality fresh meat (hump and brisket) as well as the two large horizontal sinew straps that anchor the skull to the thoracic spines of the hump. In addition, all three excavation blocks have hearths and two of the three have definite post molds, again suggesting patterning in site layout.

The differences between North block and South block occupations II and III highlight changes in site activities between these two areas and seasons of occupation. Both occupations display high quantities of bone in the North block, though occupation II is dominated by bison and III contains a broad spectrum of animals, including bison. Bison bone processing in the North block of both occupations is tied to marrow extraction. The South block bone distribution is significantly different from that in the North block, both in terms of quantity of bones and the treatment of bones. South block occupation II contains a low density of bones and bison continue to dominate. South block occupation III is also dominated by bison bones but the treatment changes from processing bones for marrow to concentrating on the dismantling of a single bison axial skeleton and the removal of tongue and brains from two skulls. The targeting of bison in this area of occupation III stands in stark contrast to the broad-spectrum faunal assemblage during occupation III in the North block area. Part of the processing of the axial skeleton included the removal and stacking of individual ribs. The purpose of removing individual ribs from the thoracic vertebrae is not apparent, unless the ribs were needed for stakes to pin hides for tanning. One such rib driven into the ground was documented in occupation III in the North block during the 2017 excavation. No pattern of post holes or other bone staking was observed.

Shifts in activities between North and South blocks are also seen in the lithic assemblages. Lithics in the North block are dominated by a single flintknapping concentration in occupation II on the north side of a hearth. All other areas of North and South blocks during occupations II and III display low flake densities, suggesting that flintknapping was not a common activity. Flaking debris densities remain low in the South block, although occupation III has higher densities than occupation II, contrasting the reverse pattern in the North block. Another contrast is the dominance of quartzite flakes in occupation III in the South block, again reversing the trend in the North block where Alibates chert dominated.

Activities in occupation II appear associated with the winter processing of bison remains, primarily marrow extraction in the North block, along with the refurbishing of hunting equipment if the flintknapping activity is related to production of a projectile point. A distinct activity for the South block occupation II area is not readily discernable. By contrast, the summer activities identified for occupation III include the processing of a wide variety of animals in the North block and the singular dismantling of a bison carcass in the South block as well as removal of brains. The random placement of post holes suggests racks or wind breaks were built. These activities appear related to bison hide processing.

The Bull Creek camp does not exist in a vacuum. People came to this site from other places and they left this site to venture out across the Plains. Whether or not people from the same group returned to this site is beyond our capabilities to detect; however, the ~200 cal year span of late Paleoindian use of the site components suggests Bull Creek camp was a persistent place on the landscape suitable for repeated occupation during both winter and summer seasons. While in residence, the occupants visited other places to obtain the faunal resources, indicated by the animal bones deposited in the various components. A cursory site catchment review for the various components suggests Components I, II, and IV used the high Plains/Prairie zone based on the recovery of bison-dominant resources. Based on the broad-spectrum assemblage composition of Component III, these occupants extracted animal resources from the high Plains/Prairie, riparian, and riverine environs. Exactly how the Component III animal resource forays were structured is difficult to reconstruct; however, if the Bull Creek camp is viewed as a base camp, then the resources were obtained through various foraging and collecting activities.

No bison kill site has yet been found directly associated with the Bull Creek camp. Often, camps are immediately adjacent to kill sites (Mackie et al., chapter 5; Dello-Russo et al., chapter 6) or, in the case of the Folsom-age Waugh site, the camp is 100 meters upstream from the kill (Hill and Hofman 1997). Similarly, the Clovis-age Murray Springs camp is located within 150 meters of the various kill locations, including the bison kill (Haynes and Huckell 2007). The closest known bison kill to the Bull Creek camp is the Ravenscroft arroyo trap bison kill. Ravenscroft is located in a small side drainage approximately 1 km south of the Bull Creek camp. Although it may not be the kill site that contributed bison material to the Bull Creek camp, the activities at the kill serve as a comparison to those that would have been performed by the inhabitants of the Bull Creek camp. To better understand the structure of the dominant resource, bison, the Bull Creek camp bison are compared and contrasted to the bison at the nearby and contemporaneous Ravenscroft arroyo trap kill site animals.

The Ravenscroft site is a large-scale arroyo trap bison kill complex of two adjacent arroyos utilized five times to trap and kill bison. All kills occurred during the winter. For this comparison, the various Ravenscroft components are segregated on the basis of stratigraphy, bison bone attributes, and radiocarbon assay, and then paired with contemporaneous components at the Bull Creek camp. The stable carbon and nitrogen isotope values of the Bull Creek winter and summer bison are compared to the isotopes from the nearby Ravenscroft winter kill bison in an effort to discern seasonal shifts in animal availability tied to mobility, fission and fusion cycles, and hunting intensity by the Bull Creek inhabitants.

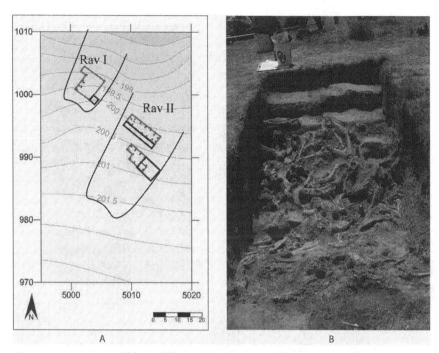

Figure 8.13. Ravenscroft bison kill site. (A) plan maps of Rav I and Rav II arroyos, looking north. (B) Main block excavation in Rav II arroyo, looking grid east.

INTER-SITE COMPARISON OF COMPONENTS

Pedestrian survey of the Bull Creek valley identified several sites ranging in age from Clovis to historic, including the Ravenscroft bison kill site approximately 1 km upstream of the Bull Creek camp (Bement, Schuster, and Carter 2007). The Ravenscroft site (34BV198) consists of two adjacent arroyos (RAV I and RAV II) containing several large-scale bison kill events (figure 8.13). The kills took place during the winter, as indicated by the recovery of young animals with tooth eruption and wear patterns attributed to animals between n + 0.5 to 0.6 years and fetuses exhibiting development stages of approximately 5 to 6 months (December through January kills) (Bement, Buehler, and Carter 2012; Muhammad 2017).

Like the Bull Creek camp, Ravenscroft is also a persistent place on the landscape. Ravenscroft was used multiple times for large-scale bison kills. The Ravenscroft bison kills can be seriated on the basis of stratigraphy, weathering stages, and radiocarbon assay. The first use (Component I) of arroyos at Ravenscroft occurred in RAV II and is indicated by the recovery of extensively weathered and trampled bison remains on the floor of the RAV II arroyo. Tooth eruption and wear patterns indicate this kill episode occurred during the winter. The winter seasonality is further supported by the recovery of a bison fetus at the five-month developmental stage, indicating a December to January kill episode (if timing of the bison rut during the early Holocene is similar to that of today). No radiocarbon dates or stable isotope data is available for this kill episode due to the lack of collagen preservation.

The second use (Component II) of Ravenscroft also occurred in RAV II and is indicated by the presence of an extensive bison bone deposit directly over the heavily weathered and trampled lower bone deposit. The bones from the second use display little weathering damage, suggesting these remains were quickly buried following the kill/butchering activities. Quick burial is also indicated by the presence of a halo of redoximorphic or reduce gley deposits directly under the skeletal remains. The gley-like deposits indicate the decomposition of organics by microorganisms in a reduced atmosphere. Tooth eruption and wear attributes as well as fetal development in this level also indicate a winter use of the site. Radiocarbon assay of two samples indicate an age of 9338 ± 21 ^{14}C BP (10,497–10,592 cal BP) and stable carbon and nitrogen isotope means of δ^{13}C = –8.6 ‰ and δ^{15}N = 10.5 ‰, respectively (table 8.3).

A third use (Component III) of the RAV II arroyo is indicated in the stratigraphic separation of another series of bison remains and accompanying radiocarbon ages significantly different from those obtained from the middle kill event. Of particular note in this level is the stacking of eight bison crania along the left side of the arroyo floor. These skulls lacked mandibles and none were articulated with atlas vertebrae. Only one of the skulls had a 10-cm diameter hole in the frontal. Closer examination of the hole suggests it resulted from a gopher burrowing into the skull and making a nest in the brain case. Tooth eruption and wear stages, as well as fetal development, indicate a winter kill event. A single radiocarbon assay of bone from this deposit yielded an age of 9210 ± 30 ^{14}C BP (10,258–10,438 cal BP) for this event (table 8.3). Stable carbon and nitrogen isotopes were δ^{13}C = –8.1 ‰ and δ^{15}N = 11.6 ‰, respectively.

The next use (Component IV) of the Ravenscroft arroyos occurred In the RAV I arroyo located 15 m west of the RAV II arroyo. Shifting to the RAV I arroyo may have been necessary since the stacking of skulls in RAV II effectively blocked entrance into the upper end of that arroyo. This lowest bison kill episode in the RAV I arroyo consisted of at least 10 bison. Again, tooth eruption and wear patterns along with a scattering of fetal material identified the season of kill during the winter, identical to the kills in the RAV II arroyo. The articulated posterior half of a bison from the third lumbar through the caudal vertebrae, as well as articulated pelvis with complete right and left appendicular elements, was found lying on its back with flexed legs splayed out to the side. In this supine or recumbent position, any fetus present would have been easily accessible. Radiocarbon assay of two samples yielded an average age of 9083 ± 21 ^{14}C BP (10,209–10,251 cal BP), and average

TABLE 8.3. Radiocarbon dates for Ravenscroft bison kills and Fulton Creek camp

Site name	Site no.	Bone no.	Element	δ13C	δ15N	%C	%N	C:N atomic	Lab #[a]	14C	±	Occ. group
Ravenscroft II	34BV198	LB628	petrous	−8.1	11.6	13.1	4.5	3.36	136071	9210	30	
	34BV198	LB692	petrous	−9.0	10.8	13.4	4.7	3.38	136072	9340	30	
	34BV198	LB724	petrous	−8.2	10.2	22.5	8.0	3.30	136077	9335	30	
	34BV198	LB711	humerus	−8.7	11.1	20.3	7.1	3.32	–	–	–	
	34BV198	LB751-1	humerus	−8.7	10.3	21.8	7.7	3.29	–	–	–	
	34BV198	1374	petrous	−8.3	11.7	–	–	2.90	A31639	9113	31	
Ravenscroft I	34BV198	150A	humerus	−9.8	10.4	9.7	3.4	3.36	–	–	–	
	34BV198	93E	femur	−8.4	9.6	20.9	7.4	3.29	–	–	–	
	34BV198	160J	femur	−8.8	10.7	23.1	8.3	3.25	–	–	–	
	34BV198	LB-55-2	petrous	−8.7	10.8	17.5	6.1	3.37	136070	8925		
	34BV198	LB26	femur	−10.3	11.5	21.2	7.5	3.32	136076	9075		
	34BV198	BN136	–	−8.1	11.1	–	–	3.42	78134	9090		
Fulton Creek	34BV178	–	charcoal	–	–	–	–	–	–	8760		

[a] No prefix letter: UCAIMS; P: Penn State; A: UGAMS

stable carbon and nitrogen isotope values of δ13C = −9.2 ‰ and δ15N = 11.3 ‰, respectively (table 8.3).

The final use (Component V) of the RAV I arroyo and of the Ravenscroft site as a whole is represented by a series of semi-articulated bison remains buried just below the modern surface and slightly down-arroyo from the older RAV I kill episode. This kill event was badly damaged by rodent activity and was also the locus of the point of discovery of this site. An MNI of 3 animals is represented in the surface collection and initial excavation assemblages from this portion of the site. A single radiocarbon assay on bison petrosal yielded an age of 8925 ± 30 14C BP (9918–10,085 cal BP) (table 8.3). This sample yielded stable carbon and nitrogen isotope values of δ13C = −8.7 ‰ and δ15N = 10.8 ‰, respectively.

In sum, the Ravenscroft bison kill site contained at least five arroyo trap bison kills. All kills occurred during the winter. The only projectile points in these

Figure 8.14. Artifacts from the Ravenscroft bison kill site: (A) lanceolate projectile point and (B) large mussel shell knife.

deposits include a complete Dakota quartzite lanceolate point that is 9.8 cm long, 2.1 cm wide, and 0.7 cm thick at its thickest portion with ground lateral basal edges and base (figure 8.14A), and the heavily ground basal ear or corner from an Alibates chert point. Additional artefactual material includes several chert flakes and a large freshwater mussel shell knife (figure 8.14B) (Muhammad 2017).

When the four Bull Creek camp components are aligned with the five Ravenscroft bison kill components, a picture emerges that chronicles the late Paleoindian summer and winter occupations of the Bull Creek drainage. At its most general level, the two sites can be aligned simply by matching the winter use of the kill with winter occupation of the camp. In this fashion, all five of the winter kills at the Ravenscroft site would potentially align with the winter occupation at the Bull Creek camp. The

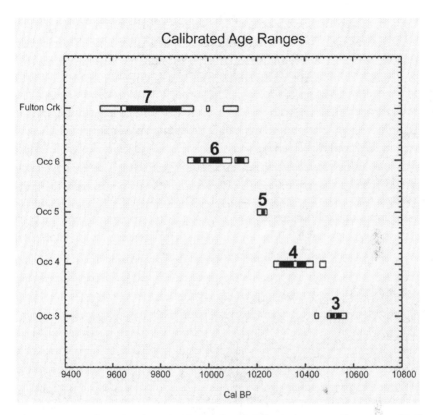

Figure 8.15. Radiocarbon box plots by combined Bull Creek camp and Ravenscroft kill components.

winter kills at Ravenscroft span the ~415 radiocarbon year period from ~9340 ± 40 ^{14}C BP to 8925 ± 30 ^{14}C BP (~578 cal year period from ~10,580 to ~10,002 cal BP). The winter component at Bull Creek camp, however, only spans the 34-radiocarbon-year period from 9305 to 9271 ^{14}C BP (~86 cal year period from 10,561 to 10,475 cal BP). Since at present there is no way to directly link the occupation of the camp with the use of the kill (no stone or bone refits between camp and kill components), the two sites perhaps better provide representational examples of what a winter camp occupation was like for each of the kill episodes and also what the potential summer occupation looked like in opposition from each winter kill episode. The following research questions summarize this situation: How many paired summer occupations and winter occupations are represented by the Bull Creek camp and Ravenscroft bison kill? To address this question, the radiocarbon record for Bull Creek camp and Ravenscroft bison kills are combined into a single set that is then segregated into statistically discrete (at 95% confidence level) temporal components. The integrity of the four camp components and five kill components is maintained while the various components are aligned according to cal BP age. The minimum criterion for grouping components is the statistical alignment of radiocarbon ages for each component. A T-test of radiocarbon ages, converted to cal BP range, provides a range of time during which matched components were occupied. The undated lowest components are included in this discussion although their temporal order cannot be determined. The results are outlined below (figure 8.15).

The undated lowest Bull Creek camp and Ravenscroft kill components are assigned to Occupations 1 and 2, respectively. The radiocarbon assays from the Bull Creek camp and Ravenscroft bison kills fall into four statistically separate groups; Occupations 3 through 6. Occupation 7 is the late Paleoindian Fulton Creek camp located along Fulton Creek, the next drainage west of Bull Creek. The Late Paleoindian occupation of the Bull Creek valley can be chronicled as follows:

Occupation 1 is represented by the undated yet stratigraphically lowest Bull Creek camp component I.

Occupation 2 is represented by the undated yet stratigraphically lowest winter kill at RAV II

Occupation 3 is represented by the winter occupation of Component II at Bull Creek camp and Component II winter kill at RAV II.

Occupation 4 is represented by the summer occupation of Component III at Bull Creek camp and Component III winter kill at RAV II.

Occupation 5 is represented by the seasonally unknown occupation of Component IV at Bull Creek camp and the Component IV winter kill at RAV I.

Occupation 6 is represented by the Component V winter kill at RAV I.

Neither of the lowest components at both the Bull Creek camp (Occupation 1) and Ravenscroft bison kill site (Occupation 2) are dated; thus, their order can be shuffled if and when radiocarbon assays become available. The remaining four grouped components provide a structure in which to interpret the late Paleoindian use of the Bull Creek drainage. Occupation 3, the earliest dated component, includes the winter Component II at Bull Creek camp and the winter Component II at RAV II and falls within the age span of ~10,492–10,570 cal BP. Occupation 4 includes the summer Component III at Bull Creek camp and winter kill Component III at RAV II and falls within the age span of ~10,272–10,433 cal BP. Occupation 5 is represented by the unknown season of occupation of Component

IV at Bull Creek camp and winter kill Component IV at RAV I and falls within the age span of ~10,221–10,239 cal BP. Occupation 6 is represented by the winter kill Component V at RAV I dating ~9915–10,096 cal BP.

Of particular interest in these defined periods of occupation is the alignment of the winter occupation at the Bull Creek camp and the large-scale winter kill at RAV II. Temporally, the two components are statistically the same, and both occur during the same season of the year. The question remains, however: is it feasible that the occupants at the Bull Creek camp conducted a kill at such a distance from the habitation site? It raises the possibility that there is a camp similar to the Bull Creek camp closer to Ravenscroft or that there is a kill closer to the Bull Creek camp, or both. All of these alternatives must address factors about transport decisions and costs, availability of other resources, such as wood for fires at a camp, available arroyos suitable for kills, and available work force, including beasts of burden, dogs, etc.

The components that make up Occupation 4 may provide clues to the answers to questions stated above. Occupation 4 includes the summer component from the Bull Creek camp and a winter component from RAV II. The seasonal disparity between these contemporaneous occupational components suggests that there exists somewhere on the landscape a camp associated with at least one winter kill component and is not the Bull Creek camp. Similarly, where were the bison killed that are represented in the summer occupation of the Bull Creek camp? Currently, there are no summer kills identified at the Ravenscroft kill site, suggesting the possibility that summertime kills are opportunistic kills of single or small groups of bison rather than large-scale, communal kills. Alternatively, summer bison kills may have also occurred in arroyos, but these arroyo traps have not yet been identified. This last possibility seems unlikely, since few summer-season, large-scale bison kills are known for the late Paleoindian period on the southern or central Plains, and the majority of large-scale kills occur during the fall and winter (Hill 2010; Hill and Knell 2013).

The stable carbon isotopes obtained from bison from the various winter kills at Ravenscroft, the winter occupation at Bull Creek camp, and the summer occupation at Bull Creek camp shed light on the structure of seasonal bison hunting in this area. A cross plot of stable carbon and nitrogen isotope values from the various components at RAV I, RAV II, and Bull Creek camp form an interesting pattern (figure 8.16). All isotopes from the winter RAV I and RAV II kills cluster in the upper right corner of the graph. The bison isotopes from the winter kill component at the Bull Creek camp also cluster with the RAV I and II winter kill isotopes. The samples from the summer occupation (Occupation 4) at Bull Creek camp are outliers that cluster to the left of the other samples, including the contemporaneous Occupation 4 winter kill at RAV II. Temporally, the summer bison are bracketed by winter kills at the Ravenscroft arroyo traps, indicating that any variances in isotopes

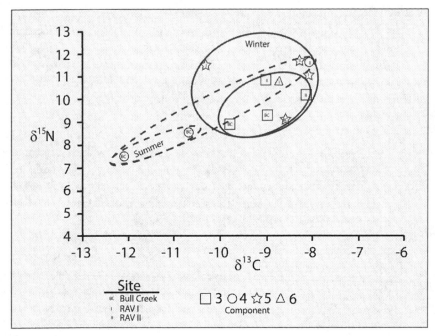

Figure 8.16. Stable isotope cross plot for defined Bull Creek camp and Ravenscroft bison kill occupations. Horizontal axis is δ¹³C values (‰) and vertical axis is δ¹⁵N values (‰).

or other bison attributes are not related to temporal shifts in climate or evolutionary trends but instead indicative of inter-herd variation, possibly related to shifts in bison mobility patterns and territories. Other researchers have shown that highly mobile bison (migrant bison) tend to display isotope values at greater in-herd variance than bison that stay within a small territory (resident herd), and that migratory and resident herds co-occur when bison population levels breech the carrying capacity of resident herds (Chisholm et al. 1986; Epp and Dyck 2002). Resident herds would be available for hunting during all seasons of the year, while migratory herds would only be available during the time they traveled through a particular area. The wintertime large-scale targeting of resident bison is opposite the pattern established during the earlier Folsom period when large-scale arroyo traps were utilized during the summer migration and small-scale kills occurred during all months of the year, including the winter (Bement 2003; Bement and Carlson 2018).

The lighter δ¹³C values (−11.4‰) and high CV (8.7) displayed by the summer bison at Bull Creek camp, compared to that displayed by the winter bison (−9.4‰ and 6.01, respectively) at Bull Creek camp, suggest the summertime bison visited areas supporting a higher percentage of C3 (cool, moist adapted) grasses relative to that occupied by the winter herds (Carlson 2015). Regions adjacent to the southern Plains with higher C3 grass composition are found to the north in the Central Plains area and to the west in the mountain foothills (Boehm 2016; Meltzer 2006; Tieszen, Stretch and Kooi 1998). Higher CV also equates to higher mobility across a broader region of variable grassland composition. Bison migration patterns during the Folsom period represented at the Cooper and Badger Hole sites followed east-west migrations across the southern Plains into the mountain foothills, placing the herds in northwest Oklahoma during the summer months. Perhaps a similar migration pattern was followed by the migrating component of early Holocene bison herds. The heavier δ^{13}C values (−8.6‰) and lower CV (5.78) displayed by the Ravenscroft animals killed in winter suggest the resident component of the early Holocene herds remained in the shortgrass prairies of northwestern Oklahoma and adjacent portions of Texas and southern Kansas.

Occupation 5 once again aligns use of Bull Creek camp with another winter kill at RAV I but does not yet provide a season of camp occupation. However, the stable carbon isotope value from the Bull Creek bison bone groups with the bison isotope values from known winter season kill events. Additional excavation into the uppermost late Paleoindian component at the Bull Creek camp may provide seasonal indicators that will help address these questions.

Occupation 6 is only found at the Ravenscroft bison kill site and adds further support to the proposition that additional late Paleoindian age camps are yet to be discovered along Bull Creek, probably including a camp closer to the Ravenscroft bison kills. The documentation of deeply buried cultural materials in other high terraces along Bull Creek, including two such terraces near Ravenscroft (Arauza et al. 2016, Conley 2010), suggests additional camps may have already been found but remain to be investigated. Site 34BV178, the Fulton Creek site, is a camp remnant located 8 km (5 miles) southwest of the Bull Creek camp in neighboring Fulton Creek drainage. The Fulton Creek camp consists of a hearth surrounded by spirally fractured bison long bones, Alibates chert bifacial reduction debris, and broken projectile point preform. A radiocarbon assay on charcoal places this occupation at 8760 ± 60 ^{14}C BP (9,550 −9,940 cal BP) (table 8.3), defining the late Paleoindian Occupation 7 in an adjacent drainage to that containing the Bull Creek camp and Ravenscroft bison kills.

Topics not covered by this discussion include the structure and distribution of resource acquisition for the wide variety of animal species identified for the summer occupation of Bull Creek camp. Whereas the winter bison hunting can be classified as communal, large-scale bison hunting, the summer-season hunting of bison and other animals is probably best classified as small-scale encounter or opportunistic hunts by individuals or small groups. With the possible exception of bison, most of these remaining animals are small-bodied and would probably be transported to camp whole. In these situations, the locus of kill or acquisition would generally not leave an archaeological signature or indication. Single bison kills, however, might manifest as partial skeletons representing low transport value elements or single animals that escaped from a lone hunter only to die elsewhere. Isolated projectile point discoveries across the landscape, particularly on playa margins, may be the archaeological expression of some of these hunting situations.

RECONSTRUCTING LATE PALEOINDIAN USE OF THE BULL CREEK DRAINAGE

Comparing the Bull Creek camp and Ravenscroft kill components draws into focus some of the problems with reconstructing overall Late Paleoindian subsistence adaptations. The arroyo trap bison kills at Ravenscroft are relatively straightforward indications that wintertime organization of some Late Paleoindian groups included large-scale bison hunting. The five preserved kill episodes bear witness to the resilient hardiness of bison bone deposits in arroyo settings during this time period. Analyses of the butchering patterns and bison stable isotope values provide a clear consensus of wintertime activities and the herds targeted.

The wintertime occupation at the Bull Creek camp nicely complements the materials from the Ravenscroft kill, including the replication of the seasonal indicators of bison tooth eruption and wear patterns as well as fetal development. The skeletal representation at the camp also fits nicely with the singular resource targeted at the kill site. Intense marrow processing and extraction of the bison brain are also indicated in the camp deposits. The refurbishing of projectile points is indicated by the discard of the heavily reworked and broken projectile point and the late-stage reduction of what was probably a projectile point preform. While it is tempting to speculate that lithic reduction was a hearth-side activity, the presence of a high density of fractured bone from marrow removal indicates this area of the site was also a discard zone. It is not clear if any activities are associated with the hearth. Cultural materials continue into unexcavated areas of the site, precluding a determination of the number of occupations and activity areas. The density of processed bone, however suggests the winter occupation area is much larger than has been documented so far in excavation. Together, these activities and site components bolster the interpretation that Late Paleoindian groups seasonally specialized in the hunting of bison.

The summertime component of the Bull Creek site contains four hearths surrounded by the butchered bones from multiple animal taxa in one area, and the secondary butchering of bison in another. Interpreting the summertime occupation at the Bull Creek camp is a bit more complicated. The murkiness surfaces when the excavation areas are compared and contrasted. The 2009 excavation area (expanded in 2015) contained a suite of animal resources indicating an extended summertime occupation and broad-spectrum foraging adaptation. Season of occupation was determined from the presence of seasonally-specific animal taxa (frogs, turtles) and developmental aspects, including young deer and neonate bison. However, had the 2016/17 areas been excavated first, then the bison-dominant aspect of the late Paleoindian subsistence adaptation would have led to a different interpretation. The lack of seasonal indicators in the 2016/17 block might have suggested the bison were from the winter kills at Ravenscroft, leading to a reconstruction that Late Paleoindian groups within the Bull Creek valley targeted or specialized in bison hunting. The disparity between the stable carbon isotope values from the Bull Creek camp and the Ravenscroft kills might, however, have led to the conclusion that the two sites were not related at all but were occupied during climatically disparate time periods. With the Ravenscroft bison kill as the only resource-acquisition referent, the conclusion of a bison-only emphasis in hunting would seem logical. It is only the presence of the 2009 and 2015 excavation blocks, replete with their 19-plus-taxa remains, that indicate both a summertime season of occupation and broad-spectrum subsistence adaptation The diversity of animal taxa in the deposits suggests an extended occupation of the site. The paucity of lithic debris, however, suggests other activity areas are yet to be discovered. At the very least, this situation at Bull Creek should alert researchers to the fallacy of interpretation brought about by small-scale excavations and how site preservation can affect overall site interpretations about regional resource adaptations.

The Bull Creek camp, and by extension, the Ravenscroft arroyo trap bison kill site, add to our understanding of the diversity of hunting and gathering groups (see Lemke 2018 and chapters within). Both camp and kill sites represent persistent places on the landscape (Carlson and Bement, chapter 1; Puckett and Graf, chapter 4; LaBelle 2010) and, as such, were occupied/used multiple times. Diversity is also seen in the seasons of occupation at the camp and in the differential use of various areas of the site as depicted by faunal remains, hearths, and lithic reduction debris. This chapter contributes to the discussion of how we establish contemporaneity of sites and activity areas—a discussion that transcends time and place in the archaeological literature (Carlson and Bement, chapter 1; Bamforth, chapter 9).

SUMMARY AND CONCLUSION

The Bull Creek camp contains four stratified Paleoindian occupations, including one winter camp dominated by bison and a summer camp representing broad-spectrum use of animal taxa. Key activities in these levels include marrow extraction, projectile point production, and bison butchery around site features that include hearths and post-supported constructs (drying racks, wind breaks, etc.). The portion of the site containing the remains of bison butchery is separate from where marrow extraction residue was uncovered. Fetal bison remains at the camp indicate fetuses were selected for transport from the kill.

One km upstream from the Bull Creek camp, resource extraction in the Bull Creek valley is represented at the large-scale bison hunting facility at the Ravenscroft site. At least five large-scale, arroyo trap bison kills are contained in the two adjacent arroyos. All kills occurred during the winter and the stable carbon isotope values across the kills depict the hunting of resident herds. Small numbers of scattered fetal remains in the kills suggest bison fetuses were brought to camps for further processing.

Radiocarbon assay of the Bull Creek camp occupations and Ravenscroft kill components indicate both sites were in use from ~10,400 cal BP to ~9,800 cal BP. Stable carbon isotope values from the winter kills and winter camp cluster together and yet are distinct from the disparate values from the summer camp bison, leading to the conclusion that winter bison were obtained from resident herds and summer bison from migrant herds. Based on the results from Bull Creek and Ravenscroft, the winter subsistence activities specialized in bison hunting while summertime subsistence was oriented toward broad-spectrum resource use. Seasonal differences in camp organization are manifest in the number of hearths, number of post holes, and dominant lithic material for tool manufacture.

The Bull Creek camp and Ravenscroft bison kill were in use simultaneously, albeit sporadically, at least by contemporaneous groups. This is not to say that people from the Bull Creek camp made the kills at Ravenscroft, or, conversely, that the people making the bison kills at Ravenscroft brought bison remains to the Bull Creek camp. It is likely that there are kill sites closer to the Bull Creek camp and camps closer to the Ravenscroft kills. What we are saying is that the activities at the Bull Creek camp represent the types of seasonal activities the users of the Ravenscroft kills are conducting at camp, and vice versa. The summer occupation of the Bull Creek camp is flanked in time by winter occupation and large-scale winter bison kill events, indicating the late Paleoindian groups used this same area during multiple seasons, perhaps negating the need for long-distance seasonal mobility patterns.

The importance of the Bull Creek site Late Paleoindian occupation is found in its potential to address questions concerning site patterning during different seasons of the year, and how site organization may have changed in response to seasonal shifts in subsistence modes from specialized bison procurement during one season to a generalist foraging pattern during another season within the same site. Addressing these questions advances our understanding of hunter-gatherer organization and diversity and promotes the contribution of Paleoindian studies in broader issues of land use, resource structure, and hunter-gatherer adaptations worldwide.

Acknowledgments. This work was funded in part by the National Geographic Society Committee for Research and Exploration Grant 9838–16, donations from Harold Courson, the Whitten-Newman Foundation, and Arnold Coldiron. Additional funding was provided by the Department of Anthropology at Augustana University, the Oklahoma Archeological Survey, the University of Oklahoma, and the Department of Plant and Soil Sciences, Oklahoma State University.

REFERENCES

Alexander, H. A. 2013. "The Stratigraphic and Geomorphic Evolution of the Bull Creek Valley, Oklahoma: Implications for Paleoclimate Studies and Nanodiamond Occurrence." MS thesis, Department of Earth Science, University of California, Santa Barbara.

Arauza, H. M., A. R. Simms, L. C. Bement, B. J. Carter, T. Conley, A. Woldergauy, W. C. Johnson, and P. Jaiswal. 2016. "Geomorphic and Sedimentary Responses of the Bull Creek Valley (Southern High Plains, USA) to Pleistocene and Holocene Environmental Change." *Quaternary Research* 85: 118–132.

Bamforth, D. B. 2002. "The Paleoindian Occupation of the Medicine Creek Drainage, Southwestern Nebraska." In *Medicine Creek: Seventy Years of Archaeological Investigations*, edited by D. Roper, 54–83. Tuscaloosa: University of Alabama Press.

Bamforth, D. B., ed. 2007. *The Allen Site: A Paleoindian Camp in Southwestern Nebraska.* Albuquerque: University of New Mexico Press.

Bement, Leland C. 2003. "Constructing the Cooper Model of Folsom Bison Kills on the Southern Plains." *Great Plains Research* 13: 27–41.

Bement, L. C. 2014. "The JS Cache: Clovis Provisioning the Southern Plains Late Pleistocene Landscape." In *Clovis Caches: Recent Discoveries and New Research*, edited by B. B. Huckell and J. D. Kilby, 61–78. Albuquerque: University of New Mexico Press.

Bement, L. C., and S. Basmajian. 1996. "Epiphyseal Fusion Rates of *Bison antiquus*." *Current Research in the Pleistocene* 13: 75–77.

Bement, L. C., and K. Carlson. 2018. "On the Significance of Cutmark Distributions at the Badger Hole Folsom Bison Arroyo Trap, Southern Plains, USA." *PaleoAmerica*, DOI: 10.1030/20555563.2017.1413531.

Bement, L., K. Buehler, and B. Carter. 2012. "Ravenscroft: A Late Paleoindian Bison Kill in the Oklahoma Panhandle." *Oklahoma Anthropological Society Bulletin* 60: 17–30.

Bement, L. C., B. J. Carter, R. A. Varney, L. S. Cummings, and J. B. Sudbury. 2007. "Paleo-Environmental Reconstruction and Biostratigraphy, Oklahoma Panhandle, USA." *Quaternary International* 169–170: 39–50.

Bement, L. C., K. Schuster, and B. Carter. 2007. "Archeologial Survey for Paleo-Indian Sites along the Beaver River, Beaver County, Oklahoma." Archeological Resource Survey Report No. 54. Norman: Oklahoma Archeological Survey.

Bement, L. C., A. S. Madden, B. J. Carter, A. R. Simms, A. L. Swindle, H. M. Alexander, S. Fine, and M. Benamara. 2014. "Quantifying the Distribution of Nanodiamonds in Pre-Younger Dryas to Recent Age Deposits along Bull Creek, Oklahoma Panhandle, USA." *Proceedings of the National Academy of Sciences* 111: 1726–1731.

Boehm, A. R. 2016. "Were Bison Predictable Prey? Using Stagle Isotopes to Examine Early Holocene Bison Mobility on the Central Great Plains." Unpublished PhD dissertation, Department of Anthropology, Dedman College, Southern Methodist University, Dallas.

Cannon, M. D., and D. J. Meltzer. 2004. "Early Paleoindian foraging: examining the faunal evidence for large mammal specialization and regional variability in prey choice." *Quaternary Science Reviews* 23: 1955–1987.

Cannon, M. D., and D. J. Meltzer. 2008. "Explaining variability in Early Paleoindian foraging." *Quaternary International* 191:5–17.

Carlson, K. 2015. "The Development of Paleoindian Communal Bison Kills: A Comparison of Northern to Southern Plains Arroyo Traps." Unpublished PhD dissertation, Department of Anthropology, University of Oklahoma, Norman.

Carlson, K., and L. C. Bement. 2013. "Organization of Bison Hunting at the Pleistocene/Holocene Transition on the Plains of North America." *Quaternary International* 297: 93–99.

Carlson, K., and L. C. Bement. 2017. "The Bull Creek Site: Late Paleoindian Encampment in the Oklahoma Panhandle." In *Plainview: The Enigmatic Paleoindian Artifact Style of the Great Plains*, edited by V. T. Holliday, E. Johnson, and R. Knudson, 122–144. Salt Lake City: University of Utah Press.

Carlson, K., L. C. Bement, B. J. Carter, B. J. Culleton, and D. J. Kennett. 2017. "A Younger Dryas Signature in Bison Bone Stable Isotopes from the Southern Plains of North America." *Journal of Archaeological Science*: Reports doi.org/10.1016/jjasrep.20.1703.001.

Casteel, R. W. 1976. *Fish Remains in Archaeology and Paleo-environmental Studies*. New York: Academic Press.

Chisholm, B., J. Driver, S. Dube, and H. P. Schwarcz. 1986. "Assessment of Prehistoric Bison Foraging and Movement Patterns via Stable-Carbon Isotopic Analysis." *Plains Anthropologist* 31 (113): 193–205.

Conley, T. O. 2010. "Buried Soils of Late Pleistocene to Holocene Ages Accented in Stacked Soil Sequences from the Southern High Plains of the Oklahoma Panhandle." MS thesis, Department of Soil Sciences, Oklahoma State University, Stillwater.

Davis, E. M. 1953. "Recent Data from Two Paleo-Indian Sites on Medicine Creek, Nebraska." *American Antiquity* 18: 380–386.

Davis, E. M. 1962. "Archaeology of the Lime Creek Site." Special Publication 3. Lincoln: University of Nebraska State Museum.

Dibble, D. S., and D. Lorrain. 1968. "Bonfire Shelter: A Stratified Bison Kill Site, Val Verde County, Texas." Miscellaneous papers No. 1. Austin: Texas Memorial Museum, The University of Texas at Austin.

Epp, H., and I. Dyck. 2002. "Early Human-Bison Population Interdependence in the Plains Ecosystem." *Great Plains Research* 12: 323–337.

Firestone, R. B. 2009. "The Case for the Younger Dryas Extraterrestrial Impact Event: Mammoth, Megafauna, and Clovis Extinction, 12,900 Years Ago." *Journal of Cosmology* 2: 256–285.

Gallagher, J. P. 1977. "Contemporary Stone Tools in Ethiopia: Implications for Archaeology." *Journal of Field Archaeology* 4: 407–414.

Gilbert, B. M. 1973. "Mammalian Osteo-Archaeology: North America." Columbia: Missouri Archaeological Society.

Gilbert, B. M., L. D. Martin, and H. G. Savage. 1981. *Avian Osteology*. Laramie, WY: Modern Printing Co.

Grayson, D. K. 1984. *Quantitative Zooarchaeology: Topics in the Analysis of Archaeological Faunas*. Orlando: Academic Press.

Grayson, D. K. 1989. "Bone Transport, Bone Destruction, and Reverse Utility Curves." *Journal of Archaeological Science* 16: 643–652.

Gustavson, T. C., R. W. Baumgardner Jr., S. C. Caran, T. T. Holliday, H. H. Mehnert, J. M. O'Neill, and C. C. Reeves Jr. 1991. "Quaternary Geology of the Southern Great Plains and an Adjacent Segment of the Rolling Plains." In *Quaternary Nonglacial Geology, Conterminous United States*, vol. K-2, edited by R. B. Morrison, 477–501. Boulder, CO: Geological Society of America, The Geology of North America.

Haynes, C. V., Jr. 1991. "Geoarchaeological and Paleohydrological Evidence for a Clovis-Age Drought in North America." *Quaternary Research* 35: 438–450.

Haynes, C. V., Jr. 2007. "Clovis Investigations in the San Pedro Valley." In *Murray Springs: A Clovis Site with Multiple Activity Areas in the San Pedro Valley, Arizona*, edited by C. V. Haynes and B. B. Huckell, 1–15. Tucson: University of Arizona Press.

Hill, M. E., Jr. 2010. "Regional Differences in Great Plains Paleoindian Occupational Intensity and Duration." In *Exploring Variability in Early Holocene Hunter-Gatherer Lifeways*, edited by S. Hurst and J. L. Hofman, 73–95. University of Kansas Publications in Anthropology 25. Lawrence: University of Kansas.

Hill, M. E., Jr., and J. L. Hofman. 1997. "The Waugh Site: A Folsom-age Bison Bonebed in Northwestern Oklahoma." In *Southern Plains Bison Procurement and Utilization from Paleoindian to Historic*, edited by L. C. Bement and K. J. Buehler, 63–83. Plains Anthropologist Memoir 29. Lincoln, NE: Plains Anthropologist.

Hill, M. E., Jr., and E. J. Knell. 2013. "Cody in the Rockies: The Mountain Expression of the Plains Culture Complex?" In *Paleoindian Lifeways of the Cody Complex*, edited by E. J. Knell and M. P. Muniz, 188–214. Salt Lake City: University of Utah Press.

Hill, M. G. 2005. "Late Paleoindian (Allen/Frederick Complex) Subsistence Activities at the Clary Ranch Site, Ash Hollow, Garden County, Nebraska." *Plains Anthropologist* 50 (195): 249–263.

Hill, M. G. 2008. "Paleoindian Subsistence Dynamics on the Northwestern Great Plains: Zooarchaeology of the Agate Basin and Clary Ranch Sites." BAR International Series 1756. Oxford: Archaeopress.

Hill, M. G., D. J. Rapson, T. J. Loebel, and D. W. May. 2011. "Site Structure and Activity Organization at a Late Paleoindian Base Camp in Western Nebraska." *American Antiquity* 76 (4): 752–772.

Hofman, J. L. 2010. "Allen Complex Behavior and Chronology in the Central Plains." In *Exploring Variability in Early Holocene Hunter-Gatherer Lifeways*, edited by S. Hurst and J. L. Hofman, 135–152. University of Kansas Publications in Anthropology 25. Lawrence: University of Kansas.

Hofman, J. L., and L. C. Todd. 1997. "Reinvestigation of the Perry Ranch Plainview Bison Bonebed, Southwestern Oklahoma." *Plains Anthropologist Memoir* 42: 101–117.

Hollenback, K. D. 2010. "Modeling Resource Procurement of Late Paleoindian Hunter-Gatherers: A View from Northwest Alabama." In *Exploring Variability in Early Holocene Hunter-Gatherer Lifeways*, edited by S. Hurst and J. L. Hofman, 13–26. University of Kansas Publications in Anthropology 25. Lawrence: University of Kansas.

Holliday, V. T. 2000. "Folsom Drought and Episodic Drying on the Southern High Plains from 10,900–10,200 [14]Cyr B.P." *Quaternary Research* 53: 1–12.

Hurst, S., and J. L. Hofman. 2010. *Exploring Variability in Early Holocene Hunter-Gatherer Lifeways*. University of Kansas Publications in Anthropology 25. Lawrence: University of Kansas.

Jepson, G. 1953. "Ancient Buffalo Hunters of Northwestern Wyoming." *Southwestern Lore* 19: 19–25.

Johnson, E. 1987. *Lubbock Lake: Late Quaternary Studies on the Southern High Plains*. College Station: Texas A&M University Press.

Johnson, A. M., and B. O. K. Reeves. 2013. "Summer on the Yellowstone Lake 9,300 Years Ago: The Osprey Beach Site." *Plains Anthropologist* Memoir 41, volume 58, nos. 227–228.

Kennett, D. J., J. P. Kennett, A. West, C. Mercer, S. S. Que Hee, L. Bement, T. E. Bunch, M. Sellers, and W. S. Wolbach. 2009. "Nanodiamonds in the Younger Dryas Boundary Sediment Layer." *Science* 323: 94.

Knell, E. J., and M. P. Muniz. 2013. *Paleoindian Lifeways of the Cody Complex*. Salt Lake City: University of Utah Press.

LaBelle, J. M. 2010. "Reoccupation of Place: Late Paleoindian Land Use Strategies in the Central Plains." In *Exploring Variability in Early Holocene Hunter-Gatherer Lifeways*, edited by S. Hurst and J. L. Hofman, 37–72. University of Kansas Publications in Anthropology 25. Lawrence: University of Kansas.

Larson, M. L., M. Kornfeld, and G. C. Frison. 2009. *Hell Gap: A Stratified Paleoindian Campsite at the Edge of the Rockies*. Salt Lake City: University of Utah Press.

Lemke, A. K. 2018. *Foraging in the Past: Archaeological Studies of Hunter-Gatherer Diversity*. Louisville: University Press of Colorado.

Leonard, A. B. 1959. "Handbook of Gastropods in Kansas." Miscellaneous Publication No. 20. Topeka: Department of Zoology and State Biological Survey, University of Kansas.

Lyman, R. L. 1994. *Vertebrate Taphonomy*. Cambridge: Cambridge University Press.

Lyman, R. L. 2015. "North American Paleoindian Eyed Bone Needles: Morphometrics, Sewing, and Site Structure." *American Antiquity* 80 (1): 146–160. doi.org/10.7183/0002-7316.79.4.146.

Mallouf, R. J., and R. D. Mandel. 1997. "Horace Rivers: A Late-Plainview Component in the Northeastern Texas Panhandle." *Current Research in the Pleistocene* 14: 50–52.

May, D. W., M. G. Hill, A. C. Holven, T. J. Loebel, D. J. Rapson, H. A. Semken Jr., and J. L. Theler. 2008. "Geoarchaeology of the Clary Ranch Paleoindian Sites, Western Nebraska." *The Geological Society of America Field Guide* 10: 265–293.

Meltzer, David J. 2006. *Folsom: New Archaeological Investigations of a Classic Paleoindian Bison Kill*. Berkeley: University of California Press.

Muhammad, F. S. 2017. "The Ravenscroft II Site: A Late Paleo-Indian Winter Bison Kill Event in the Oklahoma Panhandle." Unpublished MA thesis, Department of Anthropology, University of Oklahoma, Norman.

Mulloy, W. T. 1959. "The Jimmy Allen Site near Laramie, Wyoming." *American Antiquity* 25 (1): 112–116.

Pitblado, B. L. 2003. *Late Paleoindian Occupation of the Southern Rocky Mountains*. Boulder: University Press of Colorado.

Puseman, K. 2004. "Protein Residue Analysis of a Plainview Projectile Point from site 34BV177, Oklahoma." Paleo Research Institute Technical Report 04-23 on file at the Oklahoma Archeological Survey, Norman.

Reimer, P. J., E. Bard, A. Bayliss, J. W. Beck, P. G. Blackwell, C. Bronk Ramsey, C. E. Buck, H. Cheng, R. L. Edwards, M. Friedrich, P. M. Grootes, T. P. Guilderson, H. Haflidason, I. Hajdas, C. Hatté, T. J. Heaton, A. G. Hogg, K. A. Hughen, K. F. Kaiser, B. Kromer, S. W. Manning, M. Niu, R. W. Reimer, D. A. Richards, E. M. Scott, J. R. Southon, C. S. M. Turney, and J. van der Plicht. 2013. "IntCal13 and MARINE13 Radiocarbon Age Calibration Curves 0–50,000 Years cal BP." *Radiocarbon* 55 (4). DOI: 10.2458/azu_js_rc.55.16947.

Roper, D. C. 2002. *Medicine Creek: Seventy years of Archaeological Investigations.* Tuscaloosa: University of Alabama Press.

Sellards, E. H., G. L. Evans, and G. E. Meade. 1947. "Fossil Bison and Associated Artifacts from Plainview, Texas." *Bulletin of Geological Society of America* 58: 927–954.

Sellet, F., J. Donohue, and M. G. Hill. 2009. "The Jim Pitts Site: A Stratified Paleoindian Site in the Black Hills of South Dakota." *American Antiquity* 74: 735–758.

Sudbury, J. B. 2010. "Quantitative Phytolith Analysis: The Key to Understanding Buried Soils and to Reconstructing Paleoenvironments." Unpublished PhD dissertation, Department of Plant and Soil Sciences, Oklahoma State University, Stillwater.

Tieszen, L. L., L. Stretch, and J. V. Kooi. 1998. "Stable Isotopic Determination of Seasonal Dietary Patterns in Bison at Four Preserves across the Great Plains." In *Bison Ecology and Management in North America*, edited by L. R. Irby and J. E. Knight, 130–140. Bozeman: Montana State University.

Von den Dreisch, A. 1976. "A Guide to the Measurement of Animal Bone from Archaeological Sites." Peabody Museum Bulletin 1. Cambridge, MA: Peabody Museum of Archaeology and Ethnology, Harvard University.

Wheat, J. B. 1972. "The Olsen-Chubbuck Site: A Paleo-Indian Bison Kill." *Society for American Archaeology Memoir* 26: 1–180.

Wheat, J. B. 1979. "The Jurgens Site." *Plains Anthropologist* Memoir 15, vol. 24: 1–153.

Widga, C., J. D. Walker, and L. D. Stockli. 2010. "Middle Holocene Bison Diet and Mobility in the Eastern Great Plains (USA) Based on $\delta^{13}C$, $\delta^{18}O$, and $^{87}Sr/^{86}Sr$ Analyses of Tooth Enamel Carbonate." *Quaternary Research* 73: 449–463.

Wilmsen, E. N., and F. H. H. Roberts Jr. 1978. "Lindenmeier, 1934–1974 Concluding Report on Investigations." Smithsonian Contributions to Anthropology Number 24. Washington, DC: Smithsonian.

Woldearegay, A. F., P. Jaiswal, A. R. Simms, H. Alexander, L. C. Bement, and B. J. Carter. 2012. "Ultrashallow Depth Imaging of a Channel Stratigraphy with First-Arrival Traveltime Inversion and Prestack Depth Migration: A Case History from Bull Creek, Oklahoma." *Geophysics* 77: B87–B96.

9

Where Are the Activity Areas?

An Example at the Allen Site

DOUGLAS B. BAMFORTH

We all do different kinds of things in different places, and archaeologists understand that knowing how we do those things can provide important information about the human past. Since at least the 1970s, studying the spatial arrangement of human activities both within sites and across the landscape have been important streams of research in hunter-gatherer archaeology. My emphasis here is on the first of these streams. I will argue that decades of research have taught us a lot about fundamentally important aspects of the ways in which hunter-gatherers (and human beings in general) structure their use of residential space, about the archaeological implications of that use, and that taking this rich and deep body of knowledge explicitly into account will significantly improve our understanding of the human past.

I illustrate this with an example from the Early Holocene (Paleoindian) North American Great Plains. Perhaps more than any other branch of archaeology, Paleoindian archaeology focuses its attention on a single kind of site: large-mammal (usually bison) kill sites. In the larger context of thinking about ancient people, this focus has the obvious effect of spectacularly biasing our evidence and interpretations toward one aspect of the many things Paleoindian people did. In the specific context of this volume, though, it has the less obvious effect of biasing our work toward places where Paleoindians carried out very narrow ranges of activity over very short periods of time. They rarely reoccupied these places, and when they did, they reoccupied them at intervals of perhaps 20 years (i.e., Cooper; Carlson et al. 2016). As I discuss here, locations where people did more of the things that all

https://doi.org/10.5876/9781646422265.c009

humans do, where they did those things over long periods of time, and where they came and went as they did them, create much more complex patterns than those evident in kill sites, along with more complex interpretive issues. Dealing with these issues on their own terms instead of through the lens of bison kill sites also rewards us with a far richer understanding of ancient human lives.

THINKING ABOUT HUNTER-GATHERER RESIDENTIAL SITES

Hunter-gatherer archaeologists began to think about how people used residential spaces as they tried to make sense out of detailed information about artifact distributions in the sites they excavated—particularly sites that produced few or no kinds of material other than flaked stone tools and production debris. Early approaches to this used a variety of techniques to search for patterning in the distribution of different types of tools. These were often statistical techniques (Carr [1984] gives an overview of this work). This early work rested substantially on the assumptions that the "types" of tools archaeologists define have direct functional meaning and that different kinds of tools occurred together in sites because ancient people used them together to carry out fairly specific activities. This second assumption led archaeologists to argue that the places where they found sets of tools were "activity areas," or places where people used those tools to do specific jobs.

We know now that neither of these assumptions is correct. Most important for my purposes, the places where people did things and the places where we find the tools used to do those things are almost never the same, especially in residential sites. Human beings create an archaeological record by discarding objects, not by using them, and we discard the objects we use in the places where we use them only under unusual circumstances (Schiffer 1986; Yellen 1977). We therefore need to think about the relation between where we do things and where we throw objects away if we want to make sense out of the spatial patterns we see in hunter-gatherer sites.

Over decades, ethnoarchaeological research has documented strong patterns in this relation. Hunter-gatherer residential sites are not all the same. They reflect the lives of the human communities that occupied them and they vary in size, housing styles, spacing between adjacent households, formality of community arrangements, and other characteristics. This kind of variation is why we are interested in spatial patterns within sites. Despite their variability, hunter-gatherer residential sites all share common fundamental characteristics, and the differences among them seem to be structured understandably. Research on living people (not to mention our common sense) tells us unambiguously that activity areas really do exist at any given moment in the occupation of a given place, in the sense that individuals or groups of people do particular things in particular locations. But research on living people also tells us that distributions of features and the discard locations of artifacts mark these areas in complex and variable ways (I draw here on Binford 1978a, 1978b, 1982, 1983; David and Kramer 2001; Fisher and Strickland 1989, 1991; Friesem et al. 2017; Friesem and Lavi 2017; Gamble and Boismier 1991; Hitchcock 1987; Hudson 1990; Jones 1993; Kent 1991; Kroll and Price 1991; Lancelotti et al. 2017; O'Connell 1987, 1995; Svoboda et al. 2011; Yellen 1977).

In good weather, hunter-gatherers in residential camps carry out a wide range of activities (preparing and eating meals, socializing, manufacturing many items, etc.) in a central open area adjacent to the shelters that they use for shade and sleeping. In this part of the site, "activity areas"—in the sense that we generally visualize them—are ephemeral and changeable because people use the same space at different times for many different purposes. Activities move from location to location within and around this space for many reasons, including weather, social issues, comfort, and the demands of a particular task, although reliance on a specific constructed facility can tether them in place.

People keep the main central area clean, moving the debris they generate within it to dumps on the peripheries of the camp. They also use these peripheral areas for activities in addition to trash disposal, especially messy, time-consuming, or dangerous activities like heavy butchery, tasks that require large fires, and preparing poisoned arrows. Activities in these areas can shift from location to location, although they can be tethered to specific places when they need special facilities, just as they can be in central residential areas. Work-groups in peripheral areas and particular locations within those areas can also be segregated by age or by gender. Archaeologists often take the presence of hearths as automatic evidence of residential activities, but these can occur in central residential and peripheral areas of a camp. People use hearths for cooking, warmth, light, and as needed in craftwork in the central generalized area. People occupying peripheral areas may use hearths for similar purposes as well as for an array of more specialized purposes (for example, smoking hides). Many activities move inside dwellings in bad weather and dwellings themselves are sometimes more substantial when bad weather, particularly cold weather, is persistent.

Whether people use interior or exterior spaces for their primary living area, though, cleaning residential areas profoundly affects the distributions of the artifacts we recover in our excavations. On permeable surfaces, cleaning up tends to move objects larger than about 2.0 cm to peripheral dumps (often located downwind of the residential area; O'Connell 1987) and leaves smaller objects in place, along with chemical and other residues. Different objects used together at the same time may be moved farther than others because they are more "unsightly" or simply more inconvenient (Binford 1978a: 349). The result of this is a mixed and size-sorted distribution of discarded objects, with the open areas in the centers of residential sites dominated by small debris along with subtle chemical and other residues of the diverse set of activities carried out there. Middens on the site peripheries are dominated by larger debris moved from activity locations to trash heaps (especially see O'Connell 1987). Larger debris linked to activities carried out in peripheral areas may stay in place there, fairly close to the locations where people generated it. However, when it does remain in place, it is generally mingled with material generated elsewhere in a variety of different activities. The frequencies of different kinds of objects left behind in activity areas as a result of this vary together not because people used them together but because they are similar in size (O'Connell 1987: 95).

Note, though, that "debris" in this sense most often means the useless by-products of a task, not the implements used to carry out that task. Using a hammer to smash bison long bones to get marrow generates large bone fragments that people rarely leave in the middle of their homes, along with tiny bone fragments that they may miss during cleanup. However, people rarely discard the hammer used to smash those bones directly in the place where they used it, even if the hammer breaks. Still-useful tools move with their owners from camp to camp, and broken or worn-out tools or parts of tools go out with the trash, although not necessarily with trash produced when people decided to discard those tools.

However, the kinds of patterns that ethnoarchaeologists record observing living people over the course of single occupations of residential sites are rarely what we see archaeologically. This matters. The short time-scales of ethnoarchaeological research have often focused attention on detailed artifact distributions like Binford's (1978a) endlessly popular "drop zone" and "toss zone" distinction, a pattern he observed in a non-residential location used for very short periods of time by very restricted groups of people for a very limited purpose (see Stevenson [1991] for a more realistic discussion of this). Searching for these kinds of patterns archaeologically implicitly assumes an almost Pompeii-like level of preservation that has little to do with the reality of archaeological site formation. We may sometimes encounter sites that people used only once and have remained substantially intact over time (for example, the Upper Paleolithic Meer site in Belgium [Cahen et al. 1979] or the Woodland-era Wallace site in Nebraska [Winfrey 1991]). However, sites like that are likely rare, and we always have to demonstrate that any given site is or is not one of them whether they are rare or not. To do this, we need to take account of the long-term interaction between human occupation and cultural and natural formation processes that have shaped the patterns we see. Searching for the interactions among these focuses us on what Clark (2017:1302) refers to as the "occupation histories" of sites.

Sometimes these histories were short, simple, and straightforward. Perhaps more often, though, they were complex, spanning periods of time that bear little resemblance to the time scales that ethnoarchaeology studies and reflecting the effects of an array of processes that ethnoarchaeology addresses only partially (cf. Jochim [1991] on issues of temporal scale in archaeology and ethnography in general). People occupied and reoccupied many of the localities that we see as archaeological sites over centuries and sometimes millennia, and all archaeological sites have been subject to natural processes since they were formed, regardless of how people used them. This means that we can never assume that we will be able to see the precise patterns that ethnoarchaeology documents for single occupations. Instead, working out the occupational histories of the sites we study requires us to wonder how patterns of human reoccupation and natural post-depositional forces affected those sites.

It is particularly important to consider differences in the length of time that people remain at a given site and the degree to which they reoccupy a given locality. In general, people tend to clean up more carefully and more often when they stay in place for longer periods of time, suggesting that we should expect more stable formal disposal areas in more sedentary residences. The locations of residential and peripheral spaces within camps can also change over the course of long-lived occupations, blurring size-sorted patterns, moving trash from one location to another, and further mixing together trash generated at different times and in different activities.

Natural processes also interact with patterns of human occupation and profoundly shape the distributions of material that we study (Angelucci et al. 2013; Enloe et al. 1994; Enloe 2006; Henry 2012; Mallol and Hernandez 2016; Peter 1991; Wandsnider 1996). It is especially important that the living surfaces that hunters and gatherers occupy now and occupied in the past can be stable for varying periods of time. When they are stable for long periods, the habit of returning over and over to favored camp locations can blur spatial patterns in much the same way that shifts in activity locations within ongoing camps blur them—by superimposing the remains of distinct occupations directly on top of one another. However, when occupation surfaces are not stable and sediment accumulates over time, geologic forces interact with patterns of reoccupation in complex ways. When sedimentation rates are rapid in comparison to rates of reoccupation, this interaction can create discrete archaeological levels corresponding to individual occupations. When these rates are slow relative to rates of reoccupation, they can create more continuous vertical distributions of remains. Active erosion can also, obviously, rearrange the distributions of artifacts exposed on the surface prior to burial. Other processes (for example, freeze/thaw cycles, burrowing by animals) can rearrange them after burial (Erlandson 1984; Wood and Johnson 1978).

There are thus some fairly simple lessons that we can take directly from observations of recent hunters and gatherers. One important lesson is that the kinds of visible artifact concentrations that attract our excavations are often, and probably usually, trash heaps located around the edges of residential areas. However, the larger lesson of what we know has to do with the potential complexity of the processes that affect the spatial patterns that we see. Our data inevitably show us the aggregate results of varying combinations of many factors, including human choices about where to carry out activities, the degree to which they cleaned up after those activities, patterns of shifting use of living surfaces during single occupations or over repeated occupations, and the effects of the natural processes that buried living surfaces and operated on buried assemblages of archaeological material over time. I turn now to a case study that illustrates these issues.

THE ALLEN SITE

The Allen site (25FT50) was located on Medicine Creek in southwestern Nebraska, roughly 10 km upstream from the confluence of that creek and the Republican River (figure 9.1). Radiocarbon dates indicate that people occupied the site for most of the Paleoindian period, beginning shortly after 11,000 BP and ending shortly before 7,000 cal. BP. My colleagues and I report the site in detail elsewhere (Bamforth 2007). I focus here on its spatial structure (also see Bamforth et al. 2005).

FIELDWORK AND STRATIGRAPHY

Erosion caused by a massive flood exposed deeply buried archaeological remains in three localities along Medicine and Lime Creeks in 1947. Archaeologists from the University of Nebraska excavated a substantial portion of what we now refer to as the Allen site from 1947 to 1949. Stratigraphic work in the host drainage carried out at that time and in the late 1980s and early 1990s documents the geomorphic processes operating at the site (May 2007). The site itself has been destroyed by erosion following the impounding of Harry Strunk Lake, but other sites of similar age along Lime Creek remain at least partially intact.

The Allen site formed as Paleoindian groups camped on an aggrading terrace along Medicine Creek. When people first began to use the site sometime shortly after 11,000 BP, the terrace they chose lay on the floor of a valley incised between 14,000 and 11,000 RCYBP into late Pleistocene loess. They camped within this valley on a gently sloping surface backed on its upslope edge by a steep cutbank. A combination of overbank floods and colluvial processes raised the surface of the terrace roughly a meter over the next 3,000 years. Overbank flooding dominated this process in the early parts of this interval, raising the terrace to about the level of the stream by 10,700 BP. The surface then stabilized for perhaps as long as 200 to 300 years, with stability marked by well-developed buried soil. After this time,

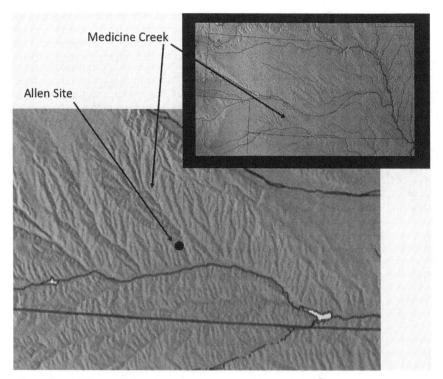

Figure 9.1. Location of the Allen Site.

colluvial deposition dominated the valley, with more or less constant sediment accumulation interrupted briefly by a period of surface stability at about 7,600 BP that was marked by a second and less distinct buried soil. Ultimately, sediment accumulated to a depth of between seven and eight meters, with evidence of Paleoindian occupation in the lowest part of this accumulation.

Erosion beginning about 3,800 years ago left the site exposed in the wall of a steep cutbank; paleontologists reported it in 1947 after burrowing roughly two meters into the bank. In 1948, archaeologists removed the overburden with bulldozers and excavated through the cultural levels, working in grid units 5.0 feet (1.53 meter) square and excavating in 0.2-foot (6.4 centimeter) levels. They recovered all the objects they saw (although they did not screen for artifacts), mapping hearths and some specific artifacts in three dimensions but generally recording provenience by grid square and excavation level. However, although the archaeologists processed most categories of material in the collection and preserved provenience information on them, they transferred unmodified animal bone to paleontologists,

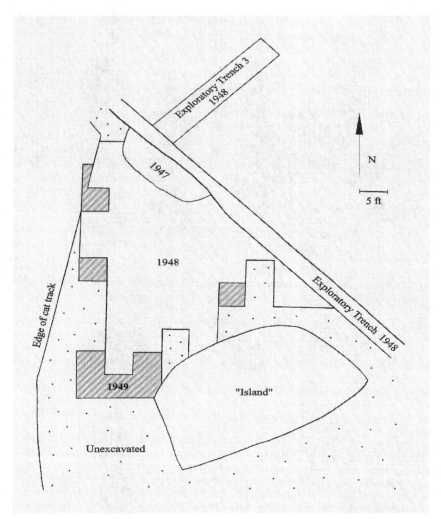

Figure 9.2. Excavated Area at the Allen Site.

who preserved only general stratigraphic information. We have fairly precise locational information on unmodified bone only for material recovered from the surface of the lower buried soil (Bamforth [2007: chapter 8] discusses this in detail). Ultimately, archaeologists excavated over 500 cubic feet of sediment from a triangular area of about 1,250 square feet (118 square meters; figure 9.2). This excavation recovered approximately 13,000 flakes and retouched pieces (virtually all made from Smoky Hill jasper, available locally within the Medicine Creek drainage), over

TABLE 9.1. Definitions of analytic stratigraphic units at the Allen Site

Unit	Definition
Above Occupation Level 2	Excavation levels with bottom depths more than 4.0 inches above the surface of Occupation Level 2.
Occupation Level 2 Upper	Excavation levels with bottom depths less than 4.0 and greater than or equal to 2.0 inches above the surface of Occupation Level 2.
Occupation Level 2 Surface	Excavation levels with bottom depths within 2.0 inches of the Occupation level 2 surface.
Occupation Level 2 Lower	Excavation levels with bottom depths more than 2.0 but less than or equal to 6.0 inches below the surface of Occupation Level 2.
Intermediate Zone	Excavation levels with bottom depths more than 6.0 inches below the surface of Occupation Level 2 and 4.0 inches or more above the surface of Occupation Level 1.
Occupation Level 1 Upper	Excavation levels with bottom depths less than 4.0 but more than 2.0 inches above the surface of Occupation Level 1.
Occupation Level 1 Surface	Excavation levels with bottom depths within 2.0 inches of the surface of Occupation Level 1.
Occupation Level 1 Lower	Excavation levels with bottom depths more than 2.0 but less than or equal to 6.0 inches below the surface of Occupation Level 1.
Below Occupation Level 1	Excavation levels with bottom depths more than 6.0 inches below the surface of Occupation Level 1

6,000 pieces of unmodified bone, 12 fragments of grinding tools, 13 hammerstones, and 125 bone tools, including eyed needles, perforating tools, and others. It also recorded 20 hearths.

The site's excavators identified three basic strata: the lower buried soil, labelled Occupation Level 1 (OL 1), the upper buried soil, labelled Occupation Level 2 (OL 2), and the unstained sediment between these, labelled the Intermediate Zone (IZ). We have lost most provenience information beyond these basic stratigraphic units for the unmodified animal bone, although we can identify bone recovered from horizontally discrete concentrations on the surface of OL 1 (concentrations that the excavators labelled "features"). The more detailed information for the rest of the assemblage lets us define vertical divisions of the site ranging in thickness from 0.4 to 1.0 feet (12.8 to 30.7 cm). Table 9.1 lists these.

SPATIAL PATTERNING AT THE ALLEN SITE

Except on the surface of OL 1, where we have limited information on the distribution of animal bone, the spatial data available for analysis at the Allen site consist of artifact densities by 5.0 foot grid squares within the vertical units defined in table 9.1. This data let us look in some detail at the distribution of material in the site, although there is no doubt that more detailed information would have let us see patterns that are invisible in density plots (cf. Enloe et al. 1994). My emphasis here is on the horizontal distribution of material, but I begin by noting two important points (Bamforth and Becker [2007:125–129] and Bamforth et al. [2005:566–567] discuss these in detail). First, although the density of artifacts varies significantly from level to level, there are no sterile levels within the excavated area of the site. Second, extensive efforts to refit the lithic assemblage document very low rates of vertical disturbance, as does the number of intact hearths scattered through the deposits. The near-absence of vertical disturbance implies strongly that the continuous vertical distribution of artifacts at the site results from the interaction between recurrent human occupation and sediment accumulation, which I return to below.

Horizontally, artifacts occur in clear concentrations throughout the sequence (figures 9.3–9.5 present examples of these patterns; Bamforth and Becker [2007: 130–132 present a full set of maps]). The excavators of the site noticed this: one field entry from 1948 mentions "a nice pile of flint chippings." Importantly, although refitting documents limited vertical disturbance and offers important insights into patterns of tool production at the site (Bamforth and Becker 2000), it also tells us unambiguously that these concentrations are *not* intact flaking clusters. Overall, we were able to refit only about 2.0 percent of the thousands of objects in the collections. None of the hundreds of flakes in the "nice pile" fit to one another. This is particularly striking because the overwhelmingly most common material in the assemblage,—Smoky Hill jasper,—is quite variable in color and texture: flakes struck from parent pieces of this material have many markers that should make it easier to fit them together.

If knappers did not generate piles of lithic debris at the Allen site while working in the locations where archaeologist recovered those piles, they must have generated that debris elsewhere and someone must have moved it to those locations. That is, someone must have cleaned this debris from other places, perhaps moving some of it more than once. Artifact concentrations at the Allen site are secondary dumps, although there is every possibility that they include at least some material generated in activities carried out around them. The concentrations mapped in figures 9.3–9.5 consist almost entirely of flaked stone tools and debitage, but maps of bone density on the surface of Occupation Level 1 (generated from field maps of bone locations)

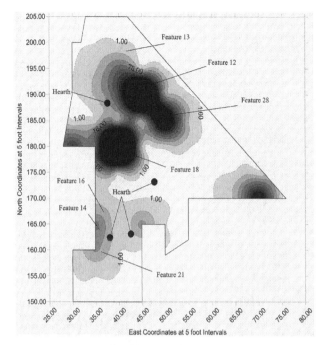

Figure 9.3. Hearth Locations and Artifact Concentrations on the Surface of Occupation Level 1 at the Allen Site. "Features" Refer to Concentrations of Artifacts and Faunal Remains Observed in the Field. Contour Interval 25 Artifacts Per Five Foot Square.

Figure 9.4. Hearth Locations and Artifact Concentrations Within the Intermediate Zone at the Allen Site. Contour Interval 25 Artifacts Per Five Foot Square.

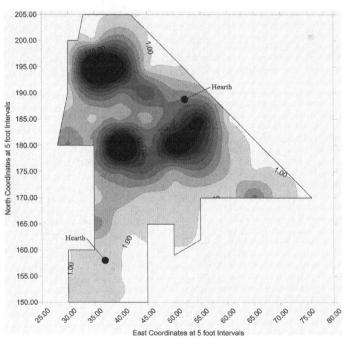

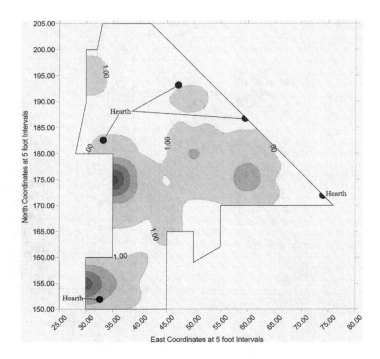

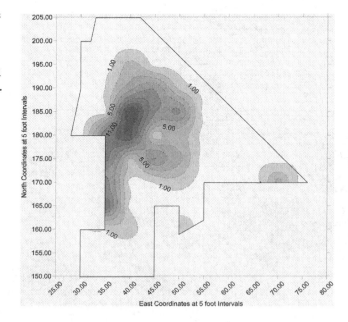

Figure 9.5.
Hearth Locations and Artifact Concentrations on the Surface of Occupation Level 2 at the Allen Site. Contour Interval 25 Artifacts Per Five Foot Square.

Figure 9.6.
Density of Point-Plotted Bone Per Five Foot Square at the Allen Site. Bone Counts Taken from Field Maps. Contour Interval Two Bones Per Five Foot Square.

suggest strongly that they are generalized trash heaps; bone on this surface overlies the flaked stone concentration (compare figure 9.3 to figure 9.6).

With this in mind, the similarity of the locations of artifact concentrations/trash piles from level to level is striking: for roughly 3,000 years, the people who came and went from the Allen site discarded their trash in roughly the same place. This is true not just in the sense that they tossed it in the same general area on the outskirts of their residential center, but also in the sense that they tossed it on the same piles, with earlier discard on piles in more northern parts of the excavation and discard locations drifting south over time.

It is difficult to explain this pattern except by the operation of what Wilk and Schiffer (1979) refer to as the "Arlo Guthrie Trash-Magnet Effect," in which people discard new material onto previously existing trash heaps (see Bamforth and Becker [2007:140–145] and Bamforth et al. [2005]). This implies that objects recovered from any given level within the site may or may not derive directly from activities carried out when people occupied that level (or, at least, from activities other than trash disposal). On surfaces that were stable for extended periods of time (for example, the surfaces of OL 1 and OL2), debris may have been exposed for extended periods. Direct evidence of this is limited, but a number of tools show retouch through a weathered surface, implying that knappers scavenged them from material that had been on the surface for some time (Bamforth and Becker 2007:164). In addition, we can examine the frequencies of modifications to bone that result from exposure on the ground surface (weathering, carnivore gnawing, and rodent gnawing) for the faunal material identified as coming from features/concentrations on the surface of OL 1. These frequencies are notably high in the north, above more deeply buried middens in lower levels, and lower in the south, beneath more shallowly buried middens in upper levels (figure 9.7; data from Hudson 2007: table 12.11).

All of this implies that Paleoindians returned to the Allen site at a rate that exceeded the rate at which sediment accumulated there, cleaned up previously existing trash and/or their own newly created trash, and discarded it onto middens from previous occupations that were still visible on the ground surface. This has implications for the pattern of human use of the site, which apparently involved repeated visits at relatively frequent intervals (Bamforth 2007: 230–242; 2009). More important for my purposes here, though, it has important implications for the locations of the hearths in the site. These show a very strong pattern relative to artifact concentrations: the people who camped at the Allen site burned fires in areas that had densities of small debris (median flake size 2.0 to 2.5 cm) and/or very low densities of debris (less than 10 to 20 objects per square meter). Burned lithic debris is common at the site, including pieces that are discolored and pieces that are damaged, but seems to derive from natural fires that burned through the Medicine

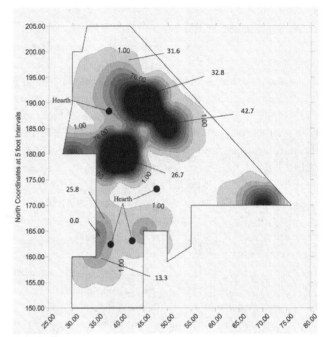

Figure 9.7.
Hearth Locations and Artifact Concentrations on the Surface of Occupation Level 1 at the Allen Site. Numbers Refer to the Percentage of Bones Within Each Feature Showing Evidence of Exposure on the Ground Surface Prior to Burial. Contour Interval 25 Artifacts Per Five Foot Square.

Creek drainage in the past rather than from people setting camp fires directly on piles of lithic debris or flintknapping directly into fireplaces (Bamforth and Becker 2007b: 167–168, 180–183). That is, rather than locating debris relative to hearths, as in Binford's (1978) "hearth-centered" artifact distributions, people at the Allen site located hearths relative to preexisting concentrations of debris. The Allen site shows an artifact-oriented hearth distribution, not a hearth-centered artifact distribution.

Hunter-gatherers do not locate hearths for residential cooking, socializing, etc., in the midst of trash middens, even in midden areas with low densities of trash. People build hearths in midden areas when they need heat or light in the context of peripheral activities, perhaps for comfort or perhaps as an integral part of carrying out those activities. Fires on the peripheries of the recent hunter-gatherer camps studied by ethnoarchaeologists were important to the people who built them, but they were not the focal centers of residential activities. Similarly, the Allen site hearths almost certainly were not focal centers of that kind of activity, and we would do well to wonder about hearths in other sites located close to substantial piles of potentially dangerous or unpleasant debris.

The patterns we can see in the Allen site tell us that the excavated area was part of a regularly reused residential site, but it was not at the center of the main residential part of that site. This area appears to have been at the upslope edge of the occupation zone, adjacent to the cutbank that marked the edge of the Medicine Creek floodplain (see Bamforth [2007: 116–117] for more detail on this), implying that the general residential area was in a downslope area destroyed by the erosion that exposed the site in 1947. Concentrations of lithic debris and animal bone at the Allen site thus mix together remains from an array of activities carried out in a variety of locations. They likely include debris discarded directly into those middens from activities carried out around the hearths located near them, but it is not obvious how we might distinguish that debris from debris swept up in other areas of the habitation and discarded on piles that had been visible on the ground for extended periods of time.

SOME IMPLICATIONS: DO ARCHAEOLOGISTS NEED ACTIVITY AREAS?

It is possible that more detailed provenience data might allow us to identify something like individual activities carried out within the excavated portion of the Allen site. However, the very low refit rates suggest that the excavated middens mix debris from many occupations fairly thoroughly, and the plain fact is that better provenience data for the site do not exist (as they do not for many sites). The activities that we know people carried out directly within the excavation area involve building campfires and dumping trash; the people who lived at the Allen site over some 3,000 years did most of the other things they did in parts of the site that are now almost certainly destroyed by erosion.

Whether or not this is a problem depends on what we want to know. We may see a very limited range of *activity areas* at the Allen site, but we can see many, many *activities* there. In fact, we can see those activities precisely because people cleaned up the residues from them and dumped them in the kinds of features that archaeologists like to dig. People made needle-shaped artifacts (and discarded the grooved abraders they used to do this) and they used needles to manufacture a variety of items (the needles in the collection vary greatly in diameter). They butchered, cooked, and ate a wide array of large and small animals. People worked animal hides, manufactured many kinds of bone and stone tools, fabricated organic items that we cannot identify, etc. They likely taught novice artisans how to do at least some of these things (Bamforth and Hicks 2008). All of this, including the pattern of cleaning up that seems to have so strongly influenced the spatial organization of the site, tells us that the Allen site was a residential base, in sharp contrast to other sites of the same age elsewhere in the Medicine Creek drainage, which seem primarily to have been workshops associated with outcrops of lithic raw material (Bamforth 2002, 2007; Hicks 2002). And if it was a residential base, the people who lived there must also have played with children, courted spouses, mourned the dead, and carried out all of the other activities that are central to being human but leave few or no archaeological traces.

It is even possible that being unable to see areas used for purposes other than lighting fires and dumping trash at the Allen site is a benefit, given the kinds of questions that underlay the work we did at Medicine Creek. That work focused on long-term human responses to terminal Pleistocene/early Holocene environmental change (Bamforth 2007). Recognizing that the artifact concentrations at the site represent debris mixed together and dumped from multiple occupations of the site lets us view them as ways of looking at aggregate patterns of activity at the site. Looking at the characteristics of this aggregate over time documents significant long-term changes in Paleoindian ways of life on the central Plains: for example, people camped more and more briefly at the site and relied less on bison and more on smaller game over time (Bamforth 2007: 227–244). Both of these changes make sense in the context of an increasingly arid Paleoindian environment. The very act of cleaning up so regularly also directly tells us something important about the way people lived at the Allen site. People do not clean up places where they do not stay long (for example, kill sites); the pattern of site maintenance that we see suggests occupation spans ranging from weeks to perhaps months, as Hudson (2007) suggested on the basis of the faunal data (the Alyawarra households that O'Connell [1987] studied lived in place for an average of two to three months).

CONCLUSIONS

The archaeology of mobile homes shows how humans organize the spaces where they dwell. Work occurs in certain areas, the dead are buried in others . . . In open air encampments, people will tend to deal with messy or potentially dangerous tasks on the edge of camp, whether butchering reindeer at Pincevent during the Upper Paleolithic or rebuilding a truck engine in central Australia in the 1970s. This is not, I repeat, because the Alyawara are representatives of the Upper Paleolithic, but because this is what humans do. (Moore 2012:47)

Ethnoarchaeology tells us that the basic factors that structure the distribution of archaeological traces in hunter-gatherer campsites seem to be universal. In fact, settled farmers in the eighteenth- and nineteenth-century American Southeast and in modern Veracruz maintain similar, generalized multipurpose residential activity areas that are themselves similar to the ones in hunter-gatherer campsites; urban Americans today leave much the same kinds of size-sorted distributions of artifacts that we see among hunters and gatherers (Killion 1990; South 1979). Today, when people remain in a place for long, when they live in places with children (especially small children), or when they need spaces for a variety of activities over a period of time, they discard malodorous, dangerous, or otherwise unpleasing things away from the areas where they live and work. Sharp or otherwise dangerous things are high on the list items that they move; in the recent past, this included discarded pop tops from aluminum cans. Ethnoarchaeology tells us that this is an unsurprising universal pattern in the modern world and it must have been equally universal in the past (Stevenson [1991] similarly emphasizes this).

This implies (perhaps ironically) that our perfectly reasonable emphasis on excavating where we can see concentrations of artifacts will inevitably lead us over and over to dig in the peripheral middens of residential activity areas. It is fair to say that *everything* that we know about human behavior tells us that concentrations of large artifacts in residential sites are almost always trash dumps, except in the most briefly occupied localities. As O'Connell (1987, 1995) argued long ago, in order to see primary activity areas, we need to turn to the smallest objects in our collection (see Keeley [1991] for examples of this) and to broad-scale excavations that extend far beyond the concentrations we often emphasize. Even when we do this, in any site occupied for very long, the residues we study will mix activities together because people use specific locations within their residential spaces for a wide variety of purposes over the time when they occupy those spaces. And we have known for decades that, except under very, very unusual circumstances, people simply do not drop the tools they use and the debris they generate in the specific locations where they use and generate them. We dump debris in the trash and we take useful tools with us when we move. We need to take this explicitly into account when we consider spatial patterns in residential sites if we hope to learn what those sites have to teach us.

I have not presented the Allen site here as a cautionary tale about why we should not be interested in activity areas. Being able to see residential space dedicated to particular tasks can provide important information about many aspects of the organization of ancient social groups, and we should work to see this when it is visible. Instead, I mean the Allen site evidence to provide an example of what we can learn about the human past when we explicitly take account of what we know about the way human beings organize work and distribute objects in and around residential spaces. *Excavation at the Allen site revealed activity areas*, even if these are not the kind of activity areas we usually hope we can see. Recognizing this makes it possible to see how we can use information on those activity areas—on the ways in which the people who lived at the site organized residential space—to understand important aspects of Paleoindian lives on the central Great Plains. Doing the same elsewhere will likely have similar benefits. These benefits will be easier to achieve if we attend explicitly to the rich body of knowledge that ethnoarchaeologists and others have generated for us over many years.

Acknowledgments. Paleoindian research at Medicine Creek was funded by the United States Bureau of Reclamation. All of our work at Medicine Creek is dedicated to the memory of Edward Mott Davis (1918–1998). Mott made archaeology a better field to work in and the world a better place to live.

REFERENCES

Angelucci, D., D. Anesin, D. Susini, V. Villaverde, J. Zapata, and J. Zilhao. 2013. "Formation Processes at a High-Resolution Middle Paleolithic Site: Cueva Antón (Murcia, Spain)." *Quaternary International* 315: 24–41.

Bamforth, D. B. 2002. "The Paleoindian Occupation of the Medicine Creek Drainage, Southwestern Nebraska." In *Medicine Creek: 70 Years of Archaeological Investigations*, edited by D. Roper, 54–83. Tuscaloosa: University of Alabama Press.

Bamforth, D. B. 2007. *The Allen Site: A Paleoindian Camp in Southwestern Nebraska.* Albuquerque: University of New Mexico Press.

Bamforth, D. B., and M. Becker. 2000. "Core/Biface Ratios, Mobility, Refitting, and Artifact Use-Lives: A Paleoindian Example." *Plains Anthropologist* 45: 273–290.

Bamforth, D. B., and M. Becker. 2007. "Spatial Structure and Refitting of the Allen Site Lithic Assemblage." In *The Allen Site*, edited by D. Bamforth, 123–147. Albuquerque: University of New Mexico Press.

Bamforth, D. B., M. Becker, and J. Hudson. 2005. "Intrasite Spatial Analysis, Ethnoarchaeology, and Paleoindian Land-Use on the Great Plains: The Allen Site." *American Antiquity* 70: 561–580.

Bamforth, D. B., and K. Hick. 2008. "Production Skill and Paleoindian Work Group Organization in the Medicine Creek Drainage, Southwestern Nebraska." In *Skillful Stones: Approaches to Knowledge and Practice in Lithic Technology*, ed. N. Finlay and D. Bamforth. *Journal of Archaeological Method and Theory* 15: 132–153.

Binford, L. R. 1978a. "Dimensional Analysis of Behavior and Site Structure: Learning from an Eskimo Hunting Stand." *American Antiquity* 43: 330–361.

Binford, L. R. 1978b. *Nunamiut Ethnoarchaeology.* New York: Academic Press.

Binford, L. R. 1982. "The Archaeology of Place." *Journal of Anthropological Archaeology* 1: 5–31.

Binford, L. R. 1983. *In Pursuit of the Past: Decoding the Archaeological Record.* London: Thames and Hudson.

Cahen, D., L. Keeley, and F. Van Noten 1979. "Stone Tools, Toolkits, and Human Behavior in Prehistory." *Current Anthropology* 20: 661–683.

Carlson, K., B. Culleton, D. Kennett, and L. Bement. 2016. "Tightening Chronology of Paleoindian Bison Kill Sites on the Northern and Southern Plains." *PaleoAmerica* 2: 90–98.

Carr, C. 1984. "The Nature of Organization of Intrasite Archaeological Records and Spatial Analytical Approaches to Their Investigation." *Advances in Archaeological Method and Theory* 7: 103–222.

Clark, A. 2017. "From Activity Areas to Occupational Histories: New Methods to Document the Formation of Spatial Structure in Hunter-Gatherer Sites." *Journal of Archaeological Method and Theory* 24: 1300–1325.

David, N., and C. Krame. 2001. *Ethnoarchaeology in Action*. Cambridge: Cambridge University Press.

Enloe, J. 2006. "Geological Processes and Site Structure: Assessing Integrity at a Late Paleolithic Open-Air Site in Northern France." *Geoarchaeology* 6: 523–540.

Enloe, J., F. David, and T. Hare. 1994. "Patterns of Faunal Processing at Section 27 of Pincevent: The Use of Spatial Analysis and Ethnoarchaeological Data in the Interpretation of Archaeological Site Structure." *Journal of Anthropological Archaeology* 13: 105–124.

Erlandson, J. 1984. "A Case Study in Faunalturbation: Delineating the Effects of the Burrowing Pocket Gopher on the Distribution of Archaeological Materials." *American Antiquity* 49: 785–790.

Fisher, J., and H. Strickland. 1989. "Ethnoarchaeology among the Efe Pygmies, Zaire: Spatial Organization of Campsites." *American Journal of Physical Anthropology* 78: 473–484.

Fisher, J., and H. Strickland. 1991. "Dwellings and Fireplaces: Keys to Efe Pygmy Campsite Structure." In *Ethnoarchaeological Approaches to Mobile Campsites*, edited by Clive S. Gamble and William A. Boismier. Ann Arbor, MI: International Monographs in Prehistory.

Friesem, D., and N. Lavi. 2017. "Foragers, Tropical Forests and the Formation of Archaeological Evidences: An Ethnoarchaeological View from South India." *Quaternary International* 448: 117–128.

Friesem, D., N. Lavi, M. Madella, P. Ajithpradad, and C. French. 2017. "Site Formation Processes and Hunter-Gatherers Use of Space in a Tropical Environment: A Geo-Ethnoarchaeological Approach from South India." *PLoS ONE* 11(10): e0164185. doi:10.1371/journal.pone.0164185.

Gamble, Clive S., and William A. Boismier. 1991. *Ethnoarchaeological Approaches to Mobile Campsites*. Ann Arbor, MI: International Monographs in Prehistory.

Henry, D. 2012. "The Palimpsest Problem, Hearth Pattern Analysis, and Middle Paleolithic Site Structure." *Quaternary International* 247: 246–266.

Hicks, K. 2002. "Local Variability in Paleoindian Lifeways: A Comparison of the Lime Creek and Allen Site Worked Stone Assemblages, Southwestern Nebraska." Master's thesis, University of Colorado Boulder.

Hitchcock, R. 1987. "Sedentism and Site Structure: Organizational Changes in Kalahari Basarwa Residential Locations." In *Method and Theory for Activity Area Research*, edited by S. Kent, 374–423. New York: Columbia University Press.

Hudson, J. 1990. "Spatial Analysis of Faunal Remains in Hunter-Gatherer Camps." In *Etnoarqueologia: Primer Cologio Bosch-Gimper*, edited by Y. Sagiura and M. Serra. Mexico City: Instituto de Investigaciones Antrologicas, Universidad Nacional Autonoma de Mexico.

Hudson, J. 2007. "Faunal Evidence for Subsistence and Settlement Patterns at the Allen Site." In *The Allen Site*, edited by D. Bamforth, 194–226. Albuquerque: University of New Mexico Press.

Jochim, M. 1991. "Archaeology as Long-Term Ethnography." *American Anthropologist* 93: 308–321.

Jones, K. 1993. "Archaeological Structure of a Short-Term Camp." In *From Bones to Behavior*, edited by Jean Hudson. Occasional Paper No. 21. Carbondale: Center for Archaeological Investigations, Southern Illinois University.

Keeley, L. 1991. "Tool Use and Spatial Patterning: Complications and Solutions." In *The Interpretation of Archaeological Spatial Patterning*, edited by E. Knoll and T. D. Price, 357–368. New York: Plenum Press.

Kent, S. 1991. "The Relationship between Mobility Strategies and Site Structure." In *The Interpretation of Archaeological Spatial Patterning*, edited by E. Knoll and T. D. Price, 33–59. New York: Plenum Press.

Killion, T. 1990. "Cultivation Intensity and Residential Site Structure: An Ethnoarchaeological Examination of Peasant Agriculture in the Sierra de los Tuxtlas, Veracruz, Mexico." *Latin American Antiquity* 1: 191–215.

Kroll E., and T. D. Price. 1991. *The Interpretation of Archeological Spatial Patterning*. New York: Plenum Press.

Lancelotti, C., A. Pecci, and D. Zurro. 2017. "Anthropic Activity Markers: Archaeology and Ethnoarchaeology." Special Issue, *Environmental Archaeology* 22: 339–446.

Mallol, C., and C. Hernandez. 2016. "Advances in Palimpsest Dissection." *Quaternary International* 417: 1–2.

May, D. 2007. "Landforms, Alluvial Stratigraphy, and Radiocarbon Chronology at Selected Paleoindian Sites around Medicine Creek Reservoir." In *The Allen Site*, edited by D. Bamforth, 17–46. Albuquerque: University of New Mexico Press.

Moore, J. 2012. *The Prehistory of Home*. Los Angeles: University of California Press.

O'Connell, J. 1987. "Alyawara Site Structure and Its Archaeological Implications." *American Antiquity* 52: 74–108.

O'Connell, J. 1995. "Ethnoarchaeology Needs a General Theory of Behavior." *Journal of Archaeological Research* 3: 205–255.

Peter, K. 1990. "Site Structural Complexity." In *Prehistoric Resource Use and Settlement in the Santa Ynez River Basin*, edited by C. Woodman, J. Rudolph, and B. Bowser, 9.4–9.60. Santa Barbara, CA: Science Applications International Corporation.

Schiffer, M. 1986. *Formation Processes of the Archaeological Record*. Albuquerque: University of New Mexico Press.

South, S. 1979. "Historic Site Content, Structure, and Function." *American Antiquity* 44: 213–247.

Stevenson, M. 1991. "Beyond the Formation of Hearth-Associated Artifact Assemblages." In *The Interpretation of Archaeological Spatial Patterning*, edited by E. Knoll and T. D. Price, 269–300. New York: Plenum Press.

Svoboda, J., S. Sazelova, P. Konsintev, V. Jankovska, and M. Holub. 2011. "Resources and Spatial Analysis at Actual Nenets Campsites: Ethnoarchaeological Implications." *Journal of Anthropological Archaeology* 30: 30–43.

Wandsnider, L. 1996. "Describing and Comparing Archaeological Spatial Structures." *Journal of Archaeological Method and Theory* 3: 319–384.

Wilk R., and M. Schiffer. 1979. "The Archaeology of Vacant Lots in Tucson, Arizona." *American Antiquity* 44: 530–536.

Winfrey, J. 1991. "Spatial Distribution of Cultural Material and Post-Depositional Disturbances at the Wallace Site (25GO2)." MA thesis, University of Nebraska, Lincoln.

Wood, W. R., and D. Johnson. 1978. "A Survey of Disturbance Processes in Archaeological Site Formation." *Journal of Archaeological Method and Theory* 1: 315–381.

Yellen, J. 1977. *Archaeological Approaches to the Present*. New York: Academic Press.

Index

Contributors

Douglas B. Bamforth, Professor, Anthropology Department, University of Colorado Boulder

Leland C. Bement, Oklahoma Archeological Survey, University of Oklahoma

Ian Buvit, Department of Anthropology, Oregon State University, Corvallis, Oregon

Kristen A. Carlson, Associate Professor of Anthropology, Augustana University

Brian J. Carter, Professor Emeritus. Department of Plant and Soil Sciences, Oklahoma State University

Robin Cordero, Office of Contract Archeology, University of New Mexico

Robert Dello-Russo, Office of Contract Archeology, University of New Mexico

George C. Frison, Department of Anthropology, University of Wyoming

Kelly E. Graf, Department of Anthropology, Center for the Study of the First Americans, Texas A&M University

Bruce B. Huckell, Department of Anthropology, University of New Mexico

Michael A. Jochim, Professor Emeritus, Department of Anthropology, University of California, Santa Barbara

Joshua D. Kapp, Ecology and Evolutionary Biology Department, University of California Santa Cruz

Robert L. Kelly, Department of Anthropology, University of Wyoming

Aleksander V. Konstantinov, Transbaikal State University, Chita, Zabaikalskii Krai, Russia

Banks Leonard, Office of Contract Archeology, University of New Mexico

Madeline E. Mackie, Department of Anthropology, University of Wyoming

Christopher W. Merriman, Department of Anthropology, University of New Mexico

Matthew J. O'Brien, Department of Anthropology, California State University, Chico

Spencer Pelton, Office of the Wyoming State Archaeologist

Neil N. Puckett, Department of Anthropology, Center for the Study of the First Americans, Texas A&M University

Beth Shapiro, Ecology and Evolutionary Biology Department, University of California Santa Cruz

Todd A. Surovell, Department of Anthropology, University of Wyoming

Karisa Terry, Department of Anthropology and Museum Studies, Central Washington University, Ellensburg, Washington

Steve Teteak, Department of Anthropology, California State University at Bakersfield

Robert Yohe, Department of Anthropology, California State University at Bakersfield